SACRED PATH OF
REIKI
HEALING AS A SPIRITUAL DISCIPLINE

ABOUT THE AUTHOR

Katalin Koda has been practicing Reiki for ten years and teaching for nine. She has given hundreds of Reiki sessions and taught many students from around the world. She studied and earned all degrees of Raku-Kei Reiki with Reiki Master and High Priestess Rowan Wilson. After learning Reiki One and Two in the spring of 1998, she spent the following year practicing earnestly on friends and family. She also volunteered at the Reiki Clinic in downtown Baltimore, where she experienced using Reiki in concert with a number of different practitioners of various lineages. A year later, she earned her Reiki Master degree. Katalin also spent a year working with Wilson, learning and perfecting the crafting arts of Wicca, contemporary paganism. This includes the art of casting sacred circles, drawing down the moon, and tarot symbolism. Over the next ten years, Katalin continued her practice and teaching of Reiki, supplementing her study with the chakra system, Hatha, and Kundalini Yoga. She is a certified Sivananda Yoga instructor and also completed an intensive two-week Kundalini Yoga course. Katalin currently divides her time between Hawaii and India. She continues to practice Reiki, teaches all degrees of her Reiki Warrior path, provides chakra and human energy field training, and runs her non-profit organization to empower women and children.

SACRED PATH OF

REIKI

HEALING AS A SPIRITUAL DISCIPLINE

KATALIN KODA

Llewellyn Publications
Woodbury, Minnesota

FIRST EDITION
First Printing, 2008

Book design by Rebecca Zins   Editing by Nicole Edman
Cover art © Staffan Andersson/age fotostock/SuperStock
Cover design by Gavin Dayton Duffy
Photos by Katalin Koda and Elizabeth Bukoski, used by permission
Illustrations on pages 7, 63, 64, 74–80, and 165 by Llewellyn art department
Llewellyn is a registered trademark of Llewellyn Worldwide, Ltd.

Library of Congress Cataloging-in-Publication Data
Koda, Katalin, 1976–
  Sacred path of Reiki : healing as a spiritual discipline / Katalin
Koda.
      p. cm.
  Includes bibliographical references and index.
  ISBN 978-0-7387-1445-5
  1. Reiki (Healing system) I. Title.
  RZ403.R45K63 2008
  615.8'51—dc22
                              2008035544
ISBN 978-0-7387-1445-5

Llewellyn Worldwide does not participate in, endorse, or have any authority or responsibility concerning private business transactions between our authors and the public.
All mail addressed to the author is forwarded but the publisher cannot, unless specifically instructed by the author, give out an address or phone number.
Any Internet references contained in this work are current at publication time, but the publisher cannot guarantee that a specific location will continue to be maintained. Please refer to the publisher's website for links to authors' websites and other sources.

Llewellyn Publications
A Division of Llewellyn Worldwide, Ltd.
2143 Wooddale Drive, Dept. 978-0-7387-1445-5
Woodbury, Minnesota 55125-2989
www.llewellyn.com

Printed in the United States of America

Contents

Reiki Three

GIVING THE GIFT OF REIKI

Acknowledgments

As with any book, this undertaking was dependent on so many people and resources. I first have to extend my deep appreciation to my first teachers on the spiritual path, who taught me to be strong as a woman, which enabled me to help begin the process of reclaiming the lost arts and power that are inherent to half the population on this earth. I am also grateful for their guidance in the art of Reiki and healing, which inevitably transcends gender and brings us all together into a place of growth and wholeness.

I am grateful to the Reiki Masters who have gone before me, especially Mikao Usui, who brought this spiritual practice to light in the form of healing, and to my own Reiki Master, who graciously seeded me with the Reiki healing light and taught me the tools I needed to make the healing grow. I hope with all my being that I am honoring the best of intentions by writing the words in this book, continuing my Reiki practice, and providing a healing space for those in need. I am thankful to all the teachers who have assisted me on the path, and especially to my current dharma teachers of the Karmu Kagyu lineage, who serve to consistently remind me of the noble importance of helping all sentient beings in the universe and beyond.

I am thankful to my dear, endlessly supportive husband, who continuously finds ways to nurture my healing and writing work and is forever cheering me on, especially during the darker hours. Also, I am eternally grateful to my parents and family, who have taught me so much and without whom none of the gifts of my life would be possible.

I wish to extend my gratitude to the most important spiritual sister in my life, Desiree Mwalimu, because without her I don't think I would have ever had the courage to step on the path as we held each other up—and continue to do so—in the trembling beginnings of learning to face who we are and our precious potential. I am also thankful to the many other teachers, friends, and people who have guided and assisted, pointed, and yelled a little to help illuminate my growth, and who continue to do so.

I am eternally grateful to all my clients and students, as each of you has taught me something new, something worthwhile, and enabled me to gain further understanding into the complexity of the human mind, body, and spirit. Each client has helped to expand my understanding of Reiki and benefited my own meditative growth process. For the students who have far surpassed my own abilities and gifts, I am forever thankful for reminding me to be humble and for shining brightly in your own wondrous, unique ways.

I distinctly thank Naomi Doumbia for all of her encouragement to write this book, her tireless editorial comments, our deep philosophical conversations and never-ending joy. I thank the editors at Llewellyn Worldwide and especially Carrie Obry for her editorial guidance, support, and clear-sightedness to bring this book into its final form. I also wish to thank Beth Bukoski, Shiby Chacko, Amina Meineker, Michele de la Menardiere, and Anna Wise, who all significantly added to the book.

And lastly, I apologize if I have made any errors in this writing; they are my own mistakes and not my teachers'. May all sentient beings find peace and lasting happiness.

OM AH HUNG

Introduction

Sacred Path of Reiki: Healing as a Spiritual Discipline is the resulting synthesis of my continuous, disciplined Reiki practice and deep study of the ancient wisdoms of India and Tibet, which I anchor in the practical applications of Wicca, a revival of the ancient system of pagan spirituality. By incorporating these different elements in a unique way, I aim to enable contemporary Reiki practitioners to flourish on all levels of body, mind, and spirit in the same way a healthy tree grows from the earth. The beginning Reiki practitioner is like an acorn seed, hard and quiet in firm ground, containing the potential of a giant oak thriving on earth and reaching up to gain the quiet wisdoms of the sky.

The tools taken from my Wiccan training are the necessary ground that cultivates the spiritual growth of any true Reiki practitioner. These tools are not limited to those who choose Reiki as a spiritual path but can be all-inclusive of every aspect of life, whether one is a householder, businessman, healer, or farmer. In that sense, this book is written for anyone and everyone, and the wisdom from practicing Reiki can be applied to every moment of life, whether eating, painting, gardening, or raising a child. Reiki is the deep, personal honoring of the universal life force and does not exist separately from our experience. People of all walks of life may find something of value in the following written words.

I have repeatedly found that although many spiritual seekers, especially those from the West, are adept in basic concentration and effort that result from an advanced education, they often lack the necessary components of grounding, discipline, compassion, and devotion that are the fertilizers for the growth of a healer on the spiritual path. The traditional Reiki path begins when a person comes to the realization that healing oneself on all levels of body, mind, and spirit is integral to working with the deeper meanings of life. The information and exercises on the chakra system and energy field will benefit any practicing healer.

This work is compounded with my years of experience in clairvoyant "seeing," and I hope it can add to the growing amount of literature now available on the human energy field. Because spirituality aspects such as clairvoyance and energy channels are still subject to Western logical deduction, they are relegated to the seemingly less important realm of experiential. Thus, the world of reason has been slower to re-integrate spirituality, energy healing, and ancient wisdom into daily life. Yet, this is changing as some hospitals now welcome laying-on-hands healing; as thousands of people every year seek alternative therapies; and as the mainstream is becoming filled with books, teachers, and practices on alternative health, spirituality, and ancient wisdom. This is positive growth, but those interested in healing and spirituality must remember that ultimately, it is the continuous *practice* of these ancient wisdoms that will bear the true fruit of spiritual beauty and lasting peace.

Having spent the last several years living in India, I have had the unique advantage of learning various healing perspectives in addition to my work with clients and students from all over the world. Living in India and absorbing the teachings available there has increased the depths of my Reiki practice in unfathomable ways. I have had the fortunate opportunities to study Tibetan Buddhism in Dharamsala, where I attended several teachings given by the Dalai Lama; learned Vipassana, or insight, meditation from a Jain monk; spent time over the years at a Zen center cultivating the practice of sitting meditation; and completed my Yoga Teacher Training at Sivananda Ashram in Neyyar Dam, southern India. Although I have received many teachings, I have only included the ones that are directly relevant to my experience with Reiki and deliberately excluded anything beyond the basic tools needed for healing work. Even more important, all of these practices and teachings would not have made much sense to me if it were not for my basic, continuous, disciplined Reiki practice. I cannot emphasize this dedication enough and truly hope to impart upon the reader that although receiving teachings from the Dalai Lama surrounded by the majestic, soaring Himalayas (which are thought to hold the secrets of the Universe) was amazing, it was in the simple act of returning to my Reiki room, practicing my intentions, and laying hands on myself and others in a very basic and grounded way that the true process of integration happened.

Thus, the archetype of the Warrior springs to mind, one who walks slowly and impeccably on this life journey, utilizing the practices in an effective manner to gain results that are life-changing and lasting. It is akin to the story of the Zen master who climbed the mountain, attained enlightenment, then went on with his life, carrying "the mountain" of his experience under his robe in the marketplace. Mikao Usui, the founder of the Reiki healing practice, also experienced *satori*, a glimpse or moment of enlightenment, on a mountain and brought it down with him to spread the truth and beauty of his experience in the form of healing.

My aim is to provide a text that can help anyone on the path, specifically through healing, without having to search for the ancient practices of Wicca or Tibet. Although those practices have certainly benefited me, this is not the only way to begin accessing our deeper potential as healers and finding the peace within, allowing the oak tree to begin its journey from seed. This book is an investigation into the cultivated philosophy of the Reiki Warrior and also, in part, a response to the short time in which one may learn the three "traditional" Reiki degrees these days and the resulting loss of substance. Because Reiki is so needed, I have no qualms with people learning to lay hands on each other in a matter of days or hours. Yet, I do believe the incredible power that lies within Reiki and its practice may be missed by the seeker who is merely collecting initiations and teachings without giving over the necessary practice time to cultivate a true relationship with Reiki. I have included many personal stories to further elucidate the experiential nature of Reiki to emphasize that the student should seek his own experiences and find a balance with the mind's ability to use logic and reasoning.

This book can benefit anyone, but it is specifically intended for Reiki practitioners of all degrees. It must be emphasized that the necessary attunements are required to practice Reiki properly. Anyone who is looking at the spiritual path at any level can benefit from the various exercises and the wisdom that I share with readers. The unique approach through the archetype of the Reiki Warrior will enhance Reiki practitioners of any lineage. One does not need special training—other than the basic Reiki attunements—to start working with this book and infusing the exercises and applications into your daily practice.

I encourage Reiki practitioners of all levels to work with each segment of the book with all the knowledge you have gained. For example, Reiki One practitioners can fully use the first seven chapters as well as certain Reiki exercises from the later chapters. Although the Reiki One practitioner does not know the Reiki symbols yet, one could still practice any of the exercises that do not require that knowledge, such as the Meeting a Guide journey or the Golden Sun Healing. Likewise, I have noted, even in the basic Reiki One exercises, ways to use them with the advanced knowledge of a Reiki Two practitioner. Although you still need the proper attunements for each level, reading all of the sections and incorporating what you can into your daily self-healing and work with clients will enhance your Reiki immensely, allowing it to permeate all aspects of your life.

The book is designed to enhance each Reiki degree by section, yet the reader can either read it straight through or skip around to various sections that suit her personal growth at the time. This book aims to be both an experience for the reader and a resource for the Reiki practitioner and teacher.

A NOTE ON THE EXERCISES

The exercises in this book are specifically designed to be built upon in order to form a full practice. For example, once you have firmly established the ability to visualize your grounding cord (Exercise 1.1), you can then add the exercise in Chapter Two called Rising Earth (Exercise 2.3) and effectively do both exercises together as one. These exercises are intended to be used as a daily practice both for yourself and for every healing that you do, to gain the full benefit of the healing work. Eventually, you will become adept at establishing your grounding cord and cleansing the aura, or energy field, so that only a few minutes are necessary to practice the resultant combination of the exercises. I would like to also add that occasionally a student cannot visualize the grounding cord or visualize during other exercises. This is not important as long as you have a sense of groundedness and the intention is there to connect to earth and cleanse your energy field. You may need to include a physical activity, such as touching the earth, with your intention. Almost all people eventually see some kind of visualization, but if you can't, don't worry. The purpose of these exercises is not to have beautiful visions but to ground and connect with the body to enhance your healing practice. For the exercises throughout the book, you may find it helpful to tape record them ahead of time so you can focus more easily on the visualization.

MY PERSONAL REIKI STORY

When I was only nineteen years old, I learned I had Hodgkin's disease, a treatable cancer that grows in the lymph system. After six months of chemotherapy, practicing basic visualization techniques, dancing furiously in the late night, and being exposed to every kind of needle and blood worker in the clinic, I emerged healed, curious, and revitalized by my survival. A year later, I found myself working in a vegan/vegetarian café and grocery as a cook, learning about nutrition, health, and a preventative lifestyle. At that time, it began to dawn on me that my cancer journey was truly a spiritual transformation and somehow, it wasn't just the chemo that had cured me. I became fascinated with any and all the New Age information I could get my hands on: from herbs to amino acids to crystals to chakras. Meeting my teacher Rowan Wilson was to be a catalyst for my fusion of the spiritual practice of Reiki with the succinct Warrior path.

The following months were spent training in Wicca, contemporary paganism that celebrates the earth and the feminine, which taught me the essential tools of offerings, intention, trust, grounding, aura clearing, and protection. These elements, combined with creating sacred space, dancing to the rhythms of the moon, and exploring the chakra system, shaped my approach to the Reiki path. My Reiki Master is a former High Priestess and brought aspects of the Goddess into our Reiki attunements; with this background, I was able to successfully blend my teachings into a unique Reiki practice. After studying Wicca and Reiki for over a year, I then practiced in a Baltimore Reiki clinic, where I was exposed to various lineages of Reiki and alternative therapies. At the clinic we treated all kinds of people, including the homeless and people with chronic unknown ailments, which opened the door for strong compassion to arise within me. Also, contact with different lineages helped me not to attach to one way of using Reiki but to allow it to flow like water, as is the true nature of Reiki healing.

As my experience of Reiki evolved, I found that my Wicca training became essential in the practice of Reiki. During my Reiki Master training with Wilson, I also incorporated the use of the chakra system. Barbara Brennan's unsurpassed book *Hands of Light*, which explores the Human Energy Field, gave me more tools to practice seeing auras and exploring through feedback with my fellow Reiki students. I learned how to listen keenly to my growing powers of intuition and to take note of the various symbols and colors that appeared through the early stages of clairvoyant perception. Over time, through the use of the Reiki symbols, laying-on-hands, and distance healing, I have been able to cultivate a one-pointed concentration that aids in my clairvoyant discernment and benefits my clients.

I continued to practice and teach Reiki as I traveled extensively through India and other parts of Asia. My skills grew steadily with time as I received my first Tibetan Buddhist teachings and empowerments in Ladakh, north India, which is situated geographically on the high desert Tibetan plateau. Back in California, I studied Kundalini Yoga[1] under the direction of a

---

1 Kundalini Yoga involves specific meditation practices to develop the chakras, or energy points, within the aura. This is explained further in Chapter Five: The Chakra System.

follower of Osho's teachings and chakra meditations. Further years spent in India gave me the time to research the compelling history of the chakra system, through my Yoga Teacher Training course at Sivananda Ashram as well as by delving into such annotated texts like *Tibetan Yoga* by Evan Wentz and the ancient works from the Vedas translated by Sir John Woodroffe. My Tibetan Buddhism studies and initiations have continued with my current teachers of the Karma Kagyu lineage and supplement my work with Reiki.

The Warrior archetype has remained an invaluable tool in connecting the varied traditions within a disciplined Reiki practice. The way of the witch in Wicca, the Tibetan Buddhist Shambhala Warrior, and the methods explored by Don Juan in Carlos Castaneda's books all utilize this incredible mix of power, visionary work, and focused discipline to achieve amazing results. When this fusion is poured effectively into the container of a Reiki practitioner, a new kind of Reiki emerges, one that is truly powerful and beneficial to all sentient beings. This kind of Reiki permeates every moment of life, leading each action to be mindful, powerful, and joyous. Journeying deep into our very beings, learning the Reiki tools, and stepping more firmly onto the spiritual path enables us to become more open, more balanced, and to hold the potential for great healing.

I have now given hundreds of Reiki sessions and taught dozens of students from around the world. I hosted a weekly Reiki share for several months on the roof of my home in Kerala, south India, which enabled practitioners from all lineages and disciplines to share various techniques and methods of Reiki. My teaching has flourished in ways I never knew possible and I continue to grow and learn on the Reiki path, further opening myself to the spiritual dance on this earthy plane of life, integrating the blessings and wisdom that are found in each wondrous day.

Katalin Koda
Dharamsala, Himalayas, India
AUGUST 2007

REIKI ONE
feeling the flow

This section is for any person interested in healing and Reiki in general. It is useful for all degrees of Reiki practitioners and provides further information for teachers of Reiki. An exploration of the Reiki symbol, meaning, and the history of Reiki is provided, as well as my own personal lineage. I have cited several sources in this section so that the reader may find ways to continue exploring Reiki history. Although the main focus of this book is not scholarly, some research was done to provide a more satisfying background of the history of Reiki, which has been so vague in the past.

The six Reiki Warrior tools in Chapter Three can add to any healer's practice and specifically aid the Reiki practitioner. The focus of the first degree for Reiki Warriors is on connecting deeply to one's form through grounding and self-healing. Also introduced here is the chakra system, which provides a clear and effective map for healing the body in combination with the energy field. The hand positions provided are unique to the Reiki Warrior method and can be effectively worked with by any level Reiki practitioner to benefit healing sessions. Further techniques are provided for clearing the aura and negative thought forms, which will bring about deeper healings for the Reiki Warrior on the sacred path.

1

Earth Meeting Sky

Every time I speak with someone who has not heard of Reiki, they ask me, "What is Reiki, exactly?" I tell them Reiki is a healing art that uses hands either on the body or in the energy field. Reiki has its roots in Japan but has been practiced worldwide for centuries. Reiki is Spirit-guided energy and does not come from the practitioner but *through* the practitioner. Reiki invokes the sky wisdom of the upper chakras but utilizes the earth body to promote healing; it is the violet bridge between the heart and the mind, cultivating compassionate wisdom within the practitioner. Reiki is a way, a path, a knowing. Reiki is a way to promote healing and change on all levels—physical, emotional, mental, and spiritual. Reiki is life-affirming, bringing joy and clarity through the daily practice of self-healing and assisting the healing process in others. The person who first asked the question looks at me intrigued, but often still has no idea what Reiki is exactly. Then I suggest they experience a Reiki session, as this is the first step in truly knowing Reiki.

My first experience with Reiki came during my first attunement, in which my Master did some things around my head and around my body. I felt very peculiar during the attunement, saw a myriad of colors swirling around, and heard a faraway sound I would now say is similar to the sound of Tibetan singing bowls. Oddly enough, I didn't think much of the experience because whatever psychic awareness I had cultivated up until that point virtually disappeared after that attunement and it would be another few years before I began to "see" auras once again. Losing that psychic ability was a blessing in disguise, as it put me in a place of humility and softened the egotistic tendency that can accompany one with healing powers. Sometime in the following year someone told me about the colored bubbles Mikao Usui, the founder of Reiki, had witnessed during his culminating *satori*, or enlightenment, in Japan, which led to the incredible teaching that is Reiki. This resonated with my first experience of Reiki and

I knew that I had found something that was worth pursuing. Although I experienced very little on the psychic level for the first years of practice, people responded positively to my treatments and I progressed through Reiki Two, practiced intensively for a year, and became a Reiki Master just a year later.

Looking back ten years later, I feel I am just beginning to enter Reiki mastery. For many years I simply called myself a Reiki teacher. Although I understood and taught the three degrees and was very familiar with the energy healing that is Reiki, I don't think I began to come into a more complete knowing of Reiki until the past year or so. This was a year of synthesis in many ways, when my years of Wiccan training, meditation practice, Tibetan Buddhist studies, Yoga practice, and work with shamanic journeying all merged into an incredible fusion of various traditions in the wondrous and harmonious practice of Reiki healing. It would be impossible for me to separate the various qualities I have learned, and instead I have formed a distinctive integration of these traditions. The opportunity to write this book came at a peak moment in my life, when I dedicated myself not only to a certain spiritual tradition, but also to a certain spiritual teacher. And although this tradition comes in the cultural context of Tibet and has its certain shades or ways of doing things, I must emphasize that these are simply the "colors" that resonate with me and my path. I have not given up any of my qualities of Wicca or yoga or being a mother, but simply absorbed them into each other, which is an aspect of Buddhism. *Bodhi* or *buddha* means, simply, "awake," or "awakened one," and where I discover that awakening is within the practice of Reiki. This awareness, compounded with my personal approach to Reiki using disciplined wisdom, has led me to develop the philosophy that is Reiki Warrior.

THE REIKI WARRIOR

My development of the Reiki path into Reiki Warrior stems from my training, which coincided with a yearlong exploration in the magickal arts known as Wicca. *Wicca* means to bend or shape in accordance with one's intention. In this form of contemporary paganism, we learned to honor the feminine and its power found in the seasons of the Earth and the cycles of the moon. My Reiki Master was a former High Priestess of a coven[2] and the teachings we received were linked to specific acts, such as working with elements, creating sacred space,

2   A coven is an exclusive group of women or men and women that meets to do magickal work together.

and tapping into the Earth's energy. We learned to set intentions for our lives, to recognize the interconnectedness of all life forms on Earth, and to work with the four elements of air, fire, water, and earth and their links to the four directions. These connections, although they vary cross-culturally, are found in ancient societies everywhere as well as in the contemporary cultures of India and Tibet, where the deep connection to nature and the Earth is still honored.

Working deeply with the natural rhythms and cycles of the Earth and how they connect to my body fueled my personal connection to Reiki. This work with Earth energy helped to illuminate the particular qualities of Reiki. I knew that I felt very differently when I "drew down the moon," or called up the individual elements of water, air, or fire, than when I worked primarily with the Reiki healing energy. The Reiki was certainly more sky-like, more transcendent and ethereal. With time, I found that this was connected to the upper chakras that are seeded and activated in Reiki. This concept will be further explained in Chapter Sixteen: Giving the Gift of Reiki. The Reiki Warrior is one who combines these two qualities: the powerful life-force energy of the Earth and the transcendent healing qualities of the ether. I continuously apply my magickal training as I practice Reiki healing, which specifically includes: making offerings, setting intention, grounding, aura clearing, and protection. These practices are fully discussed in Chapter Three: Reiki Warrior Tools and can be easily learned and used by anyone to enhance their Reiki practice.

As the years passed, I have had many students benefit from these practices in staying centered and firmly rooted to the Earth. We are, after all, walking this path as a human body, trying to alleviate the pain and suffering of others. It is important to maintain an awareness of form, a connectedness to the mundane activities of our daily life. After spending so many years in India among the seekers of the "magical mystery tour," I have met people who are floating, lost in their blissful, psychic wonderland with no real anchoring to the reality of Earth, form, and matter. A few of my Reiki students were so sensitive to the attunements that they have literally passed out when trying to practice the healing session. When they came to, they felt even more spaced out instead of revitalized. Using the tools of the Reiki Warrior can alleviate such occurrences and prevent them from being an obstacle in the path of Reiki.

Oftentimes, Westerners who find a spiritual path and begin to practice find they may sense a strong disconnect with the society, friends, and family around them. This disconnect can occur because the spiritual path is so different from their mundane activities of so-called "worldly life." Especially if the spiritual discipline a student has chosen is culturally very different from her life experience, she may strongly identify with the cultural context and the special rituals associated with it, without knowing how to truly apply the wisdom to everyday life in the West. This may lead the seeker to lose herself along the way and disconnect even further from reality in an effort to escape the mundane qualities of a regular existence. For example, I have witnessed many seekers among the Tibetan Buddhist tradition who view the magic of the ceremonies, the power of the lama chanting on his special dais, and the smell of the juniper and cedar wood as an "advanced" form of existence. When the student returns to the Western world, though, she may find with these magical elements missing, that she cannot regain the "mystical experiences" felt among the Tibetans in the Himalayas.

The key to this issue is simply integration and practice. We must remember that the spiritual wisdoms applied to daily life and the mundane world provide us the perfect opportunity to practice what we have learned, regardless of whether the mystical sounds of Tibet resonate through the air or not. Sacredness is found everywhere and anywhere. The art of Reiki healing and, in particular, the Reiki Warrior path, provide a focused practice that can be used in any environment to strengthen the spiritual awareness through healing while grounding the practitioner with practical methods.

I chose the symbolic archetype of the Warrior based on Carlos Castaneda's definition of the warrior, which is a person who walks the path impeccably, one who knows with clarity the proper use of energy. "A warrior chooses a path with heart, any path with heart, and follows it; and then he rejoices and laughs. He knows because he sees that his life will be over altogether too soon. He sees that nothing is more important than anything else."[3] This means that the Reiki Warrior healer is working toward full awareness, cultivating mindfulness in each action, each spoken word, and each thought. The Reiki Warrior is not fighting against others, but instead actively lighting the path in an effort to heal himself and show others the way to follow. The Reiki Warrior uses precise tools to enhance her practice as well as to empower her clients and students. The Reiki Warrior must have determination and courage, as this path is not for the faint of heart or weak-willed. This path requires careful attention and flawlessness from the practitioner. The Warrior is one who is both precise and mindful in his actions, speech, and thoughts and who uses every opportunity to aid his spiritual development. The Reiki Warrior is one who gains an incredible degree of perception, awareness, and healing

3   Castaneda, *A Separate Reality: Further Conversations with Don Juan*, 217.

power through the careful cultivation of the Reiki practice of laying-on-hands, healing the energy field, and focused visualization of the symbols. With time, the path leads to incredible realizations of the subtle bodies, the understanding of impermanence, and the wondrous witnessing of the interconnectedness of all things.

THE REIKI SYMBOL

Reiki has its roots in Japan, both through its history and the word itself. Symbols are the most important aspect of the Reiki tradition in the sense that they are unique to Reiki and are the very seeds that allow practitioners to begin healing the self and others. By looking to the Reiki symbol, we can further investigate the deeper meaning of Reiki. The Reiki symbol is written with two Japanese *Kanji*, which is a kind of pictograph meaning that the pictures represent the word itself. Kanji is also a kind of ideograph in which the symbols represent the sounds that form its name.[4] The Reiki symbol is comprised of two Japanese words, *Rei* and *Ki* (pronounced Ray-Key). Figure 1.1 (right) depicts the modern derivative for the ancient Reiki symbol seen in Figure 1.2 (bottom right). According to Walter Lübeck[5], the second version contains more clues to the true meaning of Reiki, as the older version was later whittled down to the contemporary version through spelling changes.[6]

Figure 1.1

First we will look at *Ki*, the bottom half of the symbol which means "energy," or "vital life force." Ki is synonymous with Chi as in Tai-Chi, Prana, or life breath of the yogic path and Orgone energy.[7] Ki is the fluid, bioenergetic force that circulates through all living things. Ancient Sanskrit texts depict a carefully mapped network of energy channels that are connected to the body through major energy vortices or spinning discs, called chakras. This will be discussed further in Chapter Five: The Chakra System. Similarly, in ancient Chinese medicine, the body is connected to an energy field via an intricate system of channels called

Figure 1.2

4 Defined by Bronwen and Frans Stiene from *The Reiki Sourcebook*, 7.

5 Walter Lübeck is a spiritual teacher and Reiki Master, author of several books, including *Rainbow Reiki*.

6 Lübeck, "The Meaning of the Reiki Character," Lübeck, et al., *The Spirit of Reiki*, 44.

7 Wilhelm Reich studied the human energy field in the early 1900s and called the flow "Orgone."

meridians, which carry the necessary Ki or Chi to the vital organs and tissues of the body. Castaneda, in his study of shamanism and the Warrior path, also discusses the presence of luminous threads in the energy field. He further expands this view to incorporate the threads that not only work in our energy field and body, but interconnect us with the universe.[8]

Ki, like sunlight, is all pervasive and nourishing and gives life to all creatures and plants on earth. Ki is blocked when stagnation or disruption occurs in the energy channels of the body. When blocks or stagnation accumulate over time, they can turn into disease. If we look to unblock the Ki before it manifests as disease we can work through the process using laying-on-hands and revitalizing the body or earth through Reiki. This process is further understood when we examine the *Rei* part of *Reiki*.

Rei, the top Kanji symbol, is translated as "spirit," "vitality," "spiritual," or "consciousness." This is akin to our Higher Self, our soul or *Atma*, Sanskrit for "soul." Other meanings of *Rei* include "respect," and "honoring." In the East, the importance of respect and duty is taken very seriously. One must cultivate a sense of respect or honoring for the parents, family, community, country, and planet. As a healer, this is illuminated in the way one respects oneself and honors spirit. By holding our Ki in reverence, honoring it through spirit, we can begin to unblock the stagnation and disease that prevents us from being whole. This is meant not only in the physical body, but also the emotional, mental, and spiritual sense as well. By working deeply through honoring and revitalizing our energetic life force, we can find peace and joy within.

Interestingly, Lübeck has translated a unique alternative to the meaning of *Rei* that illuminates the connection between Reiki and the earth through the Warrior path. He indicates that the older version of the Rei symbol can also be translated as "rain-making."[9] What does this mean exactly, rain-making? If we think of the Ki as rain, or the fluid waters of life, we can see that by making rain, or practicing Reiki, we are calling forth the healing energy flow. This is reminiscent of a story told by Alberto Villoldo, a contemporary teacher of ancient Incan shamanism, who went for a walk in the mountains with his shamanic teacher.[10] They came upon a village that had suffered from drought for a long time. The people in the village asked Villoldo's teacher to call the rain. His teacher agreed and went to a hut to fast for several days.

8 Castaneda, *The Power of Silence*, 3.

9 Lübeck, "The Meaning of the Reiki Character," in Lübeck, et al., The *Spirit of Reiki*, 50.

10 Villoldo, *Mending the Past and Healing the Future with Soul Retrieval*, 129.

He then emerged and disappeared to the mountains. Hours later, the rains began. Villoldo, in astonishment, asked how he did this. The old shaman replied that the village was so out of balance that he too was also out of balance upon entering the village. Villoldo's teacher had to fast to regain balance and only then was he able to go into the mountains to pray rain. Villoldo asked him, then, "You mean you prayed for rain?" The shaman shook his head, smiling and repeated, "No, I prayed rain." He didn't pray for rain, he became the elements of earth and sky and drew the necessary life force, the Ki— rain, in this case—to the place that needed it. This is exactly what happens in successful healing; Reiki Warriors learn to "pray rain" by becoming the channel to open and allow the healing to occur. We don't pray for the energy to come, we simply open and receive the Ki, which moves through us and into our client.

Thus, when put together, Rei-Ki is the focused life force or "Spirit-guided energy" that is inherent and accessible to all living things and used for healing. Reiki is like the pyramid hanging in the window, directing the pervasive sunlight or Ki into a brilliant, focused rainbow that enhances the life force. Oftentimes, the Reiki within remains untapped until a person begins to walk the spiritual path. Then the person will begin to rise from the muck of self-delusion toward the innate clarity of self-realization. Reiki is the Tao, the Way, the Be-ing, the quiet within that takes the specific form of healing, of laying one's hands upon one's self or others to bring about wholeness.

QUALITIES OF REIKI

Reiki has very precise qualities and aspects. The first and most important is that Reiki is passed through an attunement or initiation process. In this way, the Reiki Master energetically transmits the power of Reiki through the symbols. The initiation is not merely a gesture or empty ritual but an actual transmission that has been handed down from the very first Reiki Master, Mikao Usui, through an unbroken line to the student receiving the attunement. Although healing is innate within each of us, along with our basic qualities of power, wisdom, and clarity, most of us have a hard time accessing this sky-like essence on our own. By receiving a Reiki attunement, we are given the appropriate tools to tune in to this quality. The universal life force that drifts through all living beings is transformed when it touches the energy field of a practitioner. The healing energy is activated by the Reiki symbols that have been placed in the aura by the Reiki Master.

The second aspect inherent to Reiki is that it is a lineage. Although the practice of laying-on-hands has been around for millennia, the particular shade of healing that is called Reiki stems from a traceable lineage. Reiki is passed from Master to student as water flows down streams, occasionally changing form or direction but never losing its consistency. In this way, Reiki has maintained a largely oral tradition, which is then expressed by each Master in a way that best suits her students.

Third, Reiki is different than other laying-on-hands methods because it uses the power of symbols to firstly attune the student and later to enhance and refine the healing technique. The symbols act like radio antennae to shift the Ki into an effective healing process. Symbols are learned in the second degree of Reiki and used for advanced healing work as well as sending Reiki through time and space.

Another way that Reiki is different from other methods is that the healing energy moves through the practitioner, but does not come from the healer herself. Although other healing methods may also work in this way, this is an important focus for the Reiki practitioner, which enables the healing to only be used for "good" or the well-being of the client. Again, the symbols are the activating control for the healing symbol. The Reiki practitioner learns quickly to "get out of the way" of the energy coming through them, enhancing the healing session.

In my ten years of working with Reiki, I have found that it has an ethereal quality that is often seen by students during attunements and practice as a brilliant violet color. This can be attributed to the ajna, or forehead chakra, which contains the omniscient wisdom of the larger Self, the part of oneself that is connected more deeply with knowing. In the Reiki Warrior attunement process, the student's heart, throat, and forehead chakras are seeded in Reiki One, then activated in Reiki Two to promote a direct connection between the mind and heart. This helps the practitioner to cultivate a high level of awareness founded on the compassion of the heart.

A Personal Experience

Reiki energy does have a very clear and precise quality that is different from our own energy, which I witnessed firsthand with my daughter. I rarely give her Reiki, as she has an abundance of vital life energy moving through her naturally. Yet, as her mother, I naturally identify strongly with her when she is in pain or feels sad or upset. When I hold her close, I can feel a kind of magnetic connection between us that, I later realized, is definitely not the Reiki.

One evening when she was only a year old, her new teeth were bothering her as they broke into her gums. I laid her across my belly and put my hands on her cheeks. At first I felt the normal heart connection we have, a kind of strong magnetism between mother and child that is more akin to the feeling I have with my own parents, close friends, dear ones, and the Mother Earth. This quality is similar to magickal energy: joyous, abundant, and emotional. As I felt this for my daughter, I suddenly noticed a certain shift in the energy flow, like a light turning on, and it began to move rapidly like pins and needles through my hands, vibrating very fast. I knew instantly this was the Reiki, moving in to heal her teeth. She fell asleep a few moments later, relaxed from the Reiki. The Reiki almost seems like an impersonal, laser-like intelligence turned on to activate the healing process, very different from the intense, emotional, personal connection that my daughter and I normally share.

EXERCISE 1.1: *Grounding Cord* use before & after Reiki Session

The purpose of this exercise is to form a connection to the Earth. This connection is essential for all people and especially for healers. Our Western societies have lost touch with the Earth connection and we spend a lot of time in our heads, mentally draining ourselves with memories of the past and dreams of the future. If we cannot learn to ground properly as healers and practitioners on a spiritual path, our mental fantasies will shift into the healing arena, distracting us from the work at hand. Grounding helps us to be more firmly in the here and now, to recognize the vastness of every moment that is inherent to existence, and to touch the spirit of our planet Earth who nourishes us each day that we spend here.

To do the following exercise, it is recommended that you either sit in a cross-legged position or on a straight-backed chair. Keep the spine straight and focus on a few breaths. Concentrate on where you are sitting. Notice the feeling in your buttocks, legs, and feet that press into the floor or ground beneath you. For this exercise, bring your attention down to the base of your spine, to the chakra that resides there, the root chakra or muladhara.[11] This is located just below the cervix for women and inside the perineum for men. To do this, you can drop your awareness down into the base of the spine using the exhale. Imagine your breath as an anchor falling down, down into the body, feeling the warmth at the base of your body. Keep the concentration focused on the muladhara for several moments. If possible, visualize the muladhara as a clear red orb, slowly spinning. If you can't see this, simply try to gain a sense of warmth or heaviness sitting at the base of the spine. Concentrate on the chakra for several moments.

Then visualize a clear, bright, red root or cord growing downward into the floor below. Allow the root to continue downward, into the rooms or ground below. The root or cord slowly sinks into the soil of the Earth. Imagine the roots of other plants around you, growing alongside as you allow your root or cord to grow deeper into the moist earthiness of the planet. Grow deeper into the rock of the Earth, the heavy, warm granite. Allow the cord or root to continue on, through the water below the rock and then into the minerals and ore of the deep parts of the Earth. See the crystals and minerals here, as you continue on to the Earth's fiery core. Imagine, as you reach the center, that you are plugging into the energizing core of the Earth. Feel the pulse of the planet, the heartbeat of the Mother Earth surging up through your grounding cord, into the base of your being. Spend several minutes in communion with the center of the Earth, noticing the color and form your grounding cord takes.

Notice the qualities of your grounding cord: the size, the color, and whether it goes straight down to the Earth's core or extends in another direction. Allow the energy of the Earth to intermingle with your cord, cleansing any dark or

11 *Muladhara* is Sanskrit for "foundation."

muddled spots. Notice the color of the cord, if it changes or stays red. Observe any feelings that arise as you ground. Keep the grounding cord in place, then slowly come back into awareness of your body. Touch the floor with your hands, stretch out your body as needed, and slowly open your eyes.

Write down any experiences about the grounding cord. Note its color, size, and direction. Grounding cords that are clear, free of dark spots, and that extend all the way to the Earth core show that you have no trouble with grounding and can form a solid connection with the Earth. Dark, heavy cords may indicate that you hold tension in your root chakra and legs and may have issues concerning security or are deeply rooted in the realm of the physical. Cleansing the root chakra and grounding cord will help you to focus on your well-being by balancing body, mind, and spirit. It will also help you to work through your fears. A grounding cord that strays and is not directly beneath your root chakra indicates a tendency to root or ground into the past or future, unable to fully focus on the now. Bringing the grounding cord back below you will aid in keeping you more focused on the present. The ideal grounding cord should be a clear color, four to six inches in diameter, and grow directly down. After seeing your first cord, try to realign your cord until it is clear and healthy. Use this technique before and after each Reiki session (either on yourself or others) to keep yourself grounded.

2

Reiki Roots

The Reiki story today still has few certain historical facts and many tales that surround its origin and evolution. Reiki was discovered and developed by Mikao Usui, born in a small village called Taniai in Japan on August 15, 1865. History changes as new information comes to light and much of what we know about Mikao Usui comes from the recent discovery of Usui's memorial stone and its inscription, translated by Frank Arjava Petter. Petter is a world-renowned Reiki Master who brought Reiki back to its land of origin, Japan, and authored several insightful books, including *Reiki Fire* and *Reiki: The Legacy of Dr. Usui*.

Usui was born into a Samurai family, which is a family of higher rank in the strictly structured Japanese society. He became a businessman and worked in that arena of life for many years before becoming interested in spiritual matters. He studied Kiko at a Tendai Buddhist[12] temple on the sacred Mount Kurama. (Usui would again visit Mount Kurama later in his life, which would illuminate the secrets of Reiki healing.) Kiko is a Japanese version of Qi Gong, a discipline that develops healing through meditation, exercises, and breathing practices. This form of discipline can be used for healing but requires the practitioner to first develop the energy before passing it on. Usui was very interested in this practice, as well as other spiritual matters, and became a lay Tendai priest called a *zaike* in 1914.[13] According to Bronwen and Frans Stiene's historical research, it is most likely that Usui would have been exposed to a variety of teachings that include the Buddhist precepts, Pure Land teachings, and the Lotus Sutra.[14]

---

12 Tendai Buddhism was brought to Japan in the early ninth century with its roots in the Lotus Sutra teachings as taught by Nagarjuna.

13 Stiene and Stiene, *The Reiki Sourcebook*, 56.

14 Ibid., 59.

Inspired by his practices and teachings, in March of 1922, Usui climbed Mount Kurama, where he fasted and meditated for twenty-one days. When he enrolled in a twenty-one-day program to meditate, fast, and chant, he was probably not expecting the profound shift that took place. Toward the end of the retreat "he suddenly felt the great Reiki energy at the top of his head, which led to the Reiki healing system."[15] This is described on Usui's memorial stone as an experience of *satori*[16] and is considered to be the very first Reiki attunement or initiation.

Usui's experience on the mountain can be likened to the way the Vedas[17] were "discovered" in ancient India. The Vedas are ancient texts that have no original author but were divinely revealed by the *rishis,* or seers.[18] They were revealed by sound from the cosmos, higher forces, or divine beings and were then passed down orally among spiritual seekers. Hundreds of years later, they were written down in Sanskrit.[19] I believe it is possible that Usui, like the ancient rishis of India, also heard a special kind of teaching that enabled him to both practice and pass on the special form of healing known today as Reiki. Similarly, in the teachings of Tibetan Buddhism, advanced students may receive *lung,*[20] which is a kind of oral transmission process. Transmissions are linked to particular meditative practices that have various purposes, which work toward enabling the practitioner in the process of awakening her buddha consciousness. The Tibetan tradition is not limited to the oral transmissions and contains several stories of instant mind transmissions where the master directly transmits Dharma, or the sacred teachings, to his disciple.

This may be similar to the Usui's experience on Mount Kurama, a kind of mind transmission that emanated from the collective Universal Spirit. There is no way to know for sure, but I do see certain parallels to the process of receiving mental transmissions. For example, Usui developed an almost instant ability to perform advanced healings as well as an incredible

15 Translation from Mikao Usui's memorial stone from Petter, *Reiki Fire,* 29.

16 *Satori* cannot be translated directly to mean "enlightenment," but instead as a fleeting glimpse of a higher order or sudden understanding. From Petter's notes in *Reiki Fire,* 25.

17 *Vedas* comes from the Sanskrit root "to know."

18 Seers can "see" with altered perception, such as clairvoyant or clairaudient capabilities.

19 Ancient language of India used by the Brahmin priests to record texts in secret. Also considered a divine language in which each letter of the Sanskrit alphabet has a certain sacred meaning.

20 Tibetan for "wind," or in this case, "oral transmission."

drive to spread Reiki as much as possible to help all people. This may indicate someone who had deeper experience than what we define as satori, a brief glimpse into eternity; perhaps an experience more akin to a teaching that caused a profound shift, which has come to benefit millions of people worldwide. In Usui's own words, he says that "our Reiki Ryoho is something absolutely original and cannot be compared with any other path in the world. This is why I would like to make this method available to the public for the well-being of humanity. Each of us has the potential of being given a gift by the divine, which results in the body and soul becoming unified."[21]

In April 1922, Usui moved to Tokyo and started the healing society called Usui Reiki Ryoho Gakkai, which literally translates as Usui Reiki Healing Society. There he developed six degrees of Reiki[22] and used a version of the mantras, symbols, and meditations that are still used today to aid the student in practicing healing. Usui created the *reiju,* or attunement process, to give people the tools to connect with their awake, clear nature within.[23] In 1923, there was a massive, devastating earthquake in Japan, which spurred a great level of assistance by Usui and his students using the Reiki method. In 1925, Usui opened a large healing clinic in Nakano, Tokyo, and proceeded to teach two thousand students and trained sixteen teachers. Usui died on March 9, 1926.

One of Usui's students, Chujiro Hayashi, broke away from Gakkai and formed his own clinic. He developed his own style of Reiki, including special hand positions for treating various illnesses. Hayashi went on to develop the Reiki system of healing, adding various techniques and further developing the handbook given to students. He also established the Hayashi Reiki Ryoho Kenkyukai (Hayashi Reiki Treatment Research Association), which kept detailed records of the treatments given. According to various sources, Hayashi set a standard for Reiki hand positions, and he created and implemented the formal use of a Three Degree System for Reiki initiation procedures and training program. He also cultivated a more disciplined approach and took careful notes of Reiki treatments, encouraging his students to do likewise. One of his most important students was Hawayo Takata, the person responsible for bringing Reiki to the Western world.

21 Petter, *Reiki: The Legacy of Dr. Usui,* 13. Translated from Dr. Usui's handbook.

22 Rand, "Reiki in the Eastern World," in Lübeck, et al., *The Spirit of Reiki,* 14–15.

23 Stiene and Stiene, *The Reiki Sourcebook,* 99.

Hawayo Takata was born on December 24, 1900, in Kauai, Hawaii. After her husband died, she had to work very hard to raise her two daughters alone. Five years of difficult conditions caused Takata to become ill and she developed severe abdominal pain, a lung condition, and finally had a nervous breakdown. Soon after, her sister died and when she went back to Japan to deliver the news, she came into contact with Dr. Hayashi's clinic. Takata received daily treatments and, in four months, was completely healed. Impressed with the results, she wanted to learn Reiki. At first, she was rebuffed and told that Reiki was Japanese and that it was intended to stay in Japan and could not be taught to an outsider. But Takata was so persistent that Hayashi agreed to teach her. Later she learned the degrees from Hayashi, including the final degree, when Hayashi visited her in Hawaii in 1938. She traveled in the continental United States, where she continued her healing practice and eventually trained twenty-two masters between 1970 and her death in 1980. Almost all Western lineages of Reiki today stem from these three Reiki practitioners, teachers, and Masters. Below is a timeline of the movement of Reiki from Japan to the United States.

Reiki Timeline

August 15, 1865	Birth of Mikao Usui.
March 1922	Usui climbs Mount Kurama and has satori experience, considered the first Reiki attunement.
April 1922	Usui opens healing society and begins teaching. He initiated 16 Reiki teachers.
1925	Chujiro Hayashi begins teaching Reiki using his own methods.
March 9, 1926	Death of Mikao Usui.
1935	Hawayo Takata goes to Japan for healing at Maeda Hospital in Akasaka, then to Hayashi's Reiki clinic, Shina No Machi, Tokyo. She is healed in four months.
1936	Takata receives Reiki I from Chujiro Hayashi and works in his clinic doing Reiki treatments for a year.
1937	Takata receives Reiki II from Hayashi then returns to Hawaii. She opens her first healing clinic in Kapaa.
February 21, 1938	Takata receives Shinpiden (now known as Reiki III, or Reiki Master) from Hayashi in Hawaii.

May 10, 1941	Death of Chujiro Hayashi. He made 13–16 Reiki Masters, including the first women: his wife, Chie Hayashi, and Hawayo Takata.
1970	Takata begins training others in Shinpiden, or master level, as she named it. She initiated 22 Reiki Masters.
December 11, 1980	Death of Hawayo Takata.

The timeline provides a general idea of how Reiki passed from Master to student through a lineage. Thanks to Takata's perseverance and dedication, we now have Reiki not only in the West, but throughout the world. Yet, due to the political climate of the United States after World War II, Takata passed along several false stories concerning Usui and Reiki. This was to avoid the negative view many Americans then held about Japanese people. Although this misinformation prevented students from knowing certain truths about Reiki, Takata was probably motivated by the desire to spread the necessary healing, regardless of history.

When I first learned Reiki in 1998, we were told that Mikao Usui was a Christian who traveled to the United States of America! This is now deemed highly unlikely, especially in light of Usui's cultural traditions and geographic location. Nevertheless, Usui developed a system of healing that has been passed down, mostly by oral tradition. As you have seen above, we now have more extensive evidence regarding the history of Reiki and Usui's life. Each year more information, such as the translated manuals used by Reiki teachers in Japan, becomes more accessible to the Reiki student.

While all of this is certainly of importance to the Reiki student, it is also very important to bear in mind the value of oral tradition. Reiki came as a spontaneous transmission from a divine source and has since been passed down with very little added in the way of texts or notes. Although this may seem frustrating to the Western logical mind, it is actually a blessing that has allowed Reiki to change and evolve with its unique cultural contexts without becoming static and religious. Also, oral tradition encourages each student to learn from her Master in a unique and spontaneous method, one which truly suits the student. This allows a natural and open communication to spring forth between the Master and student.

Although there is certainly a "tradition" to Reiki, it is important to note that each Master has added or changed different aspects of the teachings in correlation with the times, the culture, and the students. In this way, I believe there is no "traditional Reiki," there is simply

Reiki. After one morning meditation, I sat, contemplating Spirit and how it moves each of us in so many different ways. As a guiding force, this is the beauty of Reiki. It allows us to tap into our personal, unique, gorgeous Spirit and align ourselves with our body walking this path right here, right now. Reiki is evolving as we evolve, becoming as we become, healing as we heal. When we receive a Reiki attunement, we are choosing to become responsible for our path as healers, allowing ourselves to open up wider, to dare to live according to Spirit.

MY PERSONAL REIKI LINEAGE

Although the tradition evolves as it moves through time, there is still significance inherent to the Reiki lineage. In this way, the Reiki is like a river flowing from Master to student. Although the general form of Reiki may vary slightly in each teaching and is different from one school of thought to another, the essence has remained the same over the past decades. The Reiki Master should have an idea of her lineage and how it has been passed from Master to student over the years.

Dr. Mikao Usui

|

Dr. Chujiro Hayashi

|

Hawayo Takata

|

Iris Ishikuro

|

Arthur Robertson

|

Diane McCumber

|

Seth Goldstein & Margaret Hammitt-McDonald

|

Rowan Wilson

|

Katalin Koda

Brief Background Summary of the Reiki Warrior Lineage

Mikao Usui: Mikao Usui (or Usui Sensei, the traditional name used by Japanese students) is the founder of the Usui System of Reiki. Usui was born in Japan on August 15, 1865, in the village of Taniai. In 1922 on Mount Kurama, during the twenty-one-day fast and meditation, he spontaneously received Reiki, the first attunement or Reiki initiation. Usui later passed this knowledge through the form of attunements with healing techniques for the next several years.

Dr. Chujiro Hayashi: Dr. Hayashi, a retired naval officer, received the Reiki Master initiation from Usui in 1925 at the age of 47. Much of our Reiki practice today may be closer to Hayashi's methods than Usui's due to Hayashi's careful methods and notes.

Hawayo Takata: Takata was born at dawn on December 24, 1900, on the island of Kauai, Hawaii. After her husband's death, she went to Japan in 1935 for medical help and received extensive Reiki healing in Hayashi's clinic. In the spring of 1936, Takata received First Degree Reiki and then worked with Dr. Hayashi for a full year before receiving her Second Degree Reiki. In 1937, Takata returned to Hawaii, where Dr. Hayashi and his daughter followed to help establish Reiki in Hawaii. In the winter of 1938, Dr. Hayashi initiated Takata as a Reiki Master. She was the thirteenth and last Reiki Master Dr. Hayashi initiated. Takata then initiated twenty-two Reiki Masters between 1970 and 1980 before passing away on December 11, 1980.

Iris Ishikuro: Little information is available about Ishikuro, but we do know that she was the tenth of twenty-two masters initiated and trained by Takata. She was also a Johrei Fellowship Practitioner. Once Takata passed away, Ishikuro began charging a more moderate fee for the Master level, instead of Takata's standard of $10,000. This change is probably one of the reasons that Reiki began to spread more quickly in the mid-1980s, becoming more accessible to people of all walks of life.

Arthur Robertson: Robertson first studied Reiki in 1975 with Virginia Samdahl and then trained for two years with Iris Ishikuro. They called their Reiki system Raku-Kei, claiming a Tibetan connection, and together they are responsible for adding the techniques of "fire dragon breath" and the "hui yin breath" that are used during the Reiki attunement process. In doing this, Ishikuro and Robertson opened up the door to adding more specific techniques to the Reiki system of study. This is discussed further in

Chapter Sixteen: Giving the Gift of Reiki. Robertson also started the Omega Dawn Sanctuary organization. He died on March 5, 2001.

Diane McCumber: McCumber was trained in Raku Kei Reiki and she, like Ishikuro, aimed to help provide Reiki at more reasonable costs. She was a minister in a spiritualist church and is remembered as a warm and loving person. McCumber passed away in 2007.

Seth Goldstein & Margaret Hammitt-McDonald: Seth and his wife Margaret have been practicing Reiki since 1987. They also run Dragonheart Family Healthcare in Gresham, Oregon, an integrative health clinic offering naturopathic and classical Chinese medicine, low-force chiropractic care, and health education services to families and individuals. Seth is a 2001 graduate of the University of Bridgeport Chiropractic College, and Margaret received her Doctor of Naturopathic Medicine and Master of Science, Organizational Management degrees from the National College of Natural Medicine in 2007.

Rowan Wilson: Wilson is a former High Priestess and current Reiki Master. Her Reiki courses are a unique synthesis of Goddess, elemental magick, and the traditional Reiki healing techniques.

Katalin Koda: Katalin has been practicing Reiki along with the chakra system for the past ten years and teaching for nine years. She values the Reiki path as a means of guided discipline that she calls Reiki Warrior, an idea she cultivates into her courses.

THE REIKI PRINCIPLES

After experiencing the heightened state on Mount Kurama and coming down from the experience, Usui collected a set of principles and precepts that act as the traditional Reiki guidelines. He used the simple yet precise principles from the Meiji Emperor of the day and applied these in his Reiki teachings. These eloquent words can be put into practice immediately and honored by any person, whether Reiki practitioner or not. These principles and precepts vary slightly in different Reiki lineages but have, for the most part, held up over the decades.

Just For Today, Do Not Anger

The first two principles include the phrase, "Just for today," which reminds us to work on this part of ourselves today, right here and right now. The future is interconnected with our present and only unfolds in a way that can respond to what we do, say, or think today. By concentrating more on the wisdoms today, we bring ourselves into more concentrated mindfulness that also aids our Reiki practice.

This principle invites us to remember to be here now, to practice mindfulness of being in the moment, just for today. This is useful to repeat daily with awareness, as anger obviously does not evaporate by simply stating to ourselves not to be angry. Yet, by reminding ourselves that just for today, we will work on this emotional quality of anger, then maybe we can make some progress.

As an unpleasant feeling, anger is rooted in suffering. We all experience anger at one time or another and although it can prove to be beneficial in times of distress or threat, lashing out or acting from anger usually results in a negative outcome. I have a strong will and a passionate outlook on life that also leads to a streak of anger erupting from time to time. I found that by witnessing the anger with a quieter, more detached part of my self, I could lessen the volatile stream that was most often felt by those closest to me. This process of witnessing was very difficult at first and it took many years for me to become aware of the irritations that sometimes led to angry outbursts. At first I might only recognize the anger after it happened, looking back and resolving to do better.

After some time, I began to see a pattern: many times I felt more anger when I also felt more creative. During these high energy times when I did not have the time or solitude to create, I would say hurtful things that came from a place of anger or suffering. I made sure, then, that I always had time for my creating and solitude. The anger still appears, but as I continue to witness it, I can now feel it rising before it has even begun to manifest. With a clear mind and cultivated awareness, I can choose how to manage this stream of energy that in itself is not anger, but simply energy. Now, if I feel irritation or anger welling within, I aim to breathe deeply several times, allow spaciousness to fill the moment between myself and the other person, and watch the interplay of energy within.

Just For Today, Do Not Worry

Like anger, worry has it roots in suffering. This emotional quality is often linked to a deeper fear or insecurity that we may hold in response to the ever-changing circumstances of life. I heard a story that worrying about someone is like creating some hideous sculpture or painting filled with dull tones and bleak shadows, then sending it on as if saying, "Here, dear. I worry about you." Worry is like a burden that keeps us from letting go into the present moment of spontaneous joy. Think for a moment how it feels when someone tells us they worry about us. We feel constrained by this feeling as it cultivates an unhealthy level of attachment. This is important when we are practicing Reiki healing, to not worry about our clients. Letting go is what enables us to transform and heal. As Reiki Warriors, we must attempt to cultivate this process in our practice.

Oftentimes, I have found that many of my clients respond strongly when I have little or no emotional attachment to them. When my desire to heal the person overrides the clarity needed to pass Reiki through me, the healing is not as efficient. My husband has a bad knee at times, which is affected by his years of athletics, the weather, and constant stooping in the garden. My overwhelming desire to "fix his knee" often gets the best of me and I try too hard to ease his pain, which results in his impatience and my frustration. Other times, when we are both relaxed and it comes up naturally and spontaneously to work on his knee, the pain lessens for several days, allowing deeper healing to occur.

Honor Your Parents, Teachers, and Elders

This is a common theme throughout Asia and holds sway over many of the Eastern cultures still today. We may need to reform this concept in the West, as putting a point of focus on this simple statement is so often surrounded by complicated emotional issues. Parents give us life and although many people today do not connect with their parents, let alone honor them, we should remember the simple fact that the opportunity to experience living on the Earth at this moment truly does spring from our parents. There is a great saying that circulates the New Age circles every once in a while, which is, "If you think you're enlightened, go home for a month. Then see what happens." I laugh, because I remember returning to my parents' house countless times, telling myself over and over, "Just remain calm. Don't let them get you riled up." It takes a lot of honest self-motivation and transformation to realize that although they helped shape us, they are not responsible for our irritation and are not our source of displeasure. In fact, parents provide ample opportunity for us to practice the qualities of compassion that inhabit the Reiki Warrior.

The same respect should be held for our teachers and elders. By respecting our teachers, we open our hearts to new concepts and ideas that allow wisdom and change to move through our culture. We can also learn many things from our elders, from their experience, their trials and tribulations. This is definitely lost in the West with its obsession for youth and immortality. Elders are often seen as a burden, displaced among society. In India, the mother and father still live with their grown children, participating daily in the household, cared for as they grow old and die. There is a strong need to reintegrate the wisdom of the elders, to breathe new life into their stories. Much of their wisdom is lost with their death in the West. For example, my grandparents all had incredible skills with gardening, cooking, carpentry, and sewing. Some of this wisdom has been passed down through my parents, but how many of us have very little knowledge from our grandparents, let alone our ancestors? Although bringing elders to live with us may not be the answer in modern society, by spending time with those who are preparing to pass from the Earth experience, we can aim to learn some of the valuable lessons that come with old age, illness, and death. Time moves quickly on Earth and before we know it we too will be elders on this planet, hoping others hear our stories and experiences.

Giving Reiki to our parents, teachers, and elders provides great opportunity to enhance our practice. We learn to listen more, to move slower and with mindfulness, to open up to ways of seeing things we may have previously rejected. Reiki is also a wonderful rejuvenator for old bones, tired minds, and people who are preparing to leave the Earth journey. By participating in this process, we gain a deeper understanding of life and healing ourselves.

EXERCISE 2.1: *Building an Ancestral Altar*

This is a simple act that can be done to honor the ancestors and teachers who have passed on before you. By setting aside a sacred space for others who have left the Earth journey, you remind yourself that you too are here for a limited time and should honor each and every day. Find a corner in your home, bedroom, or meditation space and set up a small table or use a windowsill. Place on it pictures of your grandparents or items they have given you. This is also a nice place to put images of your teachers and the Reiki Masters, such as

Mikao Usui or others from your lineage in remembrance of the sacred lineage of healing light. Decorate the small altar with flowers, bowls of water, candles, incense, or crystals to your liking. Remember to clean the space every week or so and nourish it with offerings.

Earn Your Living Honestly

"What do you do for a living?" How many times are we asked this question each time we travel or meet someone new? As if living itself were not enough, we must do something for it, some way to earn our keep, to earn our rightful place to be here. We seem to spend an awful lot of time doing things for our living, but not quite enough time simply living. Practicing Reiki helps to balance the activity of doing with the quietness of being. Of course we must do something; we have energy, we are here in these bodies, ricocheting around our house, our land, our planet, and in that sense there a million possibilities open to us. By doing whatever we choose in an honest, direct, and open-hearted way, we cultivate a positive place for ourselves and for others.

Show Gratitude to Every Living Thing

Again, this is another simple concept, one that contains a deeper wisdom. We can begin to think about this word *gratitude*, or the idea of thankfulness. There are so many things to be grateful for, such as our food, water, our health, our chance to learn about Reiki and healing, our car, our children, our family . . . the list goes on and on. As for all living things, we are all interconnected with each other as human beings, with the animals, the plants, the rocks, the stars. Just because something doesn't breathe does not mean it doesn't have a living "quality" to it, and honoring that interconnectedness helps us to cultivate compassion. We can become more aware that the dish of carrots with butter in front of us is not simply butter, nor carrots, but also the soil that grew the carrots, the cow that gave the milk for the butter, the farmers who grew the crops and nurtured the cows, the truck drivers who carted the carrots across the state . . . again the list goes on and on. By spending a few moments contemplating this interconnectedness, we see, as Reiki Warriors, not only that we are the sum of so many energetic streams, but so are the clients we work on and the people we see every day.

When I was with the Reiki clinic, we worked on people who were homeless and suffering from chronic disease, some very close to death. This was a very intense time, to see that not only are some people dying, they are really suffering every day with addictions, disease, and general ill health. This experience helped me to open up my heart and feel not only compassion for those who are suffering but an immense gratitude for my own health and well-being. Those days and my time spent in India working with poverty-stricken villages remains a consistent reminder that having a certain amount of wealth and happiness enables me to take on the responsibility to try to relieve the suffering of the world.

The "Sixth" Principle

Traditionally, there are only five principles as explained above. Various Reiki lineages have differently worded the same theme, but they all contain the basic five qualities of not angering, not worrying, honoring the elders, making an honest living, and showing gratitude. These are all excellent modes of conduct that were based on Meiji Emperor's philosophy of Mikao Usui's time.

Just for Today, Be Aware

This is the sixth principle I have added to the Reiki Warrior philosophy, or way of relating to the world. Asking students to pay closer attention to each moment in life is crucial to developing concentration, clarity, and eventual insight and wisdom. Being aware of one's movement through the world each day enables the Reiki Warrior to see how each morning, hour, and minute unfolds in its own natural rhythm, allowing us to witness how each day is truly, completely different from one to another. Even if we are working the same job every day, taking the same train, seeing the same people, still each task, each interaction, each coming and going is different—this is the nature of the universe. By paying attention to life's unique moments, we can regain a joyous alertness throughout the day, without allowing the so-called doldrums to take over.

Another important aspect of being aware should be used when addressing the issue of diet and toxins. We all use or abuse something and even if we choose not to smoke cigarettes or drink alcohol, we live in a very toxic world filled with pollutants. We must use our awareness to honor our body, but also to honor exactly where we are in our path. When students ask me if they should quit smoking when learning Reiki, I encourage them not to quit anything, as I believe this will later form a subconscious association between deprivation and healing. Instead, I tell my students to become aware—deeply, intensely aware—of their need for cigarettes, caffeine, sugar, wine, pizza. When we begin to look very closely at what we think of as an addiction, we begin to see patterns and can start to watch them more carefully. When I was giving up smoking many years ago, I practiced this and felt over time my awareness grow to focus on how unsatisfying the taste of cigarettes really was. I was able to lessen my smoking to one cigarette a day, which became a meditation for me, to really focus on this one "smoke" of the day until giving them up completely. Then, I let myself grieve for them, gave myself Reiki instead, breathed deeply and completely, took the time that I was giving myself to have my smoke and replaced it with something more healthy.

I also encourage my students to try to put more of something healthy in their day, to lessen the toxicities. Adding health to our day is useful for all of us, whether we are addicted to nicotine or not. We all know by now that drinking more fresh juice, eating whole foods, drinking water, and sleeping more is better for us. If we can add a few extra minutes of quietly sitting, sipping clean water, instead of rushing about with our coffee stuck to our hands (of which I am certainly guilty many mornings), then we can begin to inhabit a clearer space over a longer period of time. Also, by adding the exercise of cultivating the witness below, along with weekly Reiki self-healing, we can lessen our exposure to toxins. This in turn will extend the quality of our time spent on Earth.

EXERCISE 2.2: *Cultivating the Witness*

This exercise is extremely simple, but as is often the case with simplicity, it can be difficult to practice at first. Cultivating the witness is an important stepping stone for the deeper process of releasing the ego, practicing deeper meditation, and discovering the inner brilliance within. We must first learn to watch our various actions, speech, and thoughts and realize how attached we are to them before we can begin to think of transcending them. This is a life-long process and not something to be cultivated in a day, week, or month.

In order to cultivate the witness you should begin with a twenty-minute sitting meditation each day. This involves finding a quiet space that will not be disturbed. Either sit in a comfortable cross-legged position or in a chair. Simply sit, close your eyes, and witness the activity of your mind. Use a clock to make sure you sit the entire twenty minutes. The first time you do this, you will probably notice the furious activity of the mind, so often deemed the "monkey-mind" by meditation teachers. After a few weeks of this daily practice, you may be able to begin watching the thoughts, fantasies, and memories that run constantly through our minds. It is important to remember that there is another part of yourself that is quiet, the part that is learning to watch the thoughts—the quiet, uncritical, non-judgmental witness.

After you begin to have moments where you are able to watch the thoughts during your sitting practice, you can apply this throughout your day. The witness not only watches thoughts, but speech when conversing with others, actions while cooking, painting, or driving a car. With time, the witness will become stronger and you will be able to use this quality more effectively when strong emotions such as anger arise and, like your thoughts, you will notice that emotion also rises and falls away whether you choose to act on it or not.

Practicing Reiki is also a natural quieting for the mind and can be used in conjunction with cultivating the witness. This will help to lessen the judgments we may cast on clients and enable more healing energy to move through us. With time, during your Reiki practice, even the witness will disappear and you will experience moments of deep, quiet peace that are a reflection of the true Self within, the part that is able to pull in the Reiki and pass the healing to others.

THE REIKI PRECEPTS

There is a story about Mikao Usui that is often told in connection with the Reiki precepts. Sometime after he came down from Mount Kurama, after his enlightening experience, Usui decided to work in the slums of Kyoto healing beggars. With time and devotion, the beggars began to heal and change their lives, looking for jobs and becoming productive members of society. Usui left feeling he had helped the people and returned to Tokyo to open his Reiki clinic. A year later he visited Kyoto, only to find to his surprise that the beggars had returned to their previous state of begging, accompanied by all the same ills and woes as before. This led him to develop the two following precepts for practicing Reiki.

First Precept: *There must be a change in consciousness for healing to occur*

Healing is synonymous with change. Healing is movement, shifting, unblocking, and repairing. Many times healings happen spontaneously when the body and mind are deeply relaxed, as one is during a Reiki session. New avenues for the Ki to move around are opened up and cellular, tissue, or organ damage can began to revitalize.

When working with chronic illnesses, emotional trauma, and mental issues, treating symptoms without the appropriate deeper consciousness change will not heal the root cause of the disease. In fact, the disease may simply resurface in another part of the body at another time. The powerful, yet often subtle, shift in consciousness is necessary for there to be not only healing in that moment, but for it to continue throughout life.

For deeper illnesses and emotional problems, this precept is important. Yet, we must also note that there does not need to be a deep shift in consciousness when treating minor ailments, such as headaches, cuts, or bruises, unless the person repeatedly has these problems, as they may then be a symptom of a deeper issue.

Second Precept: *There must be an appropriate exchange of energy,*
one that honors each

This precept enables the client to honor the healing that is happening and gives the healer sustenance for living. As you know, money is not the only way to exchange energy. I have done Reiki sessions for a variety of things in return: dinners, massage, hand-made jewelry, hugs, loving kindness. Receiving is as important as giving and we as healers should be open and receptive to the gifts that come our way from others and from the world. Reiki works no matter what amount of money we receive, and giving sessions to people who cannot afford to pay increases generosity. Accepting money is also useful to enable us to buy food and continue a healthful life. The abundance of Reiki energy, when honored, naturally spreads throughout our life and exchange becomes a way of being, instead of an expectation or a requirement.

Sometimes students tell me that ideally, they think all healing should be for free. Although this is a great concept, oftentimes, giving an offering, whether it is money or another form, is important for those who come to seek healing. Giving an offering opens our hearts, which then allows for the teaching or healing to be stronger. This is an integral aspect of indigenous cultures worldwide. Any person who visits a shaman or medicine man in the village brings some kind of offering, whether it is food, shells, or money. When I visit my spiritual teacher, I always give some offering, usually a small donation, to show my devotion to his willingness to give me teachings. This actually increases our openness to receive the healing and cultivates devotion, an important aspect of the spiritual path.

THE THREE DEGREES OF REIKI

The following is a brief description of the general way in which the three degrees of Reiki are taught today and what is included in each course. When looking for a teacher, I advise that the student look for one who has in their courses the information contained below, at a minimum. Meditation concepts and techniques are usually added to most Reiki courses along with the teacher's own personal "version" of Reiki. The cost of Reiki courses varies widely and I encourage students to find a teacher who has strong experience not only in teaching but also in their healing practice. Many teachers, including myself, offer a sliding scale that can be adjusted to how much the student can afford. That being said, Reiki is a valuable tool and should be honored with an appropriate exchange.

First Degree includes the first four attunements. (These are sometimes combined into two in my classes, depending on the number of students and class structure. See Chapter Sixteen: Giving the Gift of Reiki for more detailed information on attunement processes and their variations.) Students also learn the Reiki symbol, the history of Reiki, the personal lineage of Masters who have descended from Mikao Usui, and the Reiki precepts and principles. Students are taught how to give a complete self-healing and usually practice it in the course, along with how to give a full session to others. In the First Degree Reiki Warrior course, we also spend several hours working to map out the chakra system and its theory as well as learning techniques to begin working with the chakras, which is discussed further in Chapter Five: The Chakra System. Reiki Warriors learn the basic visualizations found in this book and students begin building an auric vocabulary. (See Chapter Eleven: The Human Energy Field.)

Second Degree includes the second degree attunements, which activate the seeds of Reiki One. Students learn three of the five traditional Reiki symbols and how to use them in healing sessions. This class focuses on sending Reiki through both time and space to oneself, others, and the Earth. In the Reiki Warrior course, we practice sending through a variety of methods, including sending elements (such as fire, water, or air), colors, colors via chakras, and the symbols. We work deeply on the interconnections between chakras and the layers in the auric field, which are discussed in Chapter Eleven: The Human Energy Field. Because Reiki Warrior Second Degree is a deeper commitment to the healing path, I have students practice for a year before going on to learn the Master degree to fully develop the necessary skills and awareness for becoming both a Reiki teacher and Master. Students must complete at the very least twenty-five full hands-on sessions with others plus another twenty sending sessions. This is easily accomplished in a year and most of my students far surpass this number in their dedication to the healing path.

Third Degree is the Master attunement and is considered a gift from the Reiki Masters. The student learns the two traditional symbols as well as any extra symbols deemed necessary for teaching and performing advanced healings. Students learn how to teach all degrees of Reiki as well as how to pass the initiations. Reiki Warrior students assist my Reiki One and Two classes to practice teaching the visualizations and hand positions.

THE REIKI WARRIOR TRADITION

Like so many Reiki Masters before me, I have merged the Reiki practice with other teachings as well. My own practice of Wicca and study of the Buddha Dharma has certainly influenced the way in which I understand, practice, and teach Reiki. The ancient honoring of the Earth and the moon and its cycles promote a quiet awareness that aids my practice. The physical connection to the Earth is ever important: the trees rustling in the breeze, the tiny violet flowers peering through snow, the layers of clouds on the horizon. All of these inhabit spaces of pure, untouched Be-ing; by honoring existence we honor our own place of Be-ing, allowing the Warrior within to unfold in her natural and spontaneous state. Reading the principles and precepts daily with the mindfulness of the Reiki Warrior, we can begin to open up to the wisdom of the Reiki path as a spiritual practice.

EXERCISE 2.3: *Rising Earth*

This exercise is used to bring up the Earth energy to revitalize the body and energy field. When you run Earth energy through the body and spine, you can aim to loosen any blocks or stagnancy in your Ki, or life force. This exercise is also a stepping stone from the Grounding Cord (Exercise 1.1) to the Auric Cleanse (Exercise 3.1).

Sit comfortably in a cross-legged position or on a chair. Keep the spine straight and focus on your breath for a few moments. Visualize the root chakra, or muladhara, at the base of your spine as a clear red orb or disc slowly spinning. Imagine the muladhara growing into the floor below, forming your grounding cord. Make sure your grounding cord runs straight down through the rooms and ground below. The average size of the grounding cord is four to six inches in diameter. Notice the color, how clear it is. If it is not straight or is too small or large, simply remove the cord by throwing it out of your aura either onto the Earth or into a "psychic fire." (A psychic fire is a visualization used outside of the aura where you can throw anything to be removed, purified, or transmuted from the energy field.) In the case of your grounding cord, it is more important to shape it so that you receive the maximum benefit, without growing attached to the way it first appears to you. Remember, this is your energy field and you can reshape it as you like at any time.

Once you have established your grounding cord connected to the center of the Earth, begin to visualize the energy of the Earth rising up from the center, through your grounding cord and into muladhara. Feel the warmth and relaxation that accompanies the Earth energy flow. As you inhale, imagine the Earth energy flowing up through your body and as you exhale, feel the warm, revitalizing energy move through your organs, tissues, and cells. Inhaling, the energy rises into the muladhara and exhaling through the legs, hips, and inner organs. Inhaling, the energy rises up through the second chakra, and exhaling through the belly and intestines. Allow the energy to rise up higher, into the solar plexus, warming and revitalizing each of the lower chakras and internal organs. As you inhale higher, feel the warmth rise up the spine, into the heart chakra. Exhale the warmth into the lungs, shoulders, and arms. Feel the energy continuously moving up through the spine, through the back, up the body and into the upper chakras. Feel the warmth in the throat, then the head and ajna, the forehead chakra. Feel the face, eyes, ears, and mouth relax. As you continue to inhale slowly, allow the Earth energy to enter the sahasrara, or crown chakra, and come out the top of your head. Imagine that the energy is a current now, running up through the grounding cord, up the spine, out the top of the head and raining back down onto the Earth, where it will neutralize. This forms a circuit of energy that will clear and revitalize both the body and energy field as well as ground you. Notice any colors or muddled spots coming out and through the crown chakra. Let the Earth reabsorb anything negative or dark. Feel the cleansing rain. Feel yourself as a channel, connecting Earth to sky for several moments.

After several minutes, come back into the awareness of body, keeping the clearness within. Slowly move your shoulders and roll out your neck. Note how your grounding cord looks now. Then, touch the Earth or ground with your hands and slowly open your eyes. Take a moment to write down any experiences you had. Did you see any colors? Feel any sensations? Note any differences or similarities that may have occurred since the first time you did the Grounding Cord visualization (Exercise 1.1). By writing down what you experience, you can begin to build what I call an auric vocabulary. This is a list of colors, symbols, and sensations that you experience while doing visualizations and practicing Reiki. You must develop an understanding of your own interpretation of these qualities so that when you see them in clients, you can better understand what is happening in their body and energy field. This is explained further in Chapter Eleven: The Human Energy Field.

3

Reiki Warrior Tools

Over time, in my Reiki practice and teaching, I have found that even with the proper attunements, a good practice, and a well-meaning heart, various obstacles do arise on the Reiki path. Although the ideal Reiki practitioner does not take on the issues, karmas, or even specific ailments of her clients, it can and does sometimes happen to us fallible human beings. Thus the use of grounding, clearing, and protecting has aided me and dozens of my students in accenting their practice with a system called Reiki Warrior to effect the most powerful healing possible.

Other obstacles arise when students have not fully developed their ability to discern between reason and intuition, which will be discussed further in Chapter Ten: Reason Versus Intuition. Also, students may not have a good understanding of where they are on the path and, instead of working carefully through the self-healing Reiki practice, they rush headlong into healing others without sensing the crucial balance of when to give Reiki and when to receive it. Thus, using certain practices, the student may alleviate obstacles on his path and benefit from enhanced awareness. The six essential tools for the Reiki Warrior practitioner are: making an offering, setting intention, grounding, trust, clearing, and protection.

MAKING AN OFFERING

Making an offering is found in a variety of forms and methods around the world. The act of offering—be it water, rice, sacred words, or a dedication—is the opening of self to receive the blessings. When we give an offering we are honoring the gratefulness toward others, our teachers, our community, our Earth for providing us with the abundant blessings that come to us. Without offering we cannot receive and we remained closed, trapped in self-delusion. In my Wicca practice we always give offerings to the four directions—incense (air) to the east, candle flame (fire) to the south, water to the west, and salt (earth) to the north. Flowers and crystals are offered to the Goddess and Earth Mother. Similarly, in Tibetan Buddhism, each practice begins with various types of offerings that will enable us to open the door to receiving the teachings. When I received my empowerments for various deities and yogic practices, each ritual initiation was preceded by a mandala offering[24] where we offered rice, performed a mudra, and chanted, which symbolizes standing at the gateway of the mandala asking to be allowed in.

Similarly, in Reiki, by giving an offering and asking the Reiki to open the door, we can then receive the abundant healing energy that can benefit ourselves and clients. We can use anything as an offering in a very simple way as long as we do it in a space of reverence and humility. Before we give a session to our self or others, simply offer a bit of incense, a flower, or a crystal. You can also make the offering in your mind, as long as it comes from the heart, but it is nice to use a physical form, as this also helps to cultivate patience by performing the act of the offering.

SETTING INTENTION

This is the most important aspect of becoming a Reiki Warrior, as setting an intention is a clear and focused point of reference for any Reiki healing. Although Reiki has its own intelligence, setting an intention brings a careful and determined focus to the practice of Reiki. Intention gives the practitioner and receiver a way in which to work with the Reiki energy. Each time I give a session, I intend a sacred space and that the healing goes for the benefit of my client. This is done simply, with little preparation. If I am working consistently on a client, over a period of time, certain physical, emotional, or mental issues will come to light. As this happens we, the client and I, find specific intentions to assist the healing process.

A Client Case History

I worked over a period of several weeks with a client who had depression and fatigue. At first, our main intention was simply to promote healing and deep relaxation. As the weeks went by, it became apparent that there was a large block and a point of leakage in her energy

---

24 *Mandala* is a "circle" or "completion" in Sanskrit, denoting a set space of having or containing. The offering is the symbolic offering of the Universe to one's teacher.

field. The intention, or focus, then turned to address these issues, in which I held the space to allow this large block to clear and dissipate and to heal the leakage. With time, we saw that the emotional, underlying issue was connected to her heart chakra and we turned our intention to this area of the aura to address the sorrow that resided there. With each session, our intention and focus shifted and realigned to what the client needed. This becomes easier with practice. In Reiki Warrior of the first degree, we are simply allowing the healing life force to move through us and this is all we need intend at first. As students become more advanced, particular intentions become apparent, and by working together with our clients we may create a powerful place of healing.

Each of my students must also determine an intention for the course when learning the Reiki Warrior degrees. This helps to shape the meaning and direction for their studies. I teach the first degree of Reiki Warrior to almost anyone who asks but reserve the second degree for students who intend to continue their healing path. This is evident by the amount of laying-on-hands practice they actually do. To train a Master I take their intentions even more seriously, as this is the time of learning how to pass the attunements to others. Teaching, along with using the advanced symbols, must be part of their intention in becoming a Master.

GROUNDING

Ideally in Reiki we are clear channels of healing energy. We become healed as we heal. We are like a straw, simply pulling the ever-abundant universal life energy through ourselves, into our clients. When we practice self-healing, we open ourselves to access more energy, just as a clear straw can pull more volume through than a blocked one. The self-healing practice enables the Reiki sessions to become even more powerful for our clients. Many healers are also empathic and during sessions can "feel" what the client is experiencing. As long as the Reiki practitioner does not take on this energy, there is no harm. Unfortunately, we oftentimes do take on others' energy unintentionally, especially when we first begin to do healing work and are unable to discern when it is time to do our self-healing. This may result in emotional instability or illness. By using the Grounding Cord (see Exercise 1.1) and Auric Cleanse (see Exercise 3.1), we can make sure that if we do take on any negative or muddled energies from our client, they will be cleared out immediately. These exercises should become a habitual practice before and after each Reiki session, along with washing hands and/or purifying them over a

Reiki candle. This way we can be sure to stay clear and grounded without taking on others' issues, diseases, or illnesses.

Other Ways to Ground

Listed below are various ways that can help you in grounding both in your life in general as well as after a healing session for yourself or others.

- **Touching the Earth** with your hands or forehead. The act of bending down and reconnecting the upper part of the body with the earth helps to bring you "down to Earth." This can also help drain out excess energy that may be flowing through your system.

- **Traditional Gassho or "Prayer Position."** This is a simple yet powerful way to reconnect your energy with the heart and center the energy flow. Bring your palms together at the heart center, thumbs touching the center of the chest. Here all ten meridians of the body are pressed together and reconnected. This position can be used to ground, set intention, and honor the self and others.

- **Practicing Reiki self-healing** is effective for a full body and energy field grounding. Set aside half an hour each week to treat yourself to a full self-healing.

- **Dancing, Yoga Asanas or stretching exercises, swimming, and/or Tai-Chi** are recommended to keep the body fit, the mind relaxed, and the Ki running smoothly. These practices are found in a multitude of resources and teachers, which are recommended in the list at the end of this book. Find a daily practice that suits your body and emotional mind set.

- **Playing an instrument, painting, sculpting, or other creative activities** help to rebalance the body and mind after a long day of Reiki sessions. When I feel spaced out or tired from spending hours with my students in an altered state of Being, picking up my guitar is a highly effective way to bring me back to a sense of balance. Find an instrument or creative method that suits you.

- **The natural movement of Earth energy** is available to us everywhere, and it helps us to get out of our mind and into our bodies. Use crystals or stones to reconnect you with Earth properties. Sit in the garden among plants, pet the dog, walk barefoot in mud, dance in sunlight, plant seeds, or visit the closest stream, ocean, or lake. The possibilities are endless. Most importantly, if you live in a city, make sure you get to the park every week, and go into the softness of Earth beauty when you can. Take a break from the mental and emotional overload of work, human interaction, and daily duties.

TRUST

Trust is a form of surrender. In other words, we are simply providing the environment for healing to occur. By trusting and opening, we become even more receptive to the Reiki flow, resulting in more powerful healings. As Reiki Warrior practitioners, we are still letting the Reiki, the intelligent Spirit-guided force, do the work. Even though we set intentions and may be using the Reiki symbols, sometimes we use our own energy to heal instead of simply letting the Reiki pass through us. In this way our ego tendencies—our habitual way of acting, motivated by self-centeredness—can become too involved with the healing process. When this happens, we become "runaway" healers and pass too much of our own life force into the family member, friend, or client. This can cause disruptions in our Ki or life force, preventing us from passing Reiki effectively.

A Personal Story

After several months of traveling through India, my partner and I decided it was time for a good, long rest in a lovely tropical village in the southern state of Kerala. I had lost several pounds by that time, as I had integrated Indian culture through my stomach as well as my senses and spirit. Although I was practicing relaxing weekly self-healing, it took more of an effort to adjust to the various creatures I ate that live in Indian waters, especially in the north, which is known for its lack of hygiene.

When we arrived in Varkala, Kerala, I was exhausted and too thin and spent days soaking up the sun and eating the clean fresh foods of south Indian cuisine. Still, I wasn't ready to give any sessions to others, but I had a harder time saying "no" to people at that time. I met a woman who wanted a session and I agreed to give it to her.

The next day before the session, I learned she was unwell and had been feeling nauseous and dizzy. I treated her with Reiki, but was not grounded; after I left, I felt immediately nauseous and dizzy. She felt better that afternoon while I was stuck in my room for two days, vomiting. It was very unpleasant and I knew I had been too open, too fragile to pass the Reiki and had simply absorbed her illness into me.

Since then, I have been very careful to take the time for my own self-healing, grounding, and auric cleansing work so as not to absorb others' illnesses into my own body. As Reiki Warriors, we should first focus on simply providing the environment for the healing to occur, giving the space to encourage healing and change, trusting that it will occur as needed.

CLEARING

Clearing the aura is an effective way to develop contact with the body's energy field and learn what affects the field. Checking in with the auric field and doing the clearing exercise will enable us to see certain patterns. For example, we may notice that we feel drained after spending time in a smoky room or with a person who talks excessively. Doing an Auric Cleanse after this encounter will help to revitalize the auric field. This also further prevents the Reiki Warrior practitioner from absorbing negative or muddled energy from the client.

EXERCISE 3.1: *Auric Cleanse*

Sit comfortably in your cross-legged position. Keep the spine straight, and focus on the breath. Again, visualize muladhara and check in with your grounding cord. Notice the color of the cord and make sure it is running smoothly to the center of the Earth. If you wish, you can take a few moments to run Earth energy up the grounding cord, through your spine, and out the crown of the head. This helps to loosen any blocks or stagnancy before doing the full Auric Cleanse.

After a few moments of running Earth energy, visualize or imagine a boundary around your body, a boundary that encompasses your aura. This boundary is usually egg-shaped, like a balloon and sits about one and a half to two feet in front of you, beside you, above you, behind you, and below you. Notice any sensations where your auric field crosses through and meshes with your grounding cord. Imagine that your aura is a bright color, forming a full sphere, like an eggshell around your body. At first you may simply imagine this boundary, but with time, you will begin to see the actual shape of your own aura. When this is possible, you can then see if you need to push out any of the edges that are too close to your body, or pull in edges that are too far away to make the field smooth. Allow your auric field to talk to you, to show you any parts that need to be smoothed out. Let your mind and/or your hands do the work.

After your field has been straightened, recheck the color. Is it the same as you first visualized or did it shift to another color(s)? What sensations did you feel as you moved and played around with the energy space surrounding your physical body?

Now, pull in the auric boundary in so it is only an inch away from your body. You are pulling in your field and squeezing out anything that is dark or muddled. Visualize your aura pushing out the unwanted or excessive energies, allowing them to flow down and out through the grounding cord. Do this for several minutes. If any images, issues, or negative words come up during the cleanse, imagine them going down through the grounding cord, taken back to the center of the Earth, where they will be neutralized.

You may or may not see negative or muddled energies flowing out of the aura and body. Maybe there is a sensation of cleansing or simply the intention to cleanse. To enhance this process, you may use a mantra, or repetitive sound, to intensify the cleansing. If you are a Reiki Two practitioner, you can use the SHK mantra and symbol to increase the level of cleansing. Otherwise, you can use the seed syllable, AUM (often seen spelled as Om[25] but pronounced with an *ah-uh-mm* sound). You can repeat this sound for several moments aloud or in your head as you cleanse your aura.

After a few moments, pop the auric boundary back to its original place and visualize your auric field filling up with a brilliant color, such as white light, brilliant blue, purple, or pink. Reshape the field as needed, aiming to visualize the aura about two feet around your body, in the front, back, below, above,

---

25 Om is the Sanskrit letter that is the Universal Sound of Creation and reverberates through the Universe underlying all of creation.

and alongside. Imagine any bright color swirling and revitalizing your aura and body. Notice the difference in your energy field, how you feel lighter and brighter.

Now, recheck the grounding cord and choose any color for your grounding cord for the day. Again, use the psychic fire to let go of a grounding cord and make a new one, if you wish. Then, come back into the awareness of the body. Touch the ground and slowly open your eyes. Write down any experiences you had. Did you see any color or have any sensations before you did the cleanse? Could you see the auric boundary and where it needed to be adjusted around the body? What colors or sensations did you experience once you were cleansed? Continue this exercise after healing sessions to be sure you are re-grounded and cleansed of any energy you may pick up from your clients.

PROTECTION

The final tool in the Reiki Warrior's pouch is protection. This is used to prevent general toxicities and negative influences from permeating our field and body. It is important to understand that we are not protecting ourselves from something in a way that promotes fear or paranoia. This is just an aspect of our intention to stay clear and focused as a Reiki Warrior practitioner. This also reminds us when to say "no." We must remember that setting clear boundaries is a form of loving kindness both to ourselves and others. Our daily protective reminder should be fluid, allowing energy to flow through, but sturdy to purify as needed. Knowing that we have the tools to ground, clear, and protect ourselves also enables us to focus even more deeply on the client during the healing session.

There are various ways to use auric protection. These include using color, psychic flowers, and the Reiki symbols. To enable auric protection, simply follow the auric cleansing technique listed above. At the end, after you have popped your auric boundary back into place, choose a brilliant color, a vivid flower, or the CK power symbol as your intended protection. Imagine the flower or symbol just in front of you at the auric boundary. You can also place flowers or symbols above, beside, and behind you or at the auric boundary for additional protection. Avoid using overly defensive protectors such as white light, a coat of armor, or fire. White light, although necessary at times, can repel almost anything and keeps us from an integrated and colorful day. This being said, use what works for you. Violet light draws people toward you in a compassionate and love-based exchange. Plants are inoffensive psychic images and work well in absorbing negative qualities. As the day progresses, check in with your auric protection and notice if the plant has wilted or the color has faded. Simply replace the old symbol with a new one and continue about your day.

The six tools of the Reiki Warrior are an essential addition to the practice of Reiki healing. They can only enhance your practice in a more meaningful and powerful way and serve to bring clarity and focus to your path as a Reiki practitioner. They are also a useful practice in themselves and can easily be applied to everyday life situations, enabling the Reiki to blossom in all aspects of your life, not just during healing sessions.

4

The Priority of Self-Healing

Self-healing is a priority for all healers. Our responsibility as Reiki Warriors is to heal ourselves. We must walk the talk and practice the Reiki that has been activated within. Only then can we begin to help heal those around us in our community and our world. We must cultivate a sense of mindfulness when we practice Reiki so that we become tuned in to when we need to rest and revitalize ourselves by doing the self-healing practice, going on retreat, and renewing our connection to the Earth and the Reiki energy.

A Personal Story

My own journey to find Reiki really began when I was nineteen and found out that I had Hodgkin's disease, a form of cancer that moves through the lymph system. After the doctors had determined that I had two major tumors, one in a neck lymph node and another in a node near my heart, I had chemotherapy for six months. Although the chemo is what reduced and eventually eliminated the cancer, the spiritual sustenance I found at that time was what nurtured me. I found out I had cancer during the dark, cold months of January. Yet, as winter turned to spring, as hair shed from my head and eyebrows, as I danced into the late night, a powerful revitalization surged through me, not only healing my body but also my mind and emotions. Cancer was certainly quite a journey and the wisdom I learned along the way was healing in itself.

Remembering that our path as Reiki Warriors is a journey integral to our power as healers. Maintaining a clear vision as we consistently heal ourselves by allowing our truer nature of wisdom and joy to spring forth is the essence of Reiki that can help to transform others. Transformation is healing. From my cancer days, I learned that healing requires one to strip away what is unnecessary, to bring forth the eternal quality of connectedness that lies within each of us.

Because I dealt with such a major illness, I was forced to face my mortality early on. This realization leads us to the idea of impermanence, that nothing lasts forever, not our family, our bodies, or even the so-called "I" that inhabits this space. By contemplating this impermanence, we also discover that we are attached to many things, people, and past memories that are inherently impermanent. Staring at my own face with a bulging cancerous lump along the left side of my neck forced me to face the realization that, indeed, my body would not be here forever. There were many dark weeks of confusion and bodily pain that evolved into a kind of inner twitching of whether to live or die. I made a kind of decision in those dark moments, a choice of "life," which then led me to become suddenly strong without thinking. As if I suddenly dropped the outer mind, my Being began to respond to change, growth, newness, and eventual wellness, which resulted in a joyous state of existence following my months of chemo.

One of the most fortunate outcomes from my experience was the seed of compassion that was planted in me. By experiencing something so dark and full of suffering, I have slowly been able to understand others' suffering during illness and, to some extent, old age. This is imperative to the Reiki Warrior path, to find this seed within us and begin to nurture it so that we may approach our clients with a level of compassion that does not judge their state of being but holds the healing space in a positive and nurturing manner.

THE ATTUNEMENT PROCESS

During the attunement process the ability to use Reiki is transferred from the Master to the student. The energy channels are then opened and cleared and the student is literally "hard-wired" with the Reiki symbols to receive the Ki that will transform into healing energy within the auric field. In the first degree of Reiki Warrior, the symbols are seeded in the energy field as well as the heart, throat, and forehead chakras. Everyone experiences the attunements differently and it is best to go into them with little or no expectation. Students have reported a variety of experiences, from seeing special colors or lights to experiencing their guides and spiritual teachers, sensing heat or cold, or feeling nothing in particular. Within days or even hours, the student will usually begin to feel the Reiki "heat" pulsing through his hands, a certain indication that the Ki is running smoothly through the body. It is important to stress that you cannot "lose" the attunement and it will stay with you for life. Yet, I have found with my students, that if they do not use the attunement responsibly—if they ignore self-healing for the next twenty-one days or do not practice laying-on-hands—the healing power will have minimal effect as time goes on. Like anything, practice is needed to strengthen the power of the attunement.

After students receive the first set of Reiki One attunements, they are able to heal themselves and others. The next twenty-one days after the initiation are a very important time for the budding Reiki practitioner. Students will go through a cleansing process that may include emotional mood swings accompanied by an overall sense of well-being and physical detoxification, such as rashes, diarrhea, minor stomach complaints, and headaches. It is very important during this time to drink lots of water, practice the self-healing every day, and eat well. I always require my students to wait twenty-one days at the very minimum before moving on to the Reiki Warrior Second Degree course. The time to practice the self-healing as well as give a few practice sessions on others is vital for the student to gain the most benefit from the initiation.

THE DEEPER WORK ON OURSELVES

As we progress as Reiki Warrior practitioners, deeper issues rise to the surface from our childhood, past traumas, or long-term karmas. In order not to drain ourselves through our Reiki practice, we must take the time to work with these intense issues and make an effort to purify them. This can be done first by cultivating a daily self practice with self-healing, sitting meditation, and the simple visualizations. When issues then come light, there is a stable ground for processing the emotional stuff that comes along with it. Also, I encourage my students to both receive and give Reiki as they see fit. Receiving from others promotes the deeper rest that helps to alleviate the emotional ups and downs of processing. Giving Reiki when we are strong heals us, as we pass the Reiki by running the higher energy through ourselves. Sometimes we must face very challenging issues relating to our past, traumas, and complicated relationships with family and friends. Remaining in close contact with your Reiki teacher is an excellent way to navigate through these rough spots while remaining grounded. As we begin to see our negative life patterns and allow them to clear, many positive, healing benefits result. We feel stronger, healed, and even more connected to Earth and our clear, brilliant nature. This, in turn, enables us to work even more deeply with our clients, to understand the many layers of human illness and disease.

A Personal Story

Several years into my Reiki practice, during one particular month, I felt a strong sense that I must not practice Reiki, but simply take time off to rest and nurture myself. As the week went on, I noticed a peculiar sensation in my throat, like a tightening or swelling. It continued to get worse and I worried a little but did my own Reiki healing on it several times a day. I met another healer who was a past-life regression therapist and I requested treatment, feeling I needed to resolve the deeper issues at work. We spent a week doing three sessions, delving into the deepest, rawest emotions I have ever felt during therapy. I faced fears, saw myself die, wept in loneliness, suffered from bitterness and regret. The final therapy session culminated in a huge release of a blocked energy that had been lodged near my throat for some time. My aura opened up and expanded and finally, my throat began to fully heal.

Now, over a year later, my throat chakra has become much clearer and brighter. Soon, I began to experience clairaudience, which is the ability to psychically "hear" certain information about my clients during my Reiki sessions. This ability has enabled me to work very precisely on my clients' body and energy fields. I also began playing an instrument, something I would have never foreseen, feeling a need to connect with sound and playing music. Since then, the Reiki sessions have become stronger, allowing me to work ever more deeply with my clients. I value the spiritual opportunity that illness can provide to work deeper on ourselves in the effort to grow more whole.

EXERCISE 4.1: *Touching Earth*

This is a simple practice that helps us to reconnect ourselves with the healing energy of the Earth. Take time one morning to go outside and walk barefoot through the grass. Try to do this at sunrise when the air is still, almost as if the winds themselves are listening to the world wake up. You can also listen to the world wake up. Walk slowly over the soil and grass, sinking your foot carefully onto the surface of the Earth. Visualize your grounding cord and feel the power of the Earth rise up into you and your body. Notice the colors of the early light changing, the clouds shifting slowly across the sky, the birds singing their morning songs. Try to see how each moment is utterly unique in itself, and you are the only one witnessing that uniqueness in that place, in that time. Walk slowly until you find a spot that feels soothing and comfortable. Sit down and practice self-healing Reiki on your heart, feeling gratitude for all the beauty of the precious world you are experiencing in this moment.

SELF-HEALING PRACTICE STEPS

Every time you give Reiki to yourself, always follow the same procedure.

1. First put your hands together in gassho, or prayer position.

2. Say aloud, or in your mind, that you are now accessing the Reiki healing energy.

3. Call on the Reiki Masters of your lineage to guide you in this practice. Intend that this practice is for the well-being of oneself.

4. Visualize your grounding cord.

5. Begin the Reiki session on your body, beginning with the hand positions on the head and working down the body. Always hold the hands relaxed, yet firm. Fingers should be pressed together, with no space between. When healing on the self, it doesn't matter if your hands touch each other or not. Apply a comfortable, moderate pressure in each position for two to five minutes.

6. Use the following diagrams to assist the self-healing hand position list.

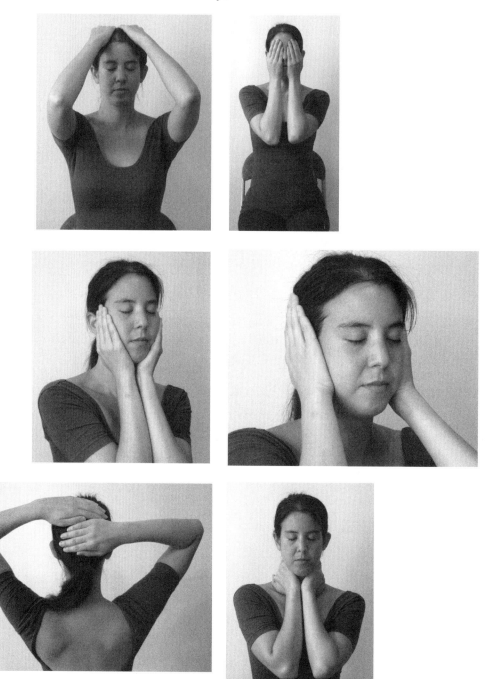

Self-Healing Hand Positions

Front of Body

1. **Top of Head:** Some traditions have you touch the top of the head and some do not. Mostly I have found that traditions that say not to touch the top of the head may have their roots in India or other Asian countries where, culturally, touching the top of the head is not acceptable. In all my years of practice, I have found no problem with direct touching on the crown chakra. This position is good for balancing the higher functions of the brain hemispheres and revitalizing the corpus callosum, the mass of neural networking between the two halves of the brain. Balancing these two hemispheres and sides of the body becomes essential for more advanced meditative practices.

2. **Over Eyes and Face:** This position starts to calm and relax the chatter in the mind. Slight pressure on the eyes provides rest for this very active organ of perception.

3. **Jaw:** We spend so much time talking that relaxing the jaw is vital for health.

4. **Ears:** This provides a rest for all the information coming in through sound.

5. **Back of Head:** This position is so important that we do it twice. Again, it helps to balance the brain hemispheres and also is the site of the Bindu[26], which holds the nectar of life that drips down from this place, nourishing our energy field during our lifetime.

6. **Neck/Throat**

---

26 *Bindu* means "point" or "dot" in Sanskrit and is a small chakra believed to produce the fluid of the life force.

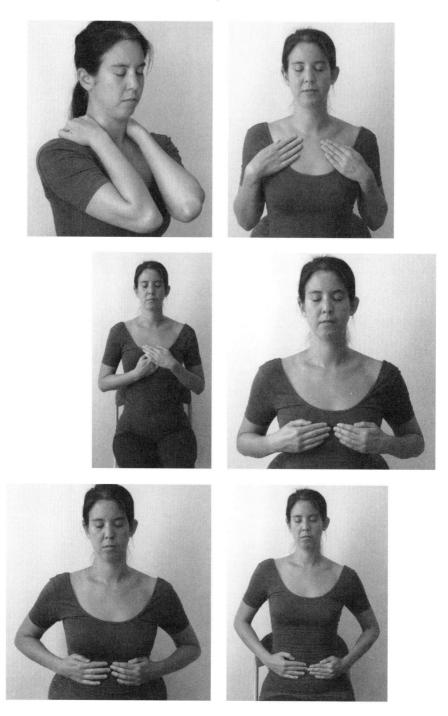

7. **Upper Shoulders**

8. **Top of Lungs**

9. **Over Heart Chakra:** Notice any sensations or colors that appear here, as by this time during the self-healing you should be sufficiently relaxed to experience the body and aura.

10. **Over Breasts:** This is essential for women, who rarely have their breasts touched in a healing, nourishing way.

11. **Over Rib Cage:** This position revitalizes several organs of the body. Stay here for a few minutes, allowing the different internal organs to absorb necessary healing Ki. When you know the placement of the organs, you can imagine them here, seeing the liver, gall bladder, pancreas, spleen, and stomach absorbing brilliant light and becoming more healed.

12. **Next to the Bellybutton:** Place hands alongside the bellybutton, over the intestines to aid in digestion.

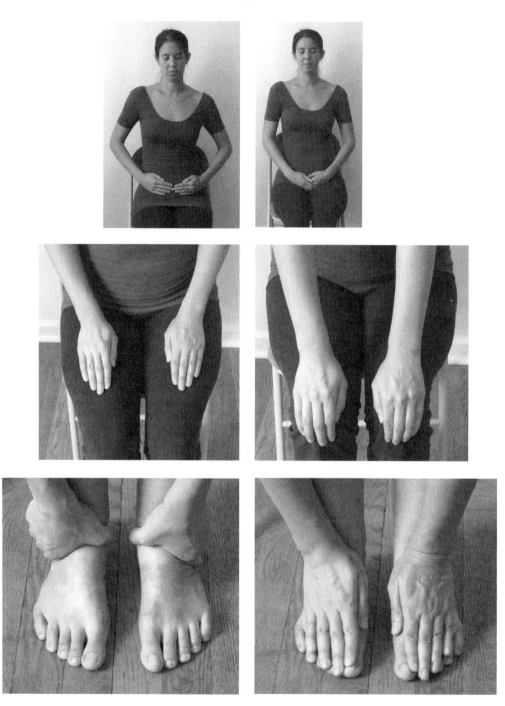

13. **Over Sacral Chakra:** The sacral or second chakra is located just four fingers below the bellybutton. Ovaries and uterus (women), bladder, lower intestines, and hips receive healing here.

14. **Genitals:** Again, this area is rarely touched in a healing, nourishing way. This is a good opportunity to touch these parts of ourselves to promote healing.

15. **Thighs**

16. **Knees**

17. **Ankles/Feet:** This can be done in two ways. You can either bend over (if you are seated in a chair) or stretch out and first do ankles together, followed by the feet. The other way is to do one ankle and foot at a time, either pulling the foot up to the thigh or as seated on the ground. (See also steps 8 and 9 on pages 58–59.)

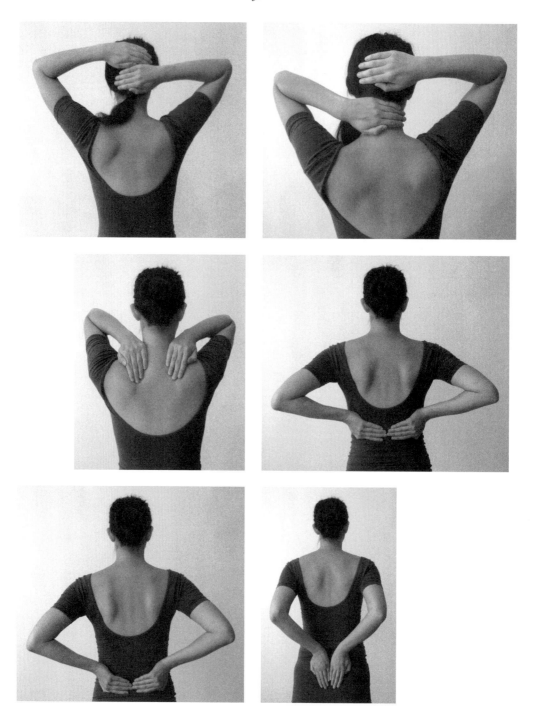

Back of Body:

1. **Back of Head:** As mentioned previously, this position is so important that we do it twice.

2. **Lower Occipital Ridge and Neck:** This is a deeply relaxing position that can aid in releasing blocks in Ki throughout the body.

3. **Upper Shoulders**

4. **Middle of Back:** This position promotes healing in the kidneys. Since you cannot reach the upper back through hands, at this stage you can send, in a general way, healing Reiki to the upper back. If you know the Reiki symbols, you can use the HSZSN, CKR, and SHK symbols to send deeper healing to this part of the body. This is important, as many people store layers of tension in their upper back and shoulders, which causes strain on the lungs and heart chakra.

5. **Lower Back**

6. **Over Sacrum:** This triangular-shaped bone at the base of the spine holds several large nerves, including the sciatic nerves that run down the legs. Relaxing and revitalizing this area helps strengthen the back.

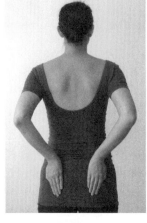

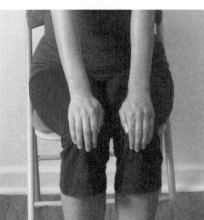

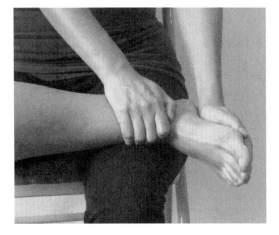

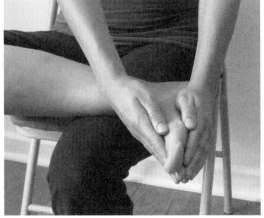

7. **Top of Buttocks:** This area helps to heal the sciatic nerve, which is often a source of back and leg pain.

8. **Knees:** We do the knees and feet again to ground out any energy that has been released in the aura. This helps stabilize or anchor the healing.

9. **Ankles/Feet**

To close the session, bring your hands again into prayer position. State, either in your mind or aloud, that the session is now over. Take a moment to feel gratitude toward yourself for honoring your healing process and toward the Reiki, your teacher, and the lineage. Visualize your grounding cord and do your Auric Cleanse (see Exercise 3.1) if you wish. The Auric Cleanse is optional, as the main function of the cleanse is to remove anything picked up from others, but it can still be done as a practice to strengthen the self-healing. Make sure to drink pure water afterwards because toxins are released in the bloodstream after healing. Write down any experiences or insights that may have occurred during the session. A full self-healing session should take 25–40 minutes, and you should always end with grounding out by giving Reiki to the feet last.

Take the time to give Reiki wherever it is needed each day. Set aside a special time and do a full self-treatment once a week. Make sure you are aware of when you need time for self-healing and nurturing. As you progress, you will naturally become more intuitive with hand placements, which is excellent. Go to the places that are calling you and simply let the Reiki flow. Once you become proficient with self-healing, you can add in the Chakra Check Visualization (see Exercise 5.1). This can be done during your self-healing by bringing focus and awareness to each chakra point to determine the overall state of health and functioning, which will greatly enhance your self-healing.

5

The Chakra System

Chakra is a Sanskrit word that translates to "wheel," or "disk," [27] yet, like many words in Sanskrit, this word has deeper esoteric meanings, including "vortex," or "wheel of light." The symbol of the loom found in the center of the Indian flag is called, similarly, a chakra and means "a spinning wheel,"[28] which evokes the more profound meaning of interconnectedness as well as the social meaning of weaving one's own cloth.

This is akin to the Vedic ancient philosophy, the yogic path of liberation through self-analysis, which derives from the root word *Yug,* meaning "to join" or "merge" by "yoking one's spirit into form."[29] This is inherent in the path of the Reiki Warrior as well. Bringing spirit into form is the very process by which Reiki works. By learning to utilize the power of self-healing and allowing the Reiki energy to move through oneself, Reiki Warriors can apply this knowledge to aid in the healing of others' bodily forms with the use of Reiki Spirit.

The chakra system has been used for thousands of years. Shamans of South America today still blow tobacco smoke into the energy points over the body to call in healing. Halos over saintly figures portray the illumination of the self-realized, a visual image of the brilliant crown, or sahasrara,[30] chakra, the energy center of a thousand petals. Tibetan Buddhists focus on the energy points found at the heart, throat, and forehead for many of their spiritual practices, the same key chakra points focused on during a Reiki Warrior attunement.

---

27 Leadbeater, *The Chakras: An Introduction*, 1.

28 Yogananda, *Autobiography of a Yogi*, 428.

29 Sivananda, *Kundalini Yoga*, xxxi.

30 *Sahasrara* means "thousand petals" and signifies the thousand energy channels that culminate in the seventh energy center located at the top of the head.

Formal, written information about the chakra system is found in the Yoga Sutras of Patanjali, an ancient Indian rishi,[31] which was written down in a Vedic text titled Sat-Cakra-Nirupam and dated 1577. This text was translated by Arthur Avalon (Sir John Woodroffe) and published in 1919.[32] The information was used by a group called the Theosophists,[33] which included revolutionary thinkers and spiritual seekers such as Madame Blavatsky, Alice Bailey, and C. W. Leadbeater. The small text called *The Chakras* by Leadbeater was one of the first sources to find its way to the Western world and, ironically, the first book to fall into my hands that talked about these mystical energy centers of the body. Later I came to find that Leadbeater's psychic, dynamic, and fluid impressions of the chakras, combined with the explanations from ancient Vedic texts, helped to make the system more accessible to the West.

Traditionally, yogic texts present the chakras as static mandalas[34] with fixed forms. Chakra mandalas are symbolic images, often circular, that contain various colors and *bijas,*[35] which are primarily used for accessing the chakras through spiritual practice.[36]

FUNCTION OF THE CHAKRA SYSTEM

The chakra system has two main functions: to vitalize the energy field and body and to aid in self-development as they are cleared and activated. According to Vedic texts, there are thousands of chakras located throughout the auric field. These are akin to the points found along meridians in Chinese medicine—small, whirling vortices that interconnect the body and the energy field. The focus of the chakra system is the seven large vortices, or major chakras, that comprise the foundation for the chakra system. Five of the major chakras correlate with the five main segments of the spine and their corresponding nerve ganglia[37] (see Diagram 5.1, right).

31 Patanjali's date is not certain but most scholars assign him to second century BCE.

32 Woodroffe, *The Serpent Power*, 2.

33 Theosophists were turn-of-the-century thinkers who aimed to blend spirituality, science, and philosophy. Their headquarters is in Chennai, south India.

34 *Mandala* is Sanskrit for "circle" and comprises a set of symbols used in meditative practice.

35 *Bija,* or seed symbol, is a sound that evokes certain frequencies that, when chanted, help the practitioner to access various levels of spiritual development. Om (pronounced AUM) is one such bija or seed symbol.

36 Swami Satyananda Saraswati's *Kundalini Tantra* from the Bihar School of Yoga is an excellent resource for the information regarding chakra mandalas and seed symbols and how to use them in meditative practice.

37 Sivananda, *Kundalini Yoga*, xxxvii.

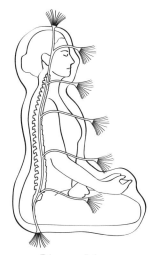

Diagram 5.1

The chakras are responsible for governing major balances in the body. The chakras pull in Ki, the vital life force, and regulate the auric field and body. This happens through a series of conduits within the aura called nadis (pronounced nod-dee). *Nadi* is a Sanskrit word that literally means "yogic nerves."[38] Nadis are found throughout the auric field and are energy channels that can be likened to the meridians found in Chinese medicine. Ki travels along the meridians, just as electrical currents travel through the nervous system. The healthiness of the Ki and its ability to move smoothly through the nadis is influenced by a variety of factors, both external and internal. The movement of the Ki then determines the overall level of functioning in the chakras. Ancient depictions show hundreds of nadis or energy channels found throughout the auric field.

Physical, emotional, and mental states; the environment; karma; and interactions with the world all play their part in affecting our auric field and the nadis found within. This in turn affects the chakra system. As energy moves through the auric field, it enters the individual chakras, energetically affecting the nervous system, which then affects the endocrine system of the body.[39] Many illnesses are linked to imbalances in the endocrine system, or glandular system, and can be alleviated if treated with the application of Reiki onto the chakras. The endocrine system has a direct affect on the blood, tissue, and organs of the body and their ability to function optimally.

38 Sivananda, *Kundalini Yoga*, 26.
39 Brennan, *Hands of Light*, 49.

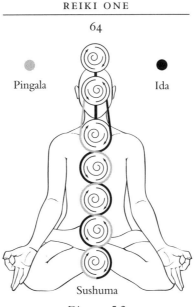

Pingala · Ida

Sushuma

Diagram 5.2

Within the auric field, three major nadis play a crucial role in the health and development of the chakras. These three nadis are: the ida, the pingala, and the sushuma[40] (see Diagram 5.2). Both the pingala and ida nadis are rooted in the base chakra, or muladhara, and then wind their way up around the spinal column through each respective chakra.

The pingala nadi, which begins on the right side of the root chakra (appears to be the left side on the diagram, as we are facing the figure), is associated with the sun, the solar activity of the day, action, force, masculine, the yang, and movement toward something. The ida nadi, beginning on the left side of the root chakra, is associated with the moon, the lunar activity of night, receptivity, stillness, feminine, the yin, and the resting point. These two nadis complement each other, as do the sun and moon, the masculine and feminine. All humans have these two complementary sides to our Being, mirrored in our complementary brain halves, our inner masculine and feminine.

In Hatha Yoga there are certain practices that aim to balance the pingala and ida nadis. In Sanskrit, *Ha* means "sun" and *Tha* means "moon"; thus the formation of Hatha Yoga, the Sun-Moon Yoga. Using yogic positions called *asanas* (postures), *pranayama* (breathing exercises), and visualization, a practitioner can begin to balance these two main nadis. Another very effective way of balancing the pingala and ida is through the Reiki self-healing. By laying

40 Sivananda, *Kundalini Yoga,* 27.

hands on oneself, the movements of these two major energy currents are energized equally and they revitalize the Ki that circulates through the major nadis and chakras.

Once these two major nadis are balanced, there is a possibility that sushuma will open and clear. Sushuma is the main current of energy that runs through the center of the spine (see Diagram 5.1), from muladhara, the root chakra located in the base of the spine, to sahasrara, the crown chakra located above the top of the head. If sushuma is fully opened, the energy that resides in muladhara, called Shakti energy,[41] can then move along the axis of the spine, clearing and activating any blocks within ida and pingala as well as the chakras.

The entire process of clearing and activating the three major nadis—ida, pingala, and sushuma—that enables the powerful movement of Shakti energy is called a Kundalini[42] awakening. Accordingly, this is a very rare event and most likely happens over a period of decades or lifetimes. If the Kundalini energy is prematurely awoken and moves through the sushuma without the proper purifications done to balance, clear, and open the ida, pingala, and chakras, the force can be too powerful and result in a variety of physical, mental, and emotional imbalances, as in the case of Gopi Krishna.[43] His story tells of various excessive sensations that moved through his body for months and years at a time, causing much distress and irritation alongside advanced psychic capabilities. The chakra system, network of nadis, and Kundalini energy is a complex system that works on many levels within the body and energy field. The true Kundalini awakening is not a minor sensation along the spine or a quiet shift, but rather an advanced form of incredible power that will organically open and rise in its own time.

When the Shakti energy begins to stir, it will pierce a *granthi*[44], or knot, in the muladhara. This knot is like a seal that only opens when the chakra is fully cleansed and activated. Once the granthi of the root chakra is opened, the Kundalini energy may then rise up from the muladhara, through the lower chakras several times before eventually piercing the granthi, or seal, that sits in the heart chakra. Thus, the lower issues of the chakras must be resolved, integrated, and activated

---

41 Shakti energy is the name given to the potential energy residing at the base of the spine. Once activated, it begins its movement along sushuma, illuminating and igniting each of the chakra centers as it travels upward.

42 Kundalini, from *kunda* meaning "coiled," and *lini* from the root *lingam* indicates a coiled energy (Shakti or feminine principle) around the lingam (Shiva or masculine principle). This potential, dynamic force is available to all humans but can only awaken fully when the human body is properly purified.

43 Krishna, *Kundalini: The Evolutionary Energy in Man,* 52.

44 *Granthi* means "knot" in Sanskrit and there are three main knots: root, heart, and forehead chakras.

before the higher wisdoms and advanced clarity of the upper chakras are truly accessed. For example, although one may have some clairvoyant abilities, usually attributed to the sixth chakra, if the "lower" aspects of self—such as desire, ego, and fear—have not been cleared and worked through, they can affect the way in which a clairvoyant both sees and uses this information. Thus it is important to balance the whole body using the Reiki Warrior tools with the brilliant seeds that are given during the Reiki attunement.

Once the granthi in the heart chakra is pierced, the Kundalini or Shakti energy will continue its evolution upward, opening and clearing the throat, forehead, and crown chakras. The ajna, or forehead chakra, also contains a granthi which, once pierced, allows the person to access unlimited wisdom. We can see the advanced qualities of unconditional love and supreme wisdom in such past Masters as the Buddha and Jesus, as well as contemporary Masters such as Amma Amritanandamayi Devi[45] and the Dalai Lama.

The spiritual, evolutionary path of humans awakens these latent energies within and will inevitably come to each of us. In terms of Reiki, the first attunement works to begin clearing these channels and seeding the aura with the potential to open and clear the energy channels in the body. This enables us to transform lower qualities of fear into love, of greed into compassion, and of anger into creativity. I advise that one work slowly and carefully with chakras to ensure proper clearing and activation is achieved within each energy center along with the balancing of the ida and pingala so that one may move along the path without harm. Finding a teacher in Kundalini Yoga is also essential so that the purifications can be done properly with care and guidance.

Besides the three major nadis, hundreds of other nadis move Ki within the auric field and into the body. Each chakra contains a certain number of nadis, illustrated by the mandalas (images) found in the chakra table below. Each mandala contains a certain number of petals, which corresponds with the number of nadis in that chakra. For example, muladhara has four nadis and is thus drawn with four petals. When a child is born, her root and crown chakras are open.[46] The muladhara, or root chakra, contains four nadis that ground down into the environment, anchoring the body onto the Earth plane. Meanwhile, the sahasrara, or crown, has a

---

45 Also known as Amma or Ammachi, she is considered an avatar, or living saint, and resides part-time in Kerala, South India, and travels the world giving hugs as her method of connection to the divine.

46 Brennan, *Hands of Light*, 63.

thousand nadis or electrical streams moving through it. The sahasrara slowly closes during the first year of the child's life, as mirrored by the soft spot upon the crown shifting and closing as millions of neurons in the brain also die off in the first year of life. The shutting down of the nadis re-forms the crown chakra into the spiritual shape of the child's path. A critical look at the first year of children's lives is a worthwhile investigation that could illuminate people's later spiritual tendencies in life.

Each additional chakra contains a certain number of nadis that ideally are open and clear, but often become blocked as the child grows due to illness, emotional imbalances, various traumas, environmental circumstances, and family situations. Our childhood pains, our gender, family, and culture all contribute to the development of the chakras. As the child grows, her level of physical, emotional, and mental development corresponds to the opening and clearing of the nadis within the chakra.

A Personal Experience

A few years ago, a contemporary and I taught a ten-day chakra workshop that included yoga, pranayama, and intensive work with the chakras. We focused each day on a particular chakra using various exercises to understand both the physical and psychological effects of each chakra. Each evening we practiced sitting meditation for thirty minutes in silence, focusing only on the breath. The course was a lot of work and I was somewhat stressed by holding the space for the class for ten days, still breastfeeding my one-year-old, and helping to manage our guest house in India.

Yet, this strain spiritually pushed me further than usual, and by the tenth night of the silent sitting meditation, I had a breakthrough. In what seemed like an instant, my left ear felt as if it popped open, louder and wider than ever before, and suddenly, like a light had been turned on, I could literally see the nadis around the upper left area of my auric field. Not only did I see the electric, brilliant currents of energy within my field, I also witnessed, for the first time, a visual image of the Reiki symbols that were seeded along the outside of my aura boundary. The symbols were three-dimensional forms and acted like tiny antennae that channeled the Ki from the surroundings into my aura and changed the quality of the energy with their shape, depth, and form, which then contributed directly to my Reiki healing power.

THE SEVEN MAJOR CHAKRAS

Muladhara

Muladhara means "foundation" and is the root chakra, the energy center that hooks into the base of the spine. It is the seat of the Kundalini energy and the point of anchoring into the Earth. When the root chakra is in balance, we feel connected to the Earth through both male and female qualities. We are secure in our form as a human being and survival is not a primary issue. We are deeply in sync with the pulse of the Earth, the heartbeat of the planet and realize we are small forms participating in an expansive universe.

We are born with an open root chakra, which enables us to connect into our new life on Earth. This energy runs to the center of the Earth, anchoring us into our form, as well as up the spine to sahasrara, the crown center at the top of the head. If some trauma occurs during our first years of life—abandonment by either or both parents, sexual trauma, illness, or any instability that is translated as a threat to survival—the child may react by partially closing the root chakra, redirecting the grounding cord, or closing it off completely. This can result in a life based in fear, rooting around for external solutions to the internal problem of feeling disconnected. Oftentimes, a blocked or closed root deeply affects the second chakra and the two work together to promote fear of the world and looking for happiness in external sources such as wealth or relationships.

We can access our root chakra through the grounding cord and help to open and activate it by running Earth energy, dancing, and drumming. The element associated with muladhara is earth and the sense is smell. Any activity in connection with the earth is beneficial for healing this part of ourselves.

Svadhisthana

Svadhisthana means "dwelling place of the self" and is the sacral chakra. It is located a hand-width below the belly button, resting just above the pubic bone. This chakra is anchored into the sushuma, the central energy channel along the spine, and corresponds with the sacrum, the triangular bone found in the lower back of the body.

The svadhisthana begins to open and connect in with the world during the second year of life, as we begin to develop a sense of self apart from the mother. This is the seat of our relationships, our way of relating with the world and others. We develop our balance, or lack thereof, between masculine and feminine here and express this through complex emotions.

This chakra is connected with sensuality, sexuality, and creativity, and when balanced enables us to have a healthy sense of sexuality and empowers us to express ourselves and relate to others.

When this chakra is out of balance it can create problems that often reflect in our emotional lives. When the second chakra is blocked, we often cannot connect emotionally to others, leaving us feeling isolated and fearful. This may result in too much energy in the root chakra, which leaves us looking for external sources like sex, wealth, and materialism to fill the emotional void that remains inaccessible in a stagnated second chakra.

If the chakra is running too much energy, or "bleeding" onto the surrounding energy field, we may be too emotional in our expression toward the world and unable to balance our masculine and feminine sides. We may look for someone who is shut down in this area to balance our overly emotional state, which results in some of the common problems found among relationships today.

The sacral chakra is connected with water, the sense of taste and the organs with fluids in the body including lymph, kidneys, bladder, ovaries, testes, and blood. Blockages in the second chakra often result in problems in these areas as they are highly sensitive to our diet and food, which is linked to emotional behavior patterns. These problems play out very closely with the root chakra and must often be continuously addressed as we grow on the spiritual path. Here desires can run amok through the need to emotionally validate ourselves and again manifest in seeking external balms to soothe our inner pain. Regaining our sense of fluidity in the world is essential and can be done through Reiki treatments, reconnecting with water through meditation, belly dancing, or creative arts. Oftentimes, deep traumas cause people to root or ground out through the second chakra, bypassing the root chakra altogether. When this happens, deeper therapy may be needed to access the traumas from the past and release them.

Manipura

Manipura means the "city of gems," and is the solar plexus, located between the heart center and the bellybutton. At this point is a massive center of nerves that directly connect into the many organs that reside in this part of the body. The element at work here is fire, like the digestive fire that is used to burn and metabolize foods. This chakra is a gateway to the mental, astral, and higher emotional forces at work within the auric field. Although primarily associated with the mental realm, this chakra also has access to the way in which we understand and mentally inform our emotional processes. The method of perception connected with the solar plexus chakra is sight, which illuminates much of our activity during the day and also what we see at night while dreaming.

This chakra begins to open during our third year of life (age two), as we are forming our will, our power to intend, and learning about boundaries. A person with a healthy solar plexus has a body and aura invigorated with healthy life force, is able to set clear boundaries, and has a strong will power. This center is full of vitality and when fully activated the person is freed from disease.

When the chakra is blocked, the person may suffer from fatigue, inability to set clear boundaries, lowered confidence, and poor digestive functioning. Over time this can have a serious effect on the surrounding organs, causing a myriad of diseases. For years, I had a weak solar plexus and I often struggled with confidence and saying "no" to people. Over the years, I've healed and integrated other parts of my energy field that kept my solar plexus from working properly. As in my case, blockages in the second or fourth chakras prevented my solar plexus from receiving the energy it needed to function fully. This center also contains psychic cords or strong energetic attachments between ourselves and others. These can be either healthy or unhealthy, depending on the type of cord and the nature of the connection. To cut unhealthy cords, refer to Exercise 14.3: Cutting Cords.

In some people the energy is too strong in the solar plexus, causing an overactive ego or will to dominate the situation around them. This often results in behavior that is aggressive and powerful and, because the solar plexus is connected to certain astral layers of the energy field, access to higher psychic awareness. We must be careful if this happens as we can act in an uncompassionate way, confusing our advanced sense of self with spiritual awakening. Learning to balance this center and integrate it with the other chakras is vital to our spiritual development as Reiki Warriors. This can be done through certain activities, such as learning martial arts through a healing perspective. This can help us to feel out the boundaries we need to set both physically and energetically as well as forming an anchor into healing. Activities that build life force are helpful in regaining Ki as well as learning how to protect ourselves properly from toxicities and draining forces.

Anahata

Anahata means "pure sound of creation" and sits in the center of our chest, between our lungs. This is our heart center, the bridge between the lower and upper chakras, and is the seat of self-love and compassion. Here the sense of self opens up to the element of air, the breath that we take in, nourished by the life-giving oxygen from the trees and plants around us. This chakra is the place where we connect more with the world and environment, opening up to the reality that we are not alone, but interconnected with the earth and the life force.

When this chakra is open and balanced we have a strong sense of self-love and a deep appreciation for natural beauty in all its forms, from the most simple to the far-reaching cosmos. When we feel deep love for someone, we connect to them through our heart center, feeling radiant, pure emotions surge between the cords that form. This is also the place where we feel pain when we disconnect with someone we've loved deeply and cords between lovers who have broken apart appear torn in the energy field.

A closed or blocked heart chakra results in low self-esteem, depression, and a general sense of low worth. This often manifests in people who have suffered a trauma and may need to be healed on several layers before it can begin to open. Also, learning about devotion and how to make offerings is a first step to opening the heart chakra. Oftentimes we are so used to taking for survival, ego, or desire and have not cultivated a pure sense of gift or are unable to truly receive gifts, compliments, or love from others. Receiving your first Reiki attunement seeds the heart chakra, planting the seed of self-love on a personal level into the energy field, which has the potential to grow and flourish in the deeper, compassionate love for the world.

A Case History

One of my interesting encounters with the anahata, or heart chakra, occurred just a year after my Reiki Master attunement. I was giving a Reiki session to a man I did not know very well at the time, and as I was working, I noticed an intense cold sensation over his heart chakra. I sensed that the chakra was completely shut down and was not working properly. The coldness was so severe and so unlike anything I had seen before or even since, that I felt surprised that he was still alive. When I investigated his aura further, it seemed that someone had kind of "rewired" his energy matrix in such a way to keep him alive until his heart could heal. This he verified after the session, saying that a Chinese medicine doctor had told him that she had moved around his energy field to prevent him from tipping over into full-blown depression. During the rest of the session, I focused on warming up the heart chakra, which resulted in powerful, yet healing, vibrations in his body. I pressed deeply into his solar plexus to anchor in the intense clearing that happened within his heart chakra, which allowed him to move ahead in his life.

Vishudda

Vishudda means "pure" and is the clear, brilliant-blue chakra of the throat. Here is the place from which the higher self communicates, not the more worldly self of the solar plexus. This chakra is a bridge between the heart and ajna, or forehead chakra, which allows for higher or psychic communication to happen based in compassion. This chakra is connected with speaking our truth and listening to our higher wisdom. When open and clear we can not only hear our intuition, we can also act on it and use that as a guiding force for communicating clearly with others.

This chakra has several nadis, or energy channels, running through it, which gives several opportunities to catch a glimpse of the higher energy at work here. I do think it is rare to have a fully cleared and activated throat chakra. This can be seen in the choices people make concerning their careers. Oftentimes, people work jobs to make money for survival without taking the time to really listen to what that deeper voice within is saying about what may be more fulfilling.

A blocked throat chakra may result in the complete inability to really hear others and what they are saying as well being unable to communicate effectively. Sometimes this manifests as disease, both in small or large ways. For example, when we have a cough or sore throat, there may be something that needs to be expressed. Years of not expressing oneself can sometimes lead to chronic ailments of the throat and ears.

Healing this chakra can be done by first spending time in silence, listening to our own mental chatter and allowing that to subside so the deeper part of ourselves emerges. Once we begin to access this chakra, we can start activating it through our Reiki attunement and practice.

Ajna

Ajna means "unlimited power" and is located at our forehead. This is the place where the two major nadis, ida and pingala, meet and connect inside our brain, near the pineal gland. This chakra is the cool, wise part of ourselves that offers powerful insight when opened, enabling us to glimpse the cosmic mind beyond. The language of this chakra comes in symbols and dreams and must be decoded to effectively communicate with others.

If this chakra is blocked, we may suffer from being unable to see clearly, lack foresight for the future, and feel disconnected from the higher parts of self. I have often suffered from this chakra being too open, receiving too much psychic information that is not relevant to my life. This can be very draining and I must be careful to slowly integrate the wisdom that comes through me and continue my grounding exercises to stay balanced.

This chakra can be cleared and activated with the Reiki attunements along with various exercises including pranayama, which aims to balance the ida and pingala. Learning symbolism and working with your dreams are excellent ways to begin accessing the higher states of wisdom that reside here.

Sahasrara

The final center is *sahasrara* or "thousand petals," the crown chakra that sits atop the head. This chakra has the ability to run the energy of a thousand nadis, or energy channels and, when fully illuminated, is reported to glow like the halos of saints from olden days. This center is a powerful and illuminated place on the body that connects us directly with the divine or cosmic energy. During Reiki attunements, this center is opened to allow the student to fully access the healing energy that can then be passed from Master to student.

Most people have some opening in this chakra and it is only blocked in severe cases of grief or strong mental imbalances such as schizophrenia. Interestingly, people who do suffer from such mental problems often experience similar states reported by advanced spiritual yogis,[47] such as spontaneously seeing mandalas or accessing incredible psychic information. Perhaps our Western culture lacks the tools and resources found in the East to give highly sensitive people a place to connect more deeply with the higher energies at work and channel them more effectively. Perhaps Reiki and the study of chakras may offer a better glimpse at the workings of the complex human body and energy field.

47 A yogi is a spiritual practitioner of yoga.

Table 5.1: *The Chakras*

MULADHARA (Root Chakra) means "foundation" or "root support"

Color: red

Element: earth

Sense: smell

Location: in the perineum in men and just below the cervix in women

Function: seat of Kundalini energy that lies dormant in the base of the spine; supplies vital energy to body and connects directly to the sahasrara (crown chakra) through the sushuma, ida, and pingala

Associated body parts: bones, teeth, spine, nails, legs, anus, intestines, prostate gland, blood, cell multiplication

Emotions: physical will to be, survival, vitality, sense of groundedness, power, aggression, violence, anger, fear

Underactive: ungrounded, "spaced out," fatigue, feeling unsafe, insecure

Overactive: relying on physical to satisfy self, focus on physical form and external world view

Balanced: feels safe on earth, ability to manifest food and shelter easily, grounded, comfortable with body and form

Diseases: ailments of the legs and feet, bone disease, skin problems

Healing: spending time witnessing the dawn or sunset, walking barefoot in fresh soil or mud, dancing, drumming

SVADHISTHANA (Sacral Chakra) means "dwelling place of the self" or "sweetness"

Color: orange, dark blue

Element: water

Sense: taste

Location: below the navel, just above the pubic bone

Function: feelings and emotions, unification of masculine and feminine energies

Associated body parts: pelvis, reproductive glands and organs, kidneys, bladder, and bodily fluids such as blood, lymph, digestive secretions, sperm, prostate gland, ovaries, estrogen, testosterone

Emotions: sexual energy, creativity, sensuality, emotional aspect of life

Underactive: emotional issues, self-acceptance regarding sexuality, inability to feel deep self-love, unable to access worthiness

Overactive: overly-emotional, "bleeding" into muladhara and manipura, addictions, grounding out through emotions instead of muladhara base

Balanced: healthy sexuality, ability to access creativity

Diseases: kidney and bladder problems, irregular menstruation, impotence, disorders of the reproductive system

Healing: spending time in the moonlight, swimming, meditating next to water, belly dancing

MANIPURA (Solar Plexus Chakra) means "city of gems"

Color: yellow, gold

Element: fire

Sense: sight

Location: just above the navel

Function: center of power and wisdom, ability to digest ideas and thought forms, purifies desires and wishes of lower chakras, mental awareness of personality, ability to concentrate, filters psychic information from world for ajna clarity

Associated body parts: lower back, abdominal cavity, digestive tract, stomach, liver, spleen, gall bladder, pancreas, insulin

Emotions: happiness, excitement, power, relief, nervousness, guilt, attachment to things or people, fear, anxiety

Underactive: fatigue, weakness, unable to access creativity, fear of being in control, fears or anxieties about external things

Overactive: manipulation or control of outer world to soothe the inner realms, mental neuroses, strong need for power over others or from others

Balanced: healthy life force, clear personal boundaries, strong will power

Diseases: cancer, arthritis, digestive problems, constipation, diarrhea, ulcer, migraine, diabetes

Healing: laying in the sunlight, laughing, spinning

ANAHATA (Heart Chakra) means "sound made without any two things striking"

Color: green, pink, gold

Element: air

Sense: touch

Location: center of the chest

Function: bridge from lower to higher chakras, compassion for self and humanity, love

Associated body parts: upper back, heart, rib cage and chest cavity, lower lungs, blood, circulatory system, skin, hands, thymus and thymus hormone

Emotions: humility, tolerance, empathy, compassion, responsibility

Underactive: inability to feel or access emotions deeply, sorrow, unable to discern positive or negative vibrations, lack of self-love

Overactive: trying to connect with everyone, "runaway" healing, love without compassion

Balanced: strong sense of self-love, love for the world without attachment

Diseases: heart diseases, high or low blood pressure, problems with circulatory system and immune system

Healing: spending time in nature, forests, or meadows, gardening, smelling flowers, practice sending "love" without attachment to each person you meet on the street

VISHUDDA (Throat Chakra) means "pure"

Color: light blue

Element: ether

Sense: hearing

Location: throat

Function: communication of the higher self, bridge between thoughts and feelings, listening to inner voice

Associated body parts: lungs, bronchial, esophagus, vocal chords, throat, nape of neck, jaw, thyroid, parathyroid, thyroxin

Emotions: love, peacefulness, trust, beauty, sorrow, connectedness

Underactive: rigidity and frustration in communication, inability to express higher self, unable to bridge compassion (anahata) with clarity (ajna)

Overactive: inability to listen to others, highly expressive and/or opinionated

Balanced: ability to hear intuition and speak one's own truth

Diseases: asthma, addictions, throat and lung cancer, problems with ear, nose, and throat

Healing: meditating on the blue sky or reflections of the water, listening carefully to sounds and to others, spending time in silence

AJNA (Third Eye Chakra) means "unlimited power"

Color: indigo

Location: between the eyebrows

Function: perception of the world beyond the five senses, developing consciousness of the higher realms, intuition, will power

Associated body parts: cerebellum, ears, nose, sinuses, eyes, nervous system, face, pituitary gland, vasopressin

Emotions: joy, foresight, clarity of mental/emotional processes, grief, gentleness, receptivity

Underactive: confusion, lack of will or motivation, inability to foresee plans

Overactive: influx of confused psychic energy, inability to concentrate on one idea or plan, overly sensitive

Balanced: foresight, connection to higher self

Diseases: hormonal imbalance, headaches, migraines, depression, vertigo, eye problems

Healing: looking at the nighttime sky, candle gazing, scrying, meditating with the full or new moon, starlight meditation, paying attention to dreams

SAHASRARA (Crown Chakra) means "thousand petals"

Color: white, lavender

Location: top of the head

Function: direct connection to the Atman or spiritual self

Associated body parts: cerebrum, cranium, pineal gland, serotonin, other neurotransmitters

Emotions: unity with all things, high consciousness, trans-personal awareness

Underactive: isolated, uncertainty and lack of purpose, inability to connect with spiritual aspects of life

Overactive: other chakras are blocked

Balanced: ability to access healing energy

Diseases: severe grief, shock, psychosis, neurotic disorders

Healing: meditating on mountains, silent retreats

WORKING WITH THE CHAKRAS

Working to clear and activate your chakras takes a dedicated practice and can be effectively combined with the Reiki discipline. In my Reiki Warrior courses I focus intensively on the chakra system because it is one of the most valuable tools to use in connection with Reiki. The chakra system works like a map that can be used to understand the interconnection between the body and energy field, how blockages and disturbances form, and possible disease progression.

It is important to understand that chakras are not merely rainbow-colored lights dancing through our aura, but very precise energetic organs that must be developed to utilize their full potential. In order to really work with the chakras, we take four clear steps: contacting, clearing, activating, and integrating.

Contacting

Contacting the chakras is the primary step and the most important. This can be done by using Exercise 5.1: Chakra Check Visualization to go through the different areas of the body that contain the chakras and allow ourselves to perceive or intuit the individual centers. In traditional Kundalini Yoga, practitioners often begin this process with ajna or the third eye, as it is fairly easy to clear and activate because it contains only two nadis. Ajna is the ending point for the ida and pingala nadis and can be cleared, activated, and developed quite sufficiently through a Reiki attunement and the practice of Reiki. The Reiki energy is often associated with this chakra and it is a good starting point for consciousness development. An advantage to beginning with ajna, as opposed to muladhara, is that one can use the highly perceptive abilities of ajna to properly perceive the other chakras. Other schools of thought recommend starting with the heart chakra first as a place of perception so that one may develop from a place of compassion. Both starting points are equally useful. In Chapter Eleven: The Human Energy Field, I will discuss more about the interrelation of the chakras within the system and self-development.

Clearing

Clearing the chakras is the next step in working effectively with the chakras on a personal level. Clearing can be done in a myriad of ways and is extremely important to do before activating the energy centers, as it will allow more Ki to flow through in a healthy and balanced manner. Once chakras are cleared, we begin to experience emotions, desires, and fear in a more balanced manner. Traumas from the past are healed and we can begin to develop healthy relationships. Our self-image improves along with confidence and trust, and we usually begin to connect deeper into life and find activities that are more fulfilling and joyous. Reiki self-healing, receiving treatments of Reiki and other kinds of therapies, crystals, smudging, running colors exercises (See Exercise 11.3: Running Colors), and practicing yoga asanas and pranayama are all ways to begin clearing the chakras and the nadis that run through them.

Activating

The next step is activating the chakra, which, in many cases, happens naturally once the chakra has been cleared. Once chakras are balanced, we can begin to experience more advanced states of consciousness that enable us to work even more deeply on the healing path. Our ability to meditate improves, the quieting of the mind becomes more natural, and certain psychic phenomena may appear, such as more powerful healings, clairvoyance, and clairaudience. Chakra activation is seeded in the heart, throat, and forehead chakras during the Reiki One attunements and following up with the twenty-one-day self-healing and clearing develops the activation process further. Also, using the Chakra Check Visualization (Exercise 5.1), additional Reiki practice, and the use of crystals will all help to further develop the chakra. In Kundalini Yoga, the use of mandala, mantra,[48] and mudra[49] meditation is used in a precise manner with the breath and specific asanas to raise the energy level in the chakras and activate them.

Integrating

Integration is the final step of working with the chakras. This involves the deep process of interconnectedness between the chakras and how they relate to one another. At first, it is good to work on clearing and activating one chakra, which will naturally lead to work with other chakras. Often certain traumas that have affected a chakra in our childhood can deeply affect other areas of the energy field and body. For example, issues that appear in the second chakra relating to sexuality and creativity may be deeply rooted in the heart chakra, which is linked

---

48 *Mantra* means "instrument of thought" in Sanskrit. It involves using the sacred power of sound to direct the mind stream. Each Reiki symbol is named with a mantra that is learned and used in Reiki Two. See Exercise 12.4: Using Mantras.

49 *Mudra* means "seal" in Sanskrit and involves certain hand positions during meditation. The hand positions affect energy channels in the body.

to self-esteem and self-love. Easing open the heart chakra through clearing and activation can later lead to a healthy flow of energy into the second chakra and help the overall balance and integration of the chakra system.

EXERCISE 5.1: *Chakra Check Visualization*

This exercise can be used for all steps of chakra development. First, use it to contact the chakras and begin to develop a sense of their current state of openness and clarity. Later, it can be used to run colors for chakra clearing and more intense focus for activation.

When you do the Chakra Check Visualization, you can use a hand and visualize each chakra individually. Place one hand over the chakra you are checking and keep the other stabilized in the auric field or resting on your knee. When you visualize each chakra, try to imagine a healthy spinning chakra of the associated color, found in the Chakra Table in this chapter. Concentrate on the color and the associated area of the body. At first you may not see anything, but with time (over the course of several days), an image of the chakra will emerge. If your chakra appears as a different color or shows you different symbols than the associations provided, it does not mean your chakra is not healthy. This is your personal energy sphere. By acknowledging the chakras and checking in with them, you can begin to build a relationship with the chakra system.

If you are also using your hand, simply rest the palm of your hand a few inches away from each chakra, allowing your hand to sense the energy or movement. Notice any warmth or coolness, vibrations, and the direction of each chakra. This can be done on others using a pendulum as well. To use a pendulum, you must find or buy an appropriate stone that comes to a point and is on a chain. These are easy to find in any local or online new age store. Choose a stone that feels right for you. Clear and charge the pendulum in salt water for a few days in the light of the full moon. Moonlight will clear any energy picked up in the store or otherwise. For the exercise, hold the pendulum over the center point of the chakra and relax your arm and hand. Allow the pendulum to move freely, following the natural rotation and size of the chakra. A clockwise spinning chakra is regarded as healthy while a counterclockwise spinning chakra is unbalanced.

As you do the visualization, you may also use your hand to give your chakras Reiki. If a chakra seems particularly unbalanced, closed, or filled with dark or muddled energies, slowly move your hand over the chakra in a clockwise direction and allow it to regain clarity. You can also give Reiki to the part of the body where the chakra is located. If you notice that the chakra does not change right away or goes back to its unbalanced state very quickly, be patient. Oftentimes it takes several days before a chakra begins to manifest changes in its spin, balance, or color. You will notice the difference and witness the effects with a weekly chakra check.

To do the chakra check, sit comfortably with the spine straight or lay down. If you lay down, make sure you are not sleepy so you don't fall asleep. Focus on your breath for a few moments, allowing your mind to become still. First, check in with muladhara and your grounding cord and perform your Auric Cleanse (Exercise 3.1). Then begin the check with the crown chakra, visualizing brilliant white light or clear lavender. Imagine the chakra spinning clockwise around your head. Notice if it begins to spin the opposite direction, showing you the true direction of its spin. Notice any other colors or symbols that may emerge.

Continue the check for each chakra, slowly moving downward. If you are using your hand, place it directly on the chakra and then slowly move it away into the energy field. You can do this simultaneously with visualization or separately. When you visualize ajna, the forehead chakra, imagine an indigo sphere between the eyebrows. If you can, try to focus on the chakra both in the front, coming out of the forehead, as well as in the back, emerging from the back of the head. Again, allow for your chakra to show itself in alternative colors or images. Then, move down to vishudda, making sure to focus on both the front and back, visualizing a clear, light blue circle. Slowly, with careful attention, move down to anahata, manipura, and svadhisthana, visualizing bright green or pink, bright yellow, and clear orange, respectively. Note any other colors, symbols, or images that appear. Remember any sensations or feelings. When you come to muladhara, visualize a clear, bright red. Finally, recheck your grounding cord and notice its color.

Come out of the meditation by bringing awareness back to the body. Move the fingers and toes, roll the neck and touch the ground. Write down any of your experiences, making special note of each chakra and its color(s), sensations, and symbols. Keep track of the chakras on a weekly basis to note any changes.

6

Reiki Warrior Discipline:
Practicing on Others

Although the First Degree of Reiki Warrior has a distinct focus on self-healing, students must also learn how to pass the Reiki to others, which enables them to develop their practice. Using Reiki healing energy consistently leads to a calmer mind, helps to cultivate compassion, and grounds one in the firm practice that gives rise to the insights of healing found in Reiki Warrior wisdom.

MIKAO USUI'S DESCENT

After twenty-one days of fasting and meditation on Mount Kurama, Mikao Usui had an experience that is likened to satori, or a glimpse of the ultimate reality, a moment of enlightenment. After this incredible experience (believed to be the first Reiki attunement), he proceeded down the mountain, where four things happened to him: He stubbed his toe and laid his hands upon it and healed it. He went to a rest house where the woman who served him had a headache; as he laid his hands on her, the headache was gone. He was able to digest a large meal with no problems, even after twenty-one days of fasting. And finally, he want back to Tokyo and began treating his teacher, who had arthritis, with good results. This story illuminates the four methods in which Reiki heals the body on the physical level: ourselves (the toe), others' minor ailments (the headache), bodily processes (digestion), and chronic disease (arthritis).

After the practice of self-healing is established, we can begin to practice more regularly on others. Reiki Warriors can start by practicing simply and spontaneously, offering Reiki to his immediate family and friends who have minor complaints. Although the first Reiki precept states that there should be an exchange, one that honors each, because we are in constant exchange with those close to us, giving a short impromptu Reiki session can be quite useful. Several times I have offered Reiki to alleviate headaches, knee and joint pain, back pain, minor cuts and bruises, infections, and burns. The Reiki activates the body's natural healing process and is highly beneficial in healing minor health complaints. By practicing short sessions on friends and family, Reiki Warriors will begin to open more deeply to the healing Universal Life Force and in turn, the Reiki will flow even more strongly. Once the Reiki Warrior practitioner has cultivated an awareness of the Reiki flow and developed more intuition, he can begin to give full sessions to people.

FEARLESSNESS

The archetypal figure of the Warrior brings to mind the quality of fearlessness. This is a crucial aspect of the healer's path. We, as multidimensional human beings, are always dealing with layers of fears based on issues around our survival, our desires, and our losses (both potential and very real). Yet, we can develop our Reiki practice in an effort to uncover and transform our fears, promoting change and healing that benefits both ourselves and our clients. Fearlessness encourages us to experience illness, old age, and death without clinging to a hopeful or expected outcome, enabling us, as healers, to be more fully present in the moment, opening and awakening into the spaciousness that helps our fears to dissolve.

One of my students struggled for many days when attempting to practice Reiki on others. He had successfully felt some shifts on himself, but when it came to others, he felt blocked and unable to pass the Reiki effectively. After several tries, he realized that in his nervousness to "perform," which was rooted in a sense of fear, he was holding his breath. This breath retention was a physical manifestation of his own self-consciousness, and it prevented the Reiki from flowing freely through his aura, body, and hands. Once he realized this he began to relax his breath continuously during the sessions. This greatly improved the Reiki flow and healing shifts began to occur within himself and those he practiced on.

EXERCISE 6.1: *Practicing on Plants, Stones, and Creatures*
An excellent way to generate the Reiki energy is to practice on the natural world. Take the time to spend a morning or afternoon in the outdoors. Find a plant—wild or in the garden—that needs some attention. Sit down in front of

the plant and follow the same procedure as you would for a self-healing practice. Call upon the Reiki energy and dedicate it to the well-being of the plant or tree. Then begin the Reiki session. With plants and trees, you can either hold your hands directly on the organism or a few inches above it, in the energy field surrounding the tree or plant. Allow the Reiki to pass for several minutes. As your mind grows quieter with practice, you can take this moment to "ask" the plant if it has anything to say. Plants, flowers, and trees can communicate with us if we are open to their messages. Just as in the Chakra Check Visualization, allow any images, colors, and sounds to come into your awareness. Sometimes the plant will tell you if it needs more or less water, more or less light, or wants to be moved. Once you are clear enough to discern the true messages of the plants, then it may advise healing properties and uses. Know that this type of clear awareness often takes some cultivation; Reiki Warrior students will benefit from the reference point of a teacher and other students to know when the messages from plants, or anything else for that matter, are truly clear and not projections. Such discernment will be discussed further in Chapter Ten: Reason Versus Intuition.

In the meantime, practicing Reiki on plants and trees often has quick, beneficial results. Soon after my Second Degree Reiki class and attunements, I found a plant that had been thrown out onto the street by its previous owner. For some strange reason (I don't usually have a strong affection toward houseplants), I lugged the half-dead-looking plant home and started giving it Reiki. In just a few days, the plant not only perked up with my attention and some water, but it even bloomed into a huge, white, lily-like flower. I have since spent many hours in the garden, passing Reiki and communicating with all the extraordinary growing things that inhabit our planet.

We can also use Reiki to benefit animals, crystals, stones, and anything in our natural environment. In shamanism, the ancient practice of connecting into the

Earth and Universe, all creatures, elements, and things on Earth contain a spirit that is interconnected with everything else. Practicing Reiki daily allows us to tap into these connections and begin to perceive the various expressions of Spirit through the endless creative manifestations on Earth. Explore this possibility. Give Reiki to your pets, to the stones around your house, even to your car. There is no limit in passing Reiki through you and into the world.

DEALING WITH EGO

Becoming a healer, becoming a Reiki Warrior, is a courageous effort that requires the practitioner to cultivate patience, learn to drop the ego tendencies within, and practice mindfulness. The best thing, for any student of Reiki who aims to become an excellent healer, is to have a teacher with whom he can practice on a continuous basis for the first year of practice, at the very least. This provides the student with a base to check his progress and learn what can be done to enhance the practice. One of the most important aspects of healing with Reiki is to remember that Reiki is doing all the "work." Even though the Reiki Warrior becomes more advanced and is able to manipulate and direct energy more precisely, the healing that is taking place is still in concert with the client's ability to deeply relax and allow healing to occur, the karma of the illness, environmental factors, and the clearness of the Reiki Warrior practitioner. Miracles will and do happen, although it is not for the Reiki Warrior to overly identify with this "success." Sometimes people do not heal, even when we try our best as Reiki Warriors.

ACCEPTANCE

Another obstacle that Reiki Warriors may encounter is something called "runaway healing," which happens when the healer desires to heal everyone and everything. This kind of attitude is based in desire—the desire for others to be well, to be happy, to be successful—and should be motivated by a positive feeling. But if this desire is rooted in fear or the inability to accept that not all beings, ourselves included, are happy at every moment, the desire may impede our Reiki practice. The aversion to what is perceived as "negative" instead of acceptance of the true reality or nature of the world can promote more fear and eventually, even lessen healing. We must remember, as healers and as human beings, that illness, old age, and death are a natural part of everyone's experience. As Reiki Warriors, we should be honored to work with those suffering from illness or about to die, as it cultivates compassion.

Oftentimes, "runaway healing" can cause a healer to experience disease and illness herself because she is giving too much of her own self and not simply allowing the Reiki to work through her. This can cause the body, emotional state, and mind set to become overworked and drained, leading to exhaustion. Again, having a teacher and other honest Reiki contemporaries in our lives helps us to check and move past these obstacles on our spiritual path.

LIMITATIONS OF REIKI

When practicing Reiki healing, it is important to recognize its limitations. Reiki in the First Degree is, very simply, a laying-on-hands healing. The later levels use symbols to enhance the practice, but it is still a basic healing art. Most Reiki workshops provide little or no anatomy and physiology information and often only a brief explanation of the energy field is given. I encourage the Reiki Warrior student to research this important part of healing work by attending an anatomy class and studying the systems of the body.

Also, Reiki is not in any way a substitute for medical advice, counseling, or therapy. A Reiki Warrior practitioner should never diagnose or give counseling advice beyond her training. Make sure, if you begin practicing regularly, to investigate the local laws concerning alternative healing. Sometimes Reiki practitioners also need a massage certificate to be able to touch clients. Also, keep track of the client's medical history with a basic form (See Appendix C). Keeping a list of local counselors, therapists, alternative doctors, and medical advice is an excellent way to inform your clients if they have problems that you, as a Reiki practitioner, cannot fully address. That being said, with careful awareness and mindfulness, it is still good to trust your basic intuition and knowledge that Reiki is used only for benefit. Balance is key here and with experience and practice, you will be able to discern the appropriate action for your clients.

There are other, more practical times when it is inappropriate to use Reiki as well. Before setting a fractured or broken bone, the practitioner should not give Reiki as it will produce healing of the bone while it is misaligned. Also, during intense detoxification, such as when a person is overcoming an addiction or is suffering from severe dysentery, the Reiki can exacerbate the detoxifying process and cause the client to suffer more. Certain illnesses also may be aggravated by Reiki, including: migraines, schizophrenia, mental disorders, and auto immune diseases. These cases should be treated gently alongside the care of a registered physician or nurse. When in doubt, ask the client clearly if they want to receive Reiki and trust them if they tell you it becomes too much during the session. If you can, simply treat the feet to provide a relaxing, grounding effect and advise them to see a suitable doctor or therapist. Reiki is a complement to first aid but should not be used as primary care in emergency situations.

CLIENT CASE HISTORY

Out of the hundreds of Reiki sessions that I have given, I can recall only a few that tested the limit of my experience. One woman came to see me and simply wanted to experience a relaxing session. The first session was very nurturing and she felt wonderful all day, revitalized by the Reiki. She came again, two days later and had a very different experience. Halfway through the session, she began to convulse and shake, crying hysterically as deep, painful emotions wound their way to the surface. I pulled her to a sitting position and just held her for a long time as she cried for several minutes, trying to catch hold of herself and her breath. After some time, she began to calm down and then explained to me she had suffered from anxiety for a few years. She had been able to control it with time, and had not experienced any for a few months; she was both shocked and overwhelmed by the sudden onset of an anxiety attack on the Reiki table.

I also was a bit overwhelmed and recognized how vitally important it is to investigate a person's background to the best of our ability. Having no previous knowledge of the background of her mental states, I was not properly prepared for the session. Also, it is important to inform the client that deeply repressed emotions and situations come to the forefront for healing when receiving Reiki. Although Reiki is generally quite gentle and revitalizing, it can have deep and powerful effects, which should be understood by clients so they may commit fully to the healing process.

PRACTICING ON OTHERS

When beginning to practice full sessions on others, we should first make sure we are feeling fairly grounded in our own self-healing process. As Barbara Brennan states, "The golden rule for the healer is: *first, the self and what nourishes the self; then, deep pause for consideration; then, the nourishment of others.*"[50]

A good way to start our practice is to find a Reiki partner with whom we can exchange several healings back and forth. This exchange allows us to deeply explore one another's auric field and observe the changes that occur over days and weeks as well as to note our own ability to work with the Reiki energy. Also, nowadays, many towns and communities hold weekly or monthly Reiki shares that bring together Reiki practitioners of all degrees to exchange healing, stories, and insights. Students can benefit greatly from participating in group work, which often enhances the practitioner's skills. My work in the Free Reiki Clinic put me into contact with Reiki practitioners of several lineages, allowed me to experience group healing and enabled me to form contacts with people who became regular clients.

When we decide to take clients, we may have some who come for just one session and others who come weekly or monthly. If a client has a particular issue she wants to work with, a series of three sessions over the course of one week is highly effective. Often new clients do not deeply relax in the first session, as they are still becoming accustomed to you, the practitioner, the environment, and the Reiki flow. By the second session, some deeper work may be done, and the final session works to ground and revitalize the field. During the week of three sessions, ask the client to pay closer attention to feelings that arise and any significant dreams. Note these in your client case history for future reference. If a client, family member, or friend has a more serious disease such as cancer, depression, or a heart ailment, it is extremely beneficial to treat the person for twenty-one days in a row. This way, each day builds successively on the previous, allowing deep healing to occur. During a twenty-one-day treatment, the sessions would tend to be shorter, about fifteen to thirty minutes, with a focus on the area of the body in which the problem occurs.

EXERCISE 6.2: *Creating Sacred Space*

This a special technique that you can use as a Reiki Warrior to enhance your practice area and, in a sense, commit deeper to each healing session. This involves working with the four directions and five elements believed to be sacred by ancient cultures worldwide. There are myriad ways of associating the

---

50 Brennan, *Hands of Light*, 200.

directions with the elements and this is just one example. Experiment with different methods and find what works best for you.

This exercise is more powerful if you use sound, such as your voice, words, song, a rattle, chimes, a Tibetan bowl, or other instrument. It is best to create your sacred space just before your client arrives or after they are lying down on the table.

First, imagine a circle in the space you wish to make sacred. Start by focusing on the breath for a few moments, calming the mind. Then stand in the east, facing outward, away from the inner circle, and visualize the wind or air that resides in the easterly direction. Say aloud or in your mind, "I call the east, the power of wind. Blow into my circle (or space) today and bring clarity of mind and focus. Help us to perceive what can be healed." Ring your bell, sound your Tibetan bowl, shake your rattle, or sing some notes that resonate with you. Then move to the south, facing outward, and visualize fire, the flames that reside in the south. Say, "I call the south, the power of fire. Burn in my circle today and transform negative qualities into positive. Illuminate our space with your warmth and healing powers." Again, make your sounds with instrument or voice. Then, move to the west and visualize water, streams, or waterfalls. Say, "I call the west, the power of water. Wash into our circle and cleanse us of tired emotions, fatigue, and sadness. Wash away what is unneeded and purify us so we may receive the healing energy." Again, make your sounds. Then, move to the north and visualize the earth, the planet, stones and ground. Say, "I call the north, the power of earth. Come into our circle and help us to ground into form, to embody spirit in this body." Again, create your song or sounds. Finally, face the middle of the circle and say, "I call the inner qualities of space from above. Help to illuminate the higher wisdom within and bring the joy that is like starlight into our healing session." Again, make your sounds. Now visualize a circle of brilliant light surrounding the space, connecting the directions. Imagine a second circle vertically, connecting the ground with the sky.

Finally, after the session is finished, you must close up the circles and release the directions. Simply reverse the order, starting with the element of space, saying, "We thank space and the higher wisdom for being in this place today. Go if you must, stay if you will," and make your sound softly this time. Stand in the north and say, "We thank the north for grounding us today. Go if you must, stay if you will." Repeat the thanks and farewell in the west, south, and finally, the east.

This exercise can be even more simply done, in the quiet of your mind, imagining the sounds to call in the directions, or it can be a very elaborate ceremony with colored candles in each direction, symbols on an altar to represent the elements, and powerful songs to invoke the power of the directions. The method is up to you and what suits your nature.

REIKI STEPS TO PRACTICE ON OTHERS

First, meet with your prospective client, even if it is a friend or family member, to explain a few things about Reiki and set the time and place for practicing. If they have never had a Reiki session, you may tell them it is a deeply relaxing treatment that uses the hands to promote healing. Tell them not to eat at least one hour before the session (as the Reiki will often be diverted to digesting food) and to wear loose, comfortable clothing.

Before the client arrives, remove all your own hand jewelry, wash your hands, and dab yourself with lavender oil or some other gentle fragrance. Then, spend some time in the space where you will give the session. Make sure the room, bed, or table is clean and comfortable and well ventilated. Cleanse the aura of the room by simply intending a clear space, giving Reiki healing to the space, or smudging with sage or cedar wood. Crystals, bowls of water, flowers, candles, and soothing images all help to facilitate a relaxed atmosphere. Spend a few moments practicing self-healing, and doing your Grounding Cord and Auric Cleanse exercises in preparation for your session. The more focused and relaxed you are, the better the session will be.

Now is also the moment to recognize that the client is, on a deep level, already healed and whole, that he is simply trying to remember and reconnect with that wholeness. Each client who comes to see you is another spirit aiming to reconnect with Spirit; Reiki is simply the method to access that connection. If you know the Reiki symbols, take a few moments to send Reiki to your client as they approach the room. This helps to deepen the intention of healing and bring your focus to the session.

When the client arrives, take note of the way he moves in the door, if he is relaxed or nervous, what he is wearing. All of these impressions help us to intuit more about the client and his approach to the world, which is reflected in the healing process. Have him sit down and fill out a client form and tell you anything he wants to focus on. Allow this focus to be your specific intention for the healing practice. Ask him if there is anything you might need to know as the practitioner. Briefly explain the process of the session: that he will lie on his back, you will move down his body, have him turn over, and then you will work on his back. Ask if he has any questions.

Then have him remove his jewelry and loosen his belt, if needed. Removing jewelry is important for two reasons. First, metal can become hot from the Reiki energy, which is often very warm. Second, jewelry, especially metal pieces, can have a minimal effect on the energy field, especially if the jewelry is older and not cleaned often. Wooden and natural items tend to have less of an effect and can be left on the client. If it is too complicated to remove an item, just let them leave it on and be mindful of it as you are giving the session (for example, nose and eyebrow piercings are a bit complicated, so I usually leave those alone).

The client then lies down on the table or bed. Begin your session as you would any other Reiki session: put hands together in prayer position, ask for the Reiki to flow, that the Masters guide the session, and that the healing energy goes for benefit for the client. You can do this either aloud or in your mind, whatever feels more comfortable. Then begin the session, following the hand positions listed below. When you are finished with the arms on the front side, do an auric sweep three times down the arms. An auric sweep involves lightly brushing in downward strokes over the body and the field. When you are finished with the back, do another auric sweep down the entire body three times. Close the session on the client's body with a heart seal. This process entails pressing the tips of the fingers over the heart chakra, with the second hand over the first. At this moment, intend the healing to work for the next few hours or days and then state in your mind that the Reiki session is now closed.

A final essential step before finishing the session is to imagine the person healed and healthy in your mind's eye. If they came to you with a particular issue, visualize that issue resolved. I always imagine the client dancing in beauty with golden sunlight all around, feeling joyous and interconnected. In this small way, you can help to seed their future with a brighter, more whole experience.

Step outside of the client's auric field, do your Grounding Cord, Auric Cleanse, and an aura boundary exercise. As a symbol of release, blow upward with cupped hands toward the sky. You may then wash your hands or cleanse them over a candle to release any leftover energy.

After this, tell the client the session is over. Help him to sit up if he needs assistance and allow him to slowly readjust to sitting up. Offer him a glass of water and encourage him to drink it as a way to cleanse any toxins that have been released. Allow him to ask any questions. In general, when first practicing, refrain from sharing any impressions you may have felt until you gain a better understanding of the meaning or importance of these impressions. Although you may have had several insights into his aura or life experience, unless it is someone you are close with, these may not be relevant at first and may even be projections from your own mind.

Hand Positions for Full Reiki Session

Listed below are all of the hand positions taught to the Reiki Warrior student. Over the course of my Reiki studies, I found it imperative to touch more points on the body than the traditional twelve Reiki hand positions. Energy channels move throughout the body, connecting the energy field or aura with the body via the chakras; the energy points can be cleared and revitalized through the Reiki touch both directly on the body and over the various parts of the body.

Overall Guidelines:

- Never touch neck, breasts, or genitals directly

- Never step over body

- Always keep contact with their energy field even when moving around body

- Make sure both their body and yours stay uncrossed as much as possible for a good energy flow

- Keep hands separate from each other, slightly cupped, fingers together

Introduction

1. Prepare the bed or massage table and space with clear intention and grounding. Offer Reiki to the space by holding up your hands and calling in the Reiki energy, asking it to vitalize the room. Use various crystals to draw in purifying energy, ground out negative energy, and enhance the quality of the space and energy. Soft, quiet music that does not have repetitive rhythms is recommended, such as Brian Eno's *Music for Airports*. Incense can be a nice touch, but may bother some clients. Use lavender or other soothing oils to scent the mattress or burn the incense before the client arrives to leave the scent in the air. This also purifies the space energetically. Using the four elements can charge the space with a special intention that enhances the Reiki session. See Exercise 6.2: Creating Sacred Space to work with the elements and four directions.

2. Make sure your hands are washed and scented with a bit of lavender or other soothing oil.

3. Watch as your client comes in the room. Notice dress, body language, etc., as this gives you an immediate sense of the person and the way he expresses himself and what he is "bringing" to the session.

4. Have the client sit down and fill out the client form (See Appendix C). This information enables you to begin a record treatment for the person and gives you important past history that may affect the healing session.

5. Have him take off any jewelry.

6. Ask if he has received Reiki before; if not, explain what Reiki is by describing what Reiki can do: "it is relaxing" and "it helps to promote healing."

7. Ask if there is anything he wants you to focus on. This question is important, as it provides a certain level of intention for the Reiki session. Focusing on an issue may promote even deeper healing. For example, if the client suffers from constipation, you can treat the large intestine for a longer period of time and alter your hand positions so that they follow the flow of the bowel movement.

8. Explain how the session will go: that you will work on the body and sometimes in the energy field, then you will have him turn over and work on his back.

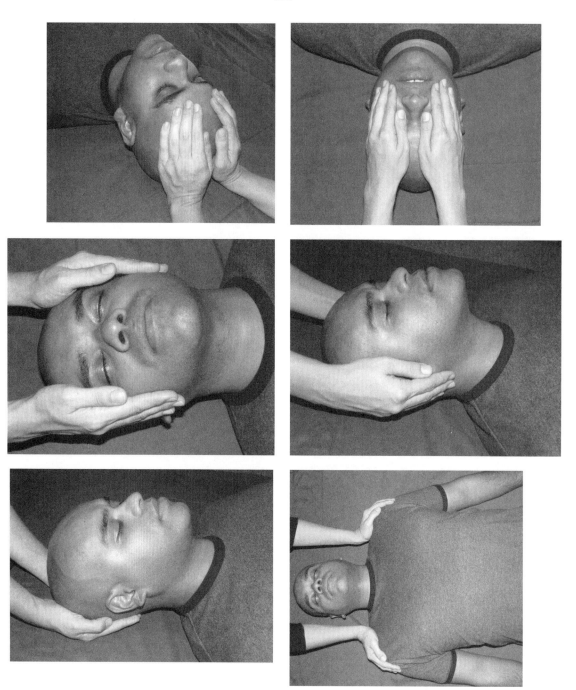

Front of Body

As you treat the various body parts, it is helpful to imagine Reiki flowing through the crown and upper chakras, into the hands and then into the client. If you are especially good at visualizing, imagine the various organs as you move down the body. You will often feel the Reiki healing you as you heal others. During the Reiki session, you may pick up on the client's emotions and physical sensations through your own body. As I provide many hand positions, spend just a few minutes on each point. The session should last about forty-five minutes to an hour and fifteen minutes.

11. **Top of head:** This position charges the crown chakra, illuminating the cerebral cortex and balancing the brain hemispheres. Here, the soul imprint is stored, and it is easiest to scan the aura with your intuition here. Ask the Reiki guides or your inner self what is important to focus on during the session. Trust your intuition but be open and surrender to the Reiki moving through as well. Also notice the breathing here and take a few deep breaths to encourage the client to relax.

12. **Eyes:** Notice the movement of the eyes here as rapid eye movement (not the dreaming state) indicates more mental activity. Usually, as the client relaxes, the eye movement becomes slower and even stills into a deep, meditative state. Visualize the optic nerve here if possible and the forehead chakra.

13. **Jaw:** This position helps to relax the throat and revitalize the throat chakra, as it is connected to communication.

14. **Ears:** Again, this affects the throat chakra, as it is connected to listening (the other half of healthy communication).

15. **Back of head:** This is one of the most important positions, as it promotes deep healing in the brain and helps to balance the two hemispheres. This balance is key in achieving deeper levels of meditation and inner peace. Spend an extra minute here to encourage further relaxation.

16. **Shoulders**

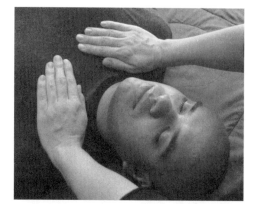

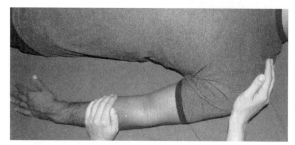

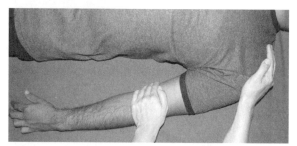

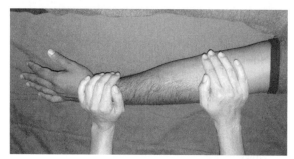

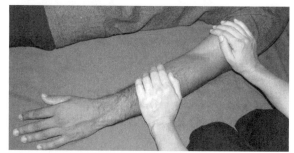

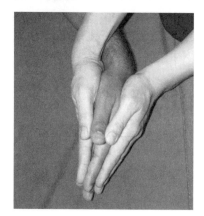

17. **Neck:** Don't press directly over the throat, as it may cause an uncomfortable sensation in the throat. Give Reiki at the base of the throat or directly over in the aura.

18. **Move to arms:** First one side, then the other (either side can be treated first). This is an important area of the body that is often overlooked when discussing the traditional Reiki positions. People use their arms and hands frequently and these locations should be given Reiki to promote deep healing. Sometimes I skip the arms and hands when I need to focus more on the internal organs; then I simply intend that the Reiki flow from the shoulders to the fingertips. It is especially important to include the arms and hands if the client suffers from arthritis or joint problems or works extensively with her hands (artist, builder, healer). The following sequence is ideal for balancing the entire arm, joints, and multitude of bones:

19. **Shoulder and forearm together**

    (19b. Alternate: **Shoulder and elbow together**)

20. **Elbow and wrist**

    (20b. Alternate: **Around elbow, upper arm, and forearm together.** This is ideal for treating tennis elbow and other problems in that joint.)

21. **Hands** (once on each side of the hand): The hands are the givers and receivers of the body and hold a direct connection with the heart chakra. Often you may notice a difference between the left and right hands. Generally speaking, this is a distinction that reflects the right side of the body, associated with active and giving qualities, while the left is associated with receptive qualities.

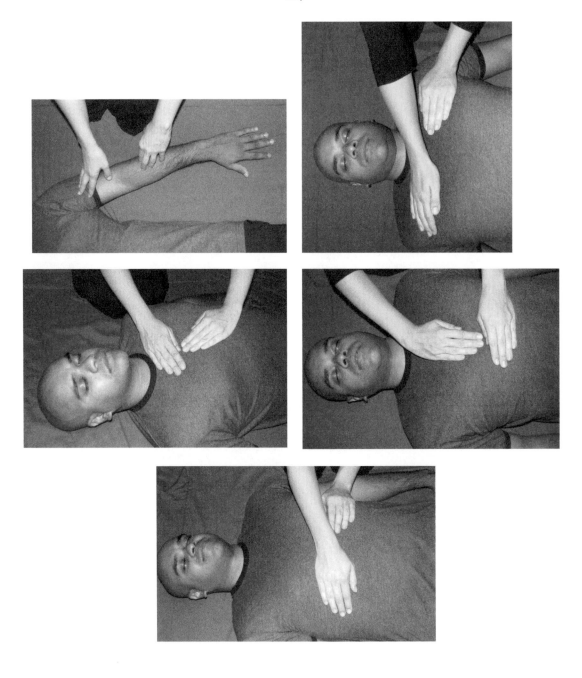

22. **Sweep** the arm three times when finished with the hands, as you will most likely not return to the arms and hands. Visualize throwing any released energy into a "psychic fire" or actually flick your hands over a real fire, as in a candle.

23. Repeat on the other arm.

— Move to the side of the body —

24. **Sternum/tops of lungs:** Visualize the lungs here, imagining the Reiki energy flowing into the alveoli, into the blood flow, and through the body.

25. **Heart center:** Above breasts or between breasts (one hand pointing up, over upper heart or one hand pointing down, over solar plexus)

26. **Beneath breasts** (over the ribs) (L/R): This is another very important point, as several internal organs benefit from the Reiki. Intend or visualize all the various organs here: the liver, gall bladder, pancreas, spleen, stomach, and intestines. Spend a few extra minutes here allowing the body to absorb the Reiki. Studying what the organs do and how they look inside the body will benefit your practice immensely. During this position, you can also focus on the solar plexus, which governs emotional and mental states as well as will power, and has a direct connection with the influx of energy between the auric layers.

I have noticed that the spleen is often very responsive to the Reiki, as it is responsible for detoxifying blood and is directly connected to the lymph system, which helps to fight infections. There is a minor chakra directly over the spleen that benefits from Reiki.

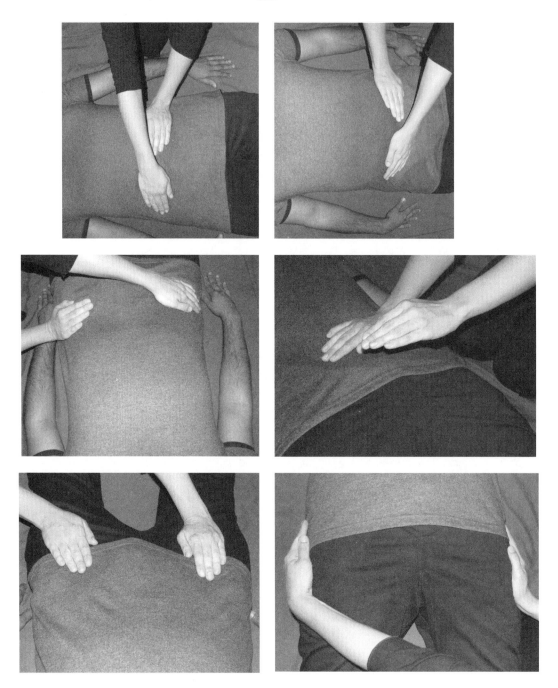

27. **Above naval** (L/R): The next two positions are important for relaxing digestion and promoting healing. Oftentimes clients' stomachs will directly respond to the Reiki treatment. If the client has eaten just before the session, the Reiki will go more toward digesting food and less toward healing the body. Recommend that the client not eat at least an hour before the session.

28. **Below naval** (L/R) at sacral chakra

29. **Pelvis** (a bit wider than above): This position treats the ovaries directly and the healing flows into the uterus and lower digestive tract, bladder, and genitals. Visualize the ovaries and second chakra here.

30. **Genitals:** For this position, you can practice a simple chakra balancing by putting one hand directly on the sacral chakra, between the hips, and the other hand above genitals, over the root chakra. Because these two are often linked energetically, it is beneficial to treat them together.

    (30b. Alternate: **Genitals.** Place hands alongside the genitals to increase flow in the root chakra and down the legs.)

— Re-check body at this point to see if you need to return to any positions in the torso. Sometimes an area needs to receive more Reiki. Trust your intuition.

31. **Hips** (side of body, L/R together): This area of the body often stores lots of tension, especially in women, and benefits greatly from the deep healing warmth of Reiki.

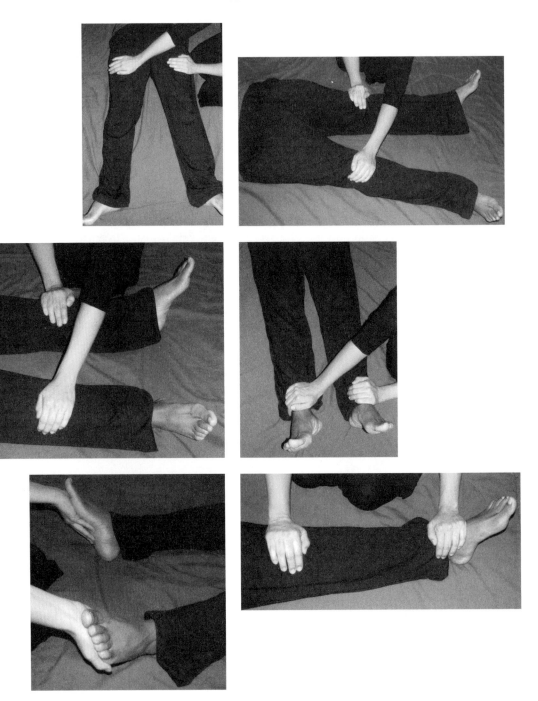

— **Legs** (both R/L together): Each position may only be one to one and a half minutes unless a specific focus is needed there.

32. **Thighs**

33. **Knees:** This area of the body often absorbs a lot of Reiki, as it supports the heavy movements of the body.

34. **Shins**

35. **Ankles**

36. **Feet:** This is another very important position, as it grounds out any energy loosened during the Reiki session. If at any point during a Reiki session the client feels overwhelmed by the emotion or physical sensations experienced and cannot continue, try to at least close the session with the feet to ground them.

    (36b. Alternatively, you may treat one leg at a time. In this case, pass Reiki to the knee and ankle together on one side, followed by the foot. Repeat with the other leg and foot to balance the body.)

37. **Sweep** the entire body three times. This brushes down the energy field and gently stimulates the client into a more awake state.

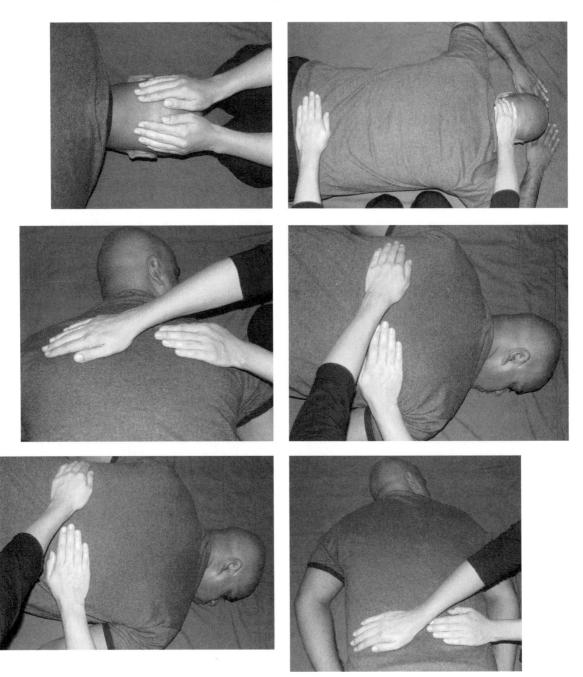

Back of Body

Ask the client to turn over slowly. Make sure you stay clear and present as the client turns over and you begin to work on the back. When you first begin giving Reiki sessions, there is a tendency for the mind to wander and it is important to bring it back to the task at hand.

38. **Back of head:** Again, this position is so important with balancing the brain that you give Reiki to this area twice.

39. **Spine balancing** (neck/sacrum, fingers pointing up): During this position, you can visualize the spine and feel the Reiki moving strongly through the back. The spine is the support for the body, the place where the spinal fluid moves, nourishing the nerves. Inside the spinal cord are the seeds of the chakras and each section of the spine corresponds with a chakra. The spine carries a lot of information here both physically and energetically, and several minutes of Reiki can help to revitalize the body and aura.

40. **Shoulder blades** (L/R sides, fingers pointing across): This area of the body often carries a lot of tension, as if people literally throw "back" energy that they don't want to deal with. The shoulder blades need deep relaxation to begin the healing process.

41. **Lungs** (L/R sides, fingers pointing across): The lungs are more accessible here and you can visualize them as you treat this area.

42. **Heart/ribs**

43. **Solar plexus:** This area contains the kidneys, which detoxify the body and often need some rebalancing.

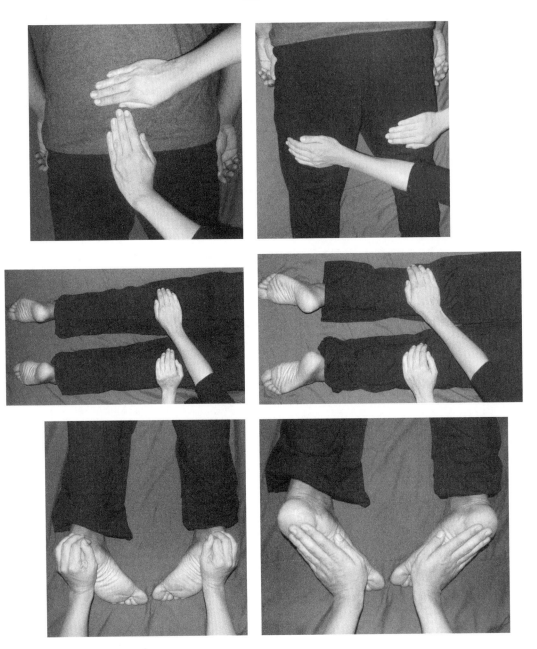

44. **Sacrum**

— Legs (both LS/RS together)

45. **Thighs**

46. **Back of knees:** Again, a lot of tension is stored here and the area benefits greatly from a few extra moments of Reiki healing.

47. **Calves**

48. **Ankles**

49. **Heels**

50. **Bottom of feet:** Again, ground out any loosened toxins or muddled energy by giving Reiki to the feet. The feet contain points that connect to all areas of the body, and the final position is very important in reconnecting the Reiki with the entire body and energy field.

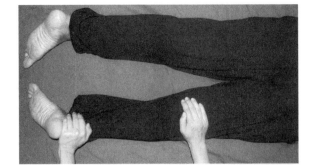

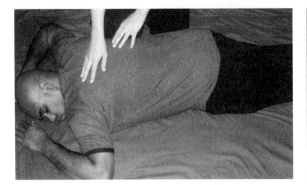

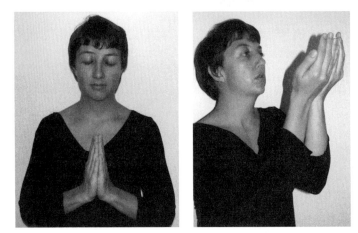

51. **Alternate treatment of legs:** Treat thigh and calf, followed by ankle and foot on one leg, right or left. Repeat with the other leg.

Completion

52. **Sweep** the body head to toes three times and throw energy into the "psychic" fire or candle flame. The "psychic" fire is an imagined fire burning on the ground, where you can throw released energy. You can also simply throw this to the surface of the Earth.

53. **Heart Seal:** Seal the Reiki session by pressing lightly onto the heart chakra and silently intending that the Reiki benefit the person for the next twenty-four hours. Take several moments to visualize the client healed and healthy. Remember that each person is, at their core, whole and full of light and just trying to remember that. This is essential to fully benefit the client.

54. Step away and out of the client's auric field and reground yourself using the Grounding Cord exercise.

55. Do your Auric Cleanse and "wash" your hands over the candle flame if possible. You can also touch the ground to reground.

56. **Thank** the Reiki energy and guides. Hold your hands in a cup and then lift them to the sky and blow on them as a final release of the Reiki session.

Tell client the session is over and to sit up slowly. If they have fallen asleep and there is time and space, let them rest. Offer the client glass of water to help with any loosened toxins in the body. This is important and should be encouraged even if the client first refuses. Ask if there is anything they'd like to say. Ask how they feel. Only tell them your experience if they ask directly. This is the general guideline when first giving Reiki sessions. Until you have had more experience reading the body and energy field and developing the auric vocabulary, I usually advise students to simply make a note of what they may have perceived. Yet, it is important to get feedback, so working with other Reiki students and practitioners and joining a Reiki share are great ways to develop the ability to use intuition and perception.

Tell the client that Reiki will continue to work for twenty-four hours and that they should rest. They should also drink lots of pure water. The last step is to honor the exchange for the session, whatever form that may take.

Additional Techniques to Aid the Reiki Session

Blowing: This is a technique that helps to loosen the muddled energy that may reside in chakras. You simply blow directly over the chakra, then follow with the Reiki energy to vitalize the area. You can also do this over organs, meridians, and specific body parts.

Chakra Scan: This technique is helpful if you are drawn to working on a particular chakra. Put your hand directly on the chakra, and keep another hand in the energy field to stabilize the aura along the outer edge (about two feet from the body). Slowly allow the hand to rise upward, away from the body, staying within the spinning vortex of the chakra. Observe any varied sensations, images, or psychic sounds that may arise. If you are drawn to give Reiki to an area in the energy field, do so while simply keeping your hand in that area above the chakra.

Light Massage: Sometimes you may feel a lot of tension in an area such as the hips or shoulder blades. By first lightly massaging the area, some of the denser energy can be released, which then allows more Reiki to enter the body, deeply relax the muscles, and revitalize the cells and energy field.

Other Types of Sessions

Short Session

When there is less time, or you are doing a twenty-one-day series, it is appropriate to give a shorter session. You can have the client lie down or sit in a chair. Give Reiki for twenty minutes on the following positions: head, shoulders, lungs, heart, solar plexus, sacral chakra, knees, and feet followed by the upper, middle, and lower back. If the client has a serious ailment, spend more time in that area of the body, giving Reiki in the field area a few inches from the skin surface. This practice can have a stronger effect on the disease.

Energizing Session

This can be done to simply wake someone up or bring a person out of a feeling of lethargy. Have the person stand up. First give Reiki on the back of the head and shoulders and then follow this with several strong auric sweeps down the back. Finish with giving Reiki to the feet.

Re-balancing

Re-balancing the body and aura is an important aspect of Reiki healing. For this, the hand positions are similar to a full session, but first one side of the body (right or left) is given Reiki, then the other. Special focus is put on the solar plexus area to balance each side of the body and the organs contained within. Body pairs are also a focus to help regain symmetry in the emotions and the body, including shoulders, arms, hips, legs, feet, and kidneys.

Pregnancy

For pregnant women, it is advised to not give Reiki before three months into the pregnancy and after that, to not lay hands directly on the womb but instead focus on the rest of the body. This is so that the Reiki won't aggravate the uterus, possibly causing early contractions. The head, shoulders, back, feet, and legs should be the primary focus of the healing session in order to provide support for carrying the weight of the baby.

Children and the Elderly

For both of these groups, shorter sessions are best. Focus on the area that needs the most attention, such as the head for a headache or the chest for a cough, and finish by grounding out with the feet. Children are often more restless and elderly people may fall asleep, so use your intuition to work with the different situations.

7

"I Share My Power with Love":
Putting Reiki into Practice

In the first degree of Reiki Warrior, the student receives the necessary attunements, learns the basics of Reiki and its history, begins to develop a self-healing practice, studies the chakra system, and learns how to give others Reiki sessions. These are the essential tools to begin a healing practice, to step onto the path of becoming attuned with Reiki, to begin to witness our true nature of love and light and beauty. This is also a time to uncover deeply rooted suffering that we may have experienced and may be continuously experiencing. Traditionally, the student goes through a twenty-one-day cleansing process after the first Reiki attunement, as certain channels in the body and aura are cleansed and revitalized. Oftentimes students experience various physical responses, emotional mood swings, fatigue, and mental shifts. During this time, self-healing is essential, as it helps the Reiki Warrior to regulate the Reiki movement within. Continuous contact with the Reiki Master and beginning to practice on others is beneficial during this time of growth.

As the Reiki Warrior practitioner becomes a clearer channel for the Reiki energy, she will notice that the Reiki flow is not only limited to practice sessions. A sense of clarity and healing work will, with time, begin to pervade other areas of life including the home, work, relationships, and family. Practicing self-healing will continue to lead one to a deeper connection with the Universe, and that connection will be reflected in the surrounding environment. Sometimes, when Reiki Warriors begin to step even more firmly on the path, old habits, unsupportive relationships, and negative behaviors begin to fall away or transform. These changes should be welcomed as an opportunity for growth and spaciousness in one's life.

I learned all three levels of Reiki over the course of one year. During that time I practiced consistently on myself and others, worked in a free Reiki clinic, and studied the Reiki arts in combination with Wicca and the art of sacred space. My life changed drastically in that year as I grew spiritually and consciously into becoming a Reiki Master. I almost entirely gave up drinking alcohol, quit smoking cigarettes, let go of certain people in my life, and formed deep spiritual friendships with others. The months following my Reiki Master training, I left the place where I grew up, traveled three thousand miles cross-country, met a wonderful man, fell in love, traveled to India, learned the basics of meditation, and received my first empowerments in Tibetan Buddhism. Of course, not all of my students go through such a dramatic transformation but some certainly do experience drastic life changes, often when they are on the path to become a Reiki Master.

PROCESS OF MEDITATION

Many of my First Degree Reiki Warrior students are new to both healing and meditation. We begin exploring the power of the mind through simple visualizations, such as the Grounding Cord and Auric Cleanse exercises. This helps students to focus and get a glimpse at the often furiously paced mind stream that many of us experience. Visualization combined with the Reiki practice is a highly beneficial starting point for looking at the process of meditation. In true meditation the mind is as still as a deep pond, where thoughts are like passing clouds in the sky or faint ripples across the surface of the pond. This actual calm and quiet exists in each of us in a natural and clear state but it can take years to begin to truly access this quiet. Practicing Reiki helps to repeatedly quiet the body, which then affects the mind. Visualization helps to focus the mind and gives us some awareness of effective calming. As one becomes more proficient as a Reiki practitioner, the mind naturally becomes calmer, which then allows deeper insights to arise.

AFFIRMATIONS

Affirmations are a useful tool to begin the deep transformative work of the mind. The main function of an affirmation is to develop a more positive way of thinking and to help alter the habitual, negative thought forms that often crowd out our deeper peacefulness within. When we catch ourselves having thoughts that we are not good enough, that everyone is against us, that no one understands, we are promoting a negative sense of self-worth that prevents us from experiencing personal growth and inner joy. This negative view is then projected outward to others in our life who may reflect back the very negativity we think, which further cements the negative thought form.

A Personal Experience

A few years ago I had a powerful healing experience with a woman who has studied shamanism for several years. We did a reading that addressed my issue, which was, at the time, a pervasive feeling that I had a deep source of power but was not fully able to connect with it. During the reading, we discovered a part of my "soul" was still connected with the traumatic loss of my baby daughter, Rubybleu Puja, a few years before. The woman decided to perform a soul retrieval, which resulted in a deep, transformative healing process. After the hour of healing work in which she shook her rattle and journeyed to other realms, she brought back a negative contract for me to void and then rewrite. The contract was that I needed to keep my power a secret, which may have kept it from others, but resulted in me keeping the power from myself as well. That moment of trying to rewrite a positive affirmation for myself was incredibly difficult, as, on another level, I was struggling to reclaim this sense of lost power. I finally managed to rewrite my work and formed the affirmation, "I share my power with love." That moment was utterly life-changing in that I went to sleep and awoke completely refreshed and more whole. I have never felt that loss of power since and used the transformative words of my affirmation to anchor me into a new sense of peace and strength for the next several months.

USING AFFIRMATIONS

Affirmations are positive phrases that have a direct effect on our mind. They can alter our perception in a way that promotes positive thinking and a balanced mind set. Choosing an affirmation that suits you is important, yet it is important to understand that simply repeating a statement over and over is not as effective as deeply feeling the power of the statement. Affirmations are the most effective when used in conjunction with a deeper level of healing, such as Clearing Negative Thought Forms (see Exercise 7.1, below).

Thought forms are statements we tell ourselves over and over that become so strong they create actual forms or structures within our auric field. (See Chapter Eleven: The Human Energy Field for further information.) For example, we may tell ourselves things like: "I am a teacher," "I hate men (women)," or "I am not worthy of love." These thoughts, which emanate from our family and culture, are developed over the years and stick within the energy field. The thought forms themselves are not necessarily good or bad, but when associated with strong emotions and after years of crystallization, they can limit our ability to be open to new ways of thinking and deeply experiencing life. By examining our habitual thinking and resulting thought forms, we can make deeper changes that will promote healing. Brennan remarks that when these thought forms, usually formed in childhood, "are uncovered, seen and released, they can be replaced by a more mature, clear view of reality, which in turn leads to the creation of positive life experiences."[51]

During Reiki sessions and other transformative healing processes such as shamanic journeying, there are often powerful shifts that happen on a deep spiritual level. When that happens, the energy field and body work to cleanse the emotions and begin to heal the body. Usually the conscious mind has a limited connection to our deeper self, which works with the symbolism of the unconscious. Affirmations can help the conscious mind to anchor in the shifts. My personal experience with Reiki is that the spirit level shifts happen regardless of the conscious mind, but using an affirmation is a wonderful tool that can bridge the mental processing with the deeper emotional releasing.

EXERCISE 7.1: *Clearing Negative Thought Forms and Creating Affirmations*
This exercise can be done for yourself or for others. This is an excellent tool that will enhance your healing practice. Reiki Warrior One practitioners can do the basic form and Reiki Two practitioners can add the use of the Reiki symbols.,

First you must choose a thought form that you want to work with. They are often second nature to us and it takes some awareness to recognize and realize the strong negative thoughts we have about ourselves. An easy first thought form to work with is one where we identify strongly with a certain role, such as "I am a writer," or "I am a father." These are not negative thought forms, exactly, but they certainly form crystallized structures in our energy field, which can be cleared. Obviously, if we are a writer or father, this doesn't

---

51 Brennan, *Hands of Light*, 94.

mean we are destroying the role, but instead we are allowing it to clear, open, and reform in a way that is more fluid and in the present moment.

After choosing which thought form you want to dissolve, then sit in a cross-legged meditative position on your chair. Close your eyes and focus on your breath for a few moments. Check in with your grounding cord (see Exercise 1.1) and do your Auric Cleanse (Exercise 3.1). When you feel quiet and calm inside, ask yourself if there is any place in your body that is associated with this thought form. It could be the solar plexus, heart, or knees. If you receive a clear answer, begin your Reiki healing session with an intention, then place your hands on that area. If you are not sure where the thought form is located, simply keep the hands on the heart center. You may feel the urge to move them during the session as you clear the thought form.

After a few moments of passing the Reiki, bring up the thought form in your mind. For example, "I am not worthy of love." Allow yourself to think and be aware of this thought for several moments. Imagine the thought form as a cloud of energy or light or sensation in the aura, just in front of you. Face your hands toward the thought form, beginning to send Reiki. If you are attuned in Reiki Two, send CK for several moments, followed by SHK. Notice any physical or emotional sensations connected with this thought form. Then release it by visualizing the thought form, written down on a paper, as an energy cloud, or simply words. Imagine that the words float out and away from your energy field, to the outside of the aura. Then visualize exploding the thought form into brilliant light, releasing it. Immediately, fill the space left behind with Reiki, particularly allowing it to be filled up with a brilliant color. The color often comes automatically but if not, you can use white, brilliant purple, or gentle pink. Any color that is bright and associated with healing for you can be used. Then, bring the hands back to the heart and do your

Auric Cleanse and protection to seal in the brightness. Close the Reiki session and slowly open your eyes and reground by touching the Earth.

If you are cleansing a role, such as the thought form "I am mother," then you are finished. Your role as mother will reestablish itself naturally with clarity and beauty, as you have given more space to your being for that. If you have cleared a thought form such as "I am not worthy of love," then this is the opportune moment to think of an affirmation that will further the clearing process. "I am worthy of love" is an obvious choice, but any affirmation that claims the clear energy you have experienced will work. Use the affirmation for several weeks after you clear a thought form to reform your energy field.

As you work with this technique, you may notice that other, deep and more negative thought forms may surface during Reiki self-healing practice. You may also notice that you have particular thoughts or emotions recurring around certain areas of the body. We store our mental associations in certain areas of the energy field, which is fed by the emotional energy of our aura. The aura, in turn, can affect the body and physical processes. Often these thoughts are connected to other people and we can do further exercises such as Cutting Cords (See Exercise 14.3) to help release more crystallizations in the energy field.

BRINGING THOUGHT INTO FORM

When I was training in Wicca, we learned how to use ritual and form to encase or capture our thoughts. This slows down the thought process and helps to crystallize our intention in a focused, sacred space. That is where the power of Wicca lies, within the art of bringing thought into form. We do this through the honoring of the moon cycles, the elements, directions and seasons of nature, and uniting the balance of feminine and masculine energies. There are infinite variations to these themes, which are found in all societies (as magick or shamanism) since the first days of human consciousness on Earth. Symbolism plays a major role in this path, as well as using objects that represent the various forces of the Earth. For example, when we give an offering to the air, we light incense, then invoke or call in the element of air in the east direction. This represents the clarity of mind and thought, new beginnings (because the sun rises in the east), and breath, the quality of air that resides in the body.

Using symbolism with the elements is an excellent way to further the release of negative thought forms and crystallize positive affirmations. Below is a simple ceremony that can be done on the new moon to aid in the practice of releasing thought forms and bringing in the new, bright, healing energy. By taking the thoughts and bringing them into the sacred space and performing an action to symbolize release, enhanced by the Reiki healing, the change will be even more powerful and effective.

EXERCISE 7.2: *A New Moon Ceremony*

To perform this ceremony or ritual, you need to choose a new moon evening. This is the time when the moon is invisible in the sky, unseen and hidden. It is a time of going within, to the symbolic void or emptiness of nothingness where you can burn away the old and plant a seed (symbolic or literal) to bring in the new.

Items needed: altar space/table, candle(s), offering (incense, flowers, water), paper, pen, seed(s).

After you have figured out when the new moon is, set aside space and time for about an hour or more. Make sure you find a place where you will not be disturbed by anyone and can give yourself the time to enter into a sacred space. Once you have found a location, set up a small table as an altar and decorate it with a few items to make the space personal. Candles, incense, flowers, a bowl of water, and anything else that can invoke a sense of beauty and respect for Earth in your space is important. This is akin to making an offering, using one of your Reiki Warrior tools. Also, for the new moon, bring one or more seeds to bless in the sacred space for planting.

Next, sit down and intend to make sacred space. This can be done as simply visualizing yourself surrounded by brilliant white light or as elaborate as calling in the directions and honoring the individual elements, directions, feminine and masculine energies. (See Exercise 6.2: Creating Sacred Space.) After you have created your space, spend a few moments doing the Grounding Cord visualization and Auric Cleanse. You can also cleanse the aura using sage smoke[52], feather, or crystal. Give yourself Reiki healing for several moments to relax and deepen the healing connection within the circle.

Next, you must empower the space to make it full of energy and potent power. This can be done by chanting, singing a song, drumming, dancing, or simply intending. Take several moments to imagine the space filled with light, to see yourself sitting in a place that is considered "between the worlds," where magic can and does happen. Open yourself up to allowing a song or sound or movement to come through you to embrace the energy of being alive in this special space. No one is there but you and this is a moment to embrace the power that flows from the Earth and sky into your body.

When you feel that you have called up your power, then choose the thought form(s) you wish to clear. Spend a moment writing on small pieces of paper the roles you wish to release or negative thoughts that are no longer needed. Then burn the papers in your candle or small bowl. As you watch them burn, you can add to the ritual by visualizing the thought form cleansing from your auric field with the Reiki healing as you did in Exercise 7.1: Clearing Negative Thought Forms and Creating Affirmations. If you have Reiki Two attunements, use the SHK symbol to aid in the cleansing process or, alternately, a color. Burn as many roles or thought forms as you wish, watching them curl up and turn to smoke in the flames. Put as much focus and intention into the clearing process as you can, to empower your own purification. When you are done burning, you will leave the ashes in a bowl for a few days and then bury them in the earth as a symbolic gesture of rebirth.

---

52 Sage is an herbaceous plant that is dried and used in certain Native American traditions to cleanse negative energy from areas that are used in sacred space.

After burning your thought forms, take a few moments to sit in the quiet darkness of the new moon. Contemplate the void of black, the womb, the labyrinthine aspects of the Earth, the caves, inner recesses of mountains, and canyons. Sit in this space with no thought, no intention, just being and allowing for a few moments, acknowledging the letting go of your roles and unneeded thought forms.

Once you feel the quiet inside running through you, then choose an affirmation that you want to work with for the next month or so. Write it down on a paper; fold the paper, and place it on your altar. Draw three CKR symbols on the paper to enhance the affirmation. You may leave it there for the next month until the following new moon and then release it back it into the fire, or keep the affirmation to work on further. Magic work is always about change, bending things and shaping them to each moment, so that you are never fixed or blocked but flowing along in life with beauty. You can also use the energy and power of the moment to "charge" your seed with something you want to call in. Choose something simple and clear. You may visualize yourself happy and dancing and open and healthy and blow this image into the seed. Use CKR to enhance the image, if you can, passing the Reiki for a few moments to the seed. Leave the seed on the altar for the night and plant it the next day to symbolize growth into wholeness.

When you are finished, take a few moments to feel gratitude for bringing yourself to this space and performing a ceremony that will help to fuel the fire of clearing. If you know how to send distant Reiki, this is a nice time to practice for a few moments after you are feeling cleansed and charged.

Finally, close the sacred space. Closing the space is an important step to release back to the Earth and Universe the power you have called in. Simply visualize the brilliant white light all around dissolving back into the ground. Thank any elements or directions that you have called in and allow them to go. Similarly, thank the qualities of masculine and feminine and release them back to sky and Earth, respectively. Blow out the candle and leave the ashes and seed for the next day to put into the Earth.

Use this ritual anytime to release not only roles or thought forms, but anything that can be let go of. The new moon is a time of letting go of the old and bringing in seeds for new projects, ideas, relationships, or healing.

REIKI TWO
across time and through space

This section focuses on the Second Degree of Reiki, which explores more deeply the path of healing others. In my courses, Reiki Warriors learn three of the five traditional Reiki symbols, how to send Reiki through time and space, and get an advanced look at the energy field layers and how they are interconnected with the chakras. All of these are included in this book except the symbols, out of respect for the sacred symbols. This section is useful for all Reiki practitioners, particularly ones who have received the attunements and teachings of Second Degree Reiki. Many techniques are accessible for beginning Reiki practitioners, including: Exercise 8.1: Deep Relaxation before Sleep, Exercise 9.2: Earth-Sky Visualization, and the exercises in Chapter Eleven, which work with the layers of the aura and developing an auric vocabulary. A healer of any level can use these to benefit their healing practice. This section also includes certain wisdom concerning deeper healing work with others, including compassion, boundaries, and ethics—all are important for further growth on the spiritual path.

8

A Deeper Commitment

Learning Second Degree Reiki requires a stronger dedication to the Reiki path. Now is the time when Reiki Warriors begin using Reiki as a discipline. Reiki One establishes the innate healing connection to the Universal Life Force and gives us the ability to practice deep self-healing. When a Reiki Warrior receives the Reiki Two attunements, the healing power is strengthened for oneself and, even more importantly, healing others. With this power comes certain responsibilities that are inherent on the healer path. A Reiki Warrior is one who respects his power, claims it as his own, and thus takes responsibility for all of his actions. These actions include continuing our personal self-healing work, speaking our truth, and practicing mindfulness. This is especially important when using the spirit-guided energy that is Reiki to assist others in the healing process.

REIKI AS A DISCIPLINE

A Reiki Warrior practitioner who continuously does the practice of self-healing finds that her life becomes more lucid and focused. When this happens, she becomes a clearer, brighter channel for the Reiki. Using more of the Universal Life Force in Reiki sessions heals us on deeper levels. In accepting Reiki as a path, we are choosing to use it as a discipline that enables us to work even more deeply on our issues regarding health, disease, emotions, psychological states, and spiritual matters. Reiki promises to bring about major life changes as we continue on the path but, like any change, requires persistence, dedication, and surrender. It cannot be said enough times that we must persist in our own self-healing and do the work on ourselves even as we help others. In Reiki Warrior Second Degree, practitioners are affirming the choice to dedicate their self to the healing of those around them, including the environment and the planet.

Yet, these actions must be balanced with the surrender to the Reiki intelligence. Surrendering also means non-attachment to the outcome of healing sessions and allowing others to heal in their own time using their own body/mind/spirit wisdom. When we integrate these ideals into our Reiki practice, we can connect with the deep, joyous, and quiet mind of the Reiki Warrior. Thus, the path becomes the goal, walking the journey of healing.

CULTIVATING COMPASSION

Continuing the Reiki Warrior practice is an excellent way to cultivate compassion. In Second Degree Reiki, the practitioner learns how to give deeper healing sessions using three of the Reiki symbols. As we continue to work on others, oftentimes a heart-to-heart connection happens between the practitioner and the client. A few minutes after beginning the session, an energetic bond forms between the heart chakra of the Reiki Warrior and that of the client. This bond allows one to view the client with a detached awareness that is rooted in compassion. When this happens, personality does not affect the healing and any mental judgments or preconceived notions will not interfere with the session. The Reiki practitioner will find that during this connection, she can more deeply align with the Reiki flow and use the Reiki symbols to better aid in the client's healing process. When the session ends, the heart connection will dissolve naturally, returning to the normal relationship with the client. Over time Reiki Warriors cultivate a compassionate view of all people, not just their clients, as individuals struggling with their own pain and lessons. This perspective allows for more freedom of connection and a way of being that is natural and open-hearted.

I have found that when I deeply care about someone, although natural energy runs between us, I may have a harder time allowing Reiki to flow through me. It is as if my own attachment and care gets in the way of the Reiki flow, preventing it from moving freely. For example, for years I have tried to help my husband heal his knees, as he suffers from chronic pain. Usually all that happens is that the Reiki assists to minimize excessive swelling. My own desire to see him healed and healthy may prevent the impersonal but powerful Reiki from flowing where it needs to. I have much better success with clients whom I am not close to, as the impartiality of my emotions enables me to conduct a highly charged flow of Reiki healing energy.

A Personal Story

During my time of living in California, I had the opportunity to attend an introductory workshop run by students of Anna Wise.[53] Wise has explored and written about the correlation between brain wave patterns (beta, alpha, theta, delta) during various human states of mental awareness or consciousness. Using a special machine that records brain waves in real time, she maps out people's consciousness states, which include levels of awareness during activities such as concentrating on math, playing music, meditating, conversing, and so forth. She has also worked with people who meditate, from beginners to masters. Intermediate practitioners often displayed a certain brain pattern that she calls "the near-awakened state," while advanced practitioners have an "awakened mind state," in which the beta brain waves are reduced greatly and rounded inward, and the alpha, theta, and delta waves were strong and in an appropriate meditation pattern.

During the workshop, after explaining the patterns of the brain, the host asked for a volunteer and I raised my hand. They put several small patches with wires on my head so they could monitor my brain wave state for a few minutes. The pattern was in the normal conversing pattern. Then I said, "Let's see what happens when I give my friend Reiki." My friend lay down on the floor, and I began the traditional sequence of asking the Reiki to flow and honoring the Masters. At that point in my Reiki development, it took a few minutes before the connection clicked open between my friend and me. That evening, four or five minutes into the Reiki session, I felt my heart open and connect with my friend's heart. At that very moment, the host of the workshop asked excitedly, "There! What did you just feel in that moment?" I stopped the Reiki and looked up at the woman and told her about the heart-to-heart connection. She showed me on the brain wave machine how the pattern had jumped markedly into the "near-awakened state" mapped out by Anna Wise. The machine works in real time so it showed that my brain wave state was directly altered by the Reiki flow. The near-awakened state found during the Reiki session is akin to deep meditation, which has the power to effectively aid in powerful healing shifts. We can see that during Reiki practice, allowing the healing energy to move through us has a very real effect on our brains, enabling deep relaxation, which in itself promotes healing.

53 Anna Wise, author of *Awakening the Mind*, deeply explores and teaches on the connection between the brain waves and consciousness.

TIME-DISTANCE HEALING

Another major technique that is used in second degree Reiki is learning to send Reiki across time and distance. In distance healing, Reiki Warriors use the Reiki symbols to activate the Reiki energy and send it across the planet to friends and family, to parts of the Earth that need environmental healing, and to the many people who are in need. When we practice this, we create something essential in our spiritual path. Distance healing is akin to the actions of a bodhisattva,[54] a being who has chosen to help all sentient beings reach enlightenment before leaving the Earth journey. Bodhisattvas have reached an elevated, transcendent experience of enlightenment but stay in earthly form to help others also reach this place of connectedness. This is true compassion, which aids all sentient beings, and it is one of the most precious gifts we can begin to access when we send healing to others across the Earth and through time.

DEVELOPING CONCENTRATION

Another important aspect of Second Degree Reiki is developing the ability to concentrate the mind. Learning the first three Reiki symbols is a fairly easy task and they can be memorized in a day. But learning to clearly visualize the symbols, especially the time-distance symbol, takes some practice. It is essential that the Reiki Warrior practitioner has achieved some degree of mental quietness and can visualize properly before learning Second Degree Reiki. If this is not developed beforehand, students will often quickly learn the symbols and then abandon them because their mind is not able to focus. Although the power of intention is certainly strong enough to generate some amount of healing energy for sending, the actual symbols themselves are used to channel the Reiki energy in a highly effective manner. Practicing the laying-on-hands of Reiki First Degree will help to cultivate the quiet concentration that can be used during the Second Degree. This will lead to a more effective practitioner and enhance the spiritual practice of the Reiki Warrior.

SETTING COMPASSIONATE BOUNDARIES

Another integral aspect of intermediate Reiki Warrior practice is the importance of keeping a clear space, both physically and aurically. When we set a compassionate boundary, we can

---

54 *Bodhisattva,* from Sanskrit, means "hero of enlightenment." Bodhisattvas are courageous individuals who dedicate their entire being to bringing welfare and peace to all sentient beings.

visually surround ourselves with violet light as an intention to work with people in a loving manner. This concept goes hand in hand with the six Reiki Warrior tools by using offering, intention, grounding, trust, clearing, and protection consistently throughout our practice. In setting boundaries, we are able to trust or surrender to the Reiki flow even more deeply during the Reiki session.

As our healing power increases, we must remain ever mindful of how open we are to perceiving our client's issues. By setting clear compassionate boundaries, we are intending to receive our clients without judgment, to allow as much Reiki as possible to move through us to aid in their healing and well-being and then let them go to process the healing in their own way. We can of course still support our clients as they work through deeper issues, but we must not become their crutch or try to answer to their life problems. Sometimes it is even necessary to refuse treating people and show them other ways or people they can work with. Oftentimes, I encourage clients to learn Reiki themselves so they can become responsible for their own healing work. This empowers others and helps to deter clients from becoming overly attached to their "healer."

Another important time to keep clear and compassionate boundaries is during our time-distance healing. Ethically, it is very important to only send Reiki to those who we know want to receive the healing. Because Reiki can have a powerful effect on others, if they are not ready to "be healed" or to change, they can perceive the Reiki has a negative force, instead of positive healing energy. Check with those to whom you want to send distant healing in order to make sure they need it. As your healing practice grows, people will ask for distance healing, so you will have plenty of opportunities to work on that level. Also, it is important that Reiki Warriors remain clear and focused during the sending Reiki session and not spaced out or distracted. We must make sure that the session is ended properly and we are not maintaining a psychic link with the people we heal. Closing the session and ending the link helps keep our compassionate boundaries intact.

EMOTIONAL SOURCES OF DISEASE

An important part of becoming a Reiki Warrior is being responsible for our actions as a Reiki healer. This means that we must allow people to be who they are, as they are. Healing is synonymous with change and such change may require nothing short of a huge leap of faith. Allowing people to proceed as carefully as they need to when sorting through the issues that arise during the healing process enables them to experience further growth and change. Sometimes, just one Reiki session may be enough to help someone become completely healed from a twelve-year illness. Certainly, these changes happen and they even happen often. On the other hand, a series of Reiki sessions may only ease the pain of a certain illness during the actual time spent laying on hands. If this is the case, it is extremely important not to judge the person and their illness. We do not want to fall into the habit of explaining away a person's disease or illness based on emotional or mental causes.

Many New Age philosophies address the connection between our emotional states and disease. Although repressed emotions and mind state are huge factors in illness, so are the environment, genes, and karma. Often the notion that a disease is an emotional imbalance is not the full picture and can even seem callous to clients. Assigning emotional connections to disease may be rooted in fear, an outlook that lacks the true compassion we aim to cultivate. As Reiki Warriors, we must use our fearlessness to understand that as human beings, we all experience versions of every kind of emotion in a myriad of ways and that illness is a normal part of the human experience. We can also remember that sometimes dealing with illness helps us to understand people in a more compassionate way.

Client Case History

Several years ago, I was visiting San Francisco and was asked to do a session for a man who had an advanced form of cancer in the spine. As I sat on the bed, preparing to pass Reiki, I remembered my own feeling of cancer, that confusion and darkness that surrounded me in the days when I found out I had a life-threatening disease. I had never treated anyone with cancer before and half-expected to see something extremely dark and vile in this man's energy field. What I found surprised me. Certainly there was some severe leakage and some very dark spots in the aura but somehow it wasn't so different from other auras I had worked on. As I worked to rebalance and vitalize his aura as best I could in just one session, I realized that we are simply on a spectrum of illness and wellness. Cancer to someone could be depression in another, which could be loss of a limb in another. One is not worse or better, they are only relative states of existence that, instead of judging, we can only hope to assist with the healing Reiki energy.

A few years later I learned this man had died, and I felt a sense of sorrow in my heart as I remembered him, lying on the bed that day after the session talking of his hopes, his fears, his dreams. I know that his pain was eased for a moment that day, which helped to ease my own suffering. I also know that we are all truly interconnected and he is a part of me, a part of all of us.

BALANCE

One of the key aspects of any spiritual path is achieving a state of balance. In the principal teachings taught by the Buddha, he addresses walking the middle path, a balanced path. When we begin to heal and feel more connected to the Earth and energy and those around us, we often feel compelled to share that with the world. This is a wonderful feeling but it must be integrated into our life in a way that promotes harmony and equilibrium. Any kind of extreme attachment is undesirable in the Buddhist mind set, even in the case of extreme diets, religious activity, or purifications. As a healer on the path for many years, I have come into contact with people who are intensely attached to their "spiritual" way of being, which they believe to be higher or better. It is important to remember that, in the end, there really is no succinct separation between materialism and spiritualism and we are all a combination of both.

In order to more fully integrate our Reiki discipline in a balanced way, we can use the self-healing practice, visualizations, and deep relaxation to aid the body in balancing emotional and mental shifts. Deep relaxation, which occurs during Reiki sessions, is an important step in the healing process. By simply incorporating this into our life, we will begin to achieve a balance with the overload of stressful living, toxic environments, and manic surroundings. Slowing down and spending time breathing deeply, relaxing the body, promotes healing on all levels and begins to permeate our daily life in positive ways. Below is an exercise to practice deep relaxation before sleep, which will benefit our dream state and, in turn, our waking life as well.

EXERCISE 8.1: *Deep Relaxation before Sleep*

This is a simple exercise to relax the body after each day's various ups and downs. At the end of day, as you lie in your bed, first think back to the day's experiences. Allow the events of the day to rise up naturally in your mind and observe when you felt you were in touch with your inner calm and joy and when you reacted maybe too strongly to those around you. Give yourself this time to truly look at how you shaped and formed your own day through your mind. Feel gratitude for all the loving kindness and support from others, the food you ate, the sunlight you felt on your face, the trees you saw, the people you helped, all in just one day, just a few hours of your life.

Then, allow the thoughts to drift away and focus on relaxing the body. Go slowly from feet upward to head. State in your mind, "my feet are now relaxed," and feel the warmth and the letting go in your feet, then say again, "my feet are completely relaxed." Repeat this simple affirmation throughout the body for your shins, calves, knees, thighs, entire legs, hips, pelvis, genitals, internal organs, lower back. As you move up the body, take several moments with each place, really feeling the deep relaxation spread through your body. Continue up the front of the body, relaxing the stomach, the intestines, the liver, the pancreas, the spleen as well as up the back, the lower back, and kidneys. Relax the heart, lungs, shoulders, arms, hands, upper back, neck, face, and head. As you move slowly up the body, you may notice strange thoughts or fleeting impressions rising into your mind. Simply watch them and let them float away as you relax ever deeper.

You will probably fall asleep at some point, but if not, finish with intending that you remember your dreams for the next morning. Dreams can be a useful tool on the healer's path and help to uncover deeper underlying issues. The more relaxed consciousness we develop as we fall asleep, the more insights we have access to as developing Reiki Warriors.

9

The Power of Symbols

Humans have been using symbols for thousands of years. From the earliest drawings etched onto cave walls to the contemporary complexities of modern language, we have consistently used and refined the symbols of communication. Vedic texts of India explain that the ancient Sanskrit letters are not only symbolic representations of sound, but also contain specific meaning when thought or spoken aloud with intention. For example, the symbol for AUM, when drawn and chanted, is not only a letter in the Sanskrit alphabet but also holds the meaning "universal consciousness." Similarly, the basis for Japanese language, which helped Mikao Usui form the Reiki symbols, is both phonetic and conceptual, in that the symbols contain meaning as well as sounds.

When studying the Reiki symbols, we must understand that (unlike modern Western alphabets) the symbols not only represent certain meanings, but also that the mantra or name associated with each one carries with it a certain quality or power. To take this a step further, the Reiki symbols themselves are the containers for a certain kind of consciousness that allows the healer to channel Reiki, to use the symbols to enhance the healing session, and, as a Reiki Master, to seed the student's aura with the symbols.

According to myriad Reiki sources, the Reiki symbols were originally derived from ancient Sanskrit texts. This idea stems from Hawayo Takata, who claimed that Mikao Usui rediscovered Reiki in a formula in a Zen temple's Sanskrit texts.[55] To the best of my knowledge, there is no precise text from which Usui derived the Reiki formula. Probably it was Usui's personal study of various Tendai Buddhist texts, combined with his life experiences and the twenty-one-day retreat on Mount Kurama that resulted in his discovered use of the Reiki

---

55 Rand, "Hawayo Takata's Reiki Story," Lübeck, et al., *The Spirit of Reiki*, 29.

symbols. Although there is much myth and mysticism surrounding the Reiki symbols, there is no substantial evidence showing that the original Reiki symbols are connected to Tibet, Atlantis, or Egypt; yet, all the symbols are recognized in Japan.[56] Today's symbols may be a watered-down version of the original symbols used by Usui. Regardless, our intention has enough power to be carried through the symbols we have available to us today. For further elucidation on the evolution of the symbols, look into Maureen J. Kelly's book *Reiki and the Healing Buddha* and www.cedarseed.com/air/reiki.html, a Web site that provides excellent images of the possible original Reiki symbols.

REIKI SYMBOLS AND BUDDHISM

Usui was a Tendai Buddhist and most likely contemplated one of the main tenets of Buddhism, *sunyata,* or "emptiness." Emptiness is the partner of form, the dancing interplay of life between absolute and relative realities. Trying to witness emptiness does not mean the student strives to become a shell of a person, devoid or absent of thought and feeling, but instead to see the emptiness that is inherent in all existence. Even if we look at life from a scientific basis, we see that objects become smaller and smaller, composed of tiny atoms, and we find that most of that composition is indeed empty space. Working toward witnessing emptiness enables us to drop our ego tendencies and see life as it truly is: impermanent and in constant flux. Within that experience is a vast resource of wisdom fueled by a perfect understanding of bliss and luminosity. This understanding enables us to connect with all things in the Universe, in both form and emptiness.

Because it is impossible for most of us to jump from our normal day-to-day existence into a deep understanding of sunyata, we need tools to aid us. Using the Reiki symbols as a stepping stone enables us to begin the process of simplifying the mental constructs built up in our mental reality. Visualizing a sacred symbol and chanting the mantra helps to purify our mind and rid it of chaotic turbulence. We can look at Usui's glimpse of sunyata, or wisdom of emptiness, as an inspiration and a way to use the Reiki symbols that he discovered all those decades ago.

56 Stiene and Stiene, *The Reiki Sourcebook*, 88.

THE REIKI SYMBOLS

The Reiki symbols are forms that are meant to be honored and used with integrity. In order to use them, one must have the appropriate Reiki Two attunements and the proper teachings that accompany them. That being said, you can find every symbol and its variations all across the Internet and in many Reiki books. My personal philosophy is that the symbols are sacred but not secret; that would be impossible in this time of "no secrets." I share the information below so that it may enhance the understanding and practice of Reiki but leave the seeker to learn the symbols in a respectful manner. It is important to note that the symbols have little power without the proper attunements and although they are easily accessible, they remain a virtual mystery until one has learned how to draw and visualize them successfully.

The Power Symbol

The first symbol is traditionally called the "power symbol," referred to as CKR, and is associated with the color white. The symbol is an ideogram, meaning that the image holds the inherent meaning in its shape. The form of a spiral around a stem invokes an ancient connection to the Earth. The chakras spin around their points of anchoring over the body, just as the Earth spins around its axis, as electrons spin around an atomic nucleus. This spinning symbol holds the power of the universe and is directly connected with the Reiki Warrior. The axis is the unifying Earth-sky image while the spiral connects us with our planet, our environment, and our auric field as Reiki Warrior practitioners.

The power symbol is used to bring energy in, to enhance the existing energy that is there. When the practitioner draws the power symbol into a chakra or over an organ, she is intending that the energy of the place is magnified by the spiral power of the universe. The power symbol is used to attract more physical healing energy to cuts, burns, infections, and fatigue. It can aid in enhancing intentions, manifestation work, increasing memory, and improving concentration.

Because it is bringing power in, the symbol may be aggravating to certain conditions and should be used with the second Reiki symbol. In my own practice, I have found that if an ailment is causing a certain amount of pain or discomfort, one should avoid the power symbol until the pain has passed. Some examples are headaches, stomach illnesses, and epilepsy. I also avoid putting the power symbol directly onto a pregnant woman's womb so the fetus is not disturbed. (Although putting it onto her back and feet to promote deep relaxation has a lovely effect.)

Over years of working with the Reiki symbols, one begins to develop a personal and unique relationship with them. I have found that changing the symbol size, visualizing the symbol in its three dimensional form, and experimenting with colors are useful ways to integrate the symbols into my Reiki practice. Often, to clear an auric block, I visualize hundreds of tiny, almost microscopic power symbols streaming around and under the block to loosen its hold and then remove it. One student of mine who is a Chinese-medicine doctor taps tiny versions of the power symbol into her needles as she applies the treatment. An excellent way to use a large power symbol is draw the axis running down the center of the body from the head to the muladhara. Then draw the spiral around the auric field, from muladhara to ajna, then to svadhisthana, spiraling on through vishudda and manipura and ending in harmonious balance at anahata.

The Emotional/Mental or Clearing Symbol

This symbol is the emotional or mental symbol and/or clearing symbol. It is often referred to as SHK and is associated with the color blue. This symbol is often harder for the Reiki student to connect with. It has a peculiar shape that is reminiscent of a small monster or dragon. This, actually, is a very appropriate image for clearing away blocks, as it represents the dragon-like quality that can absorb illness, negativity, and blockages. This symbol seems to "move" more slowly than the power symbol and works on all levels of the client.

The clearing symbol is effective for physical ailments such as headaches, infections, and toxicities. It is also used to help clear auric "sludge," blocks, and stagnant energy. I often use it for stomach problems and visualize a large clearing symbol lying along the intestine, clearing away impurities. This symbol is also an effective way to clear negative emotional blocks or thought patterns that result in addictive and negative patterns in one's life.

This symbol works extremely well with the power symbol. Together they can be used for a variety of Reiki applications in which the practitioner first cleanses the area using the second symbol, followed by the power symbol to enhance healing energy. For example, if one has a clog in the liver, the practitioner can imagine a cleansing symbol settling into the organ for a few minutes. As the light and movement of this symbol affect the area, the practitioner then puts in the power symbol to revitalize the liver functioning. The combination of these two Reiki symbols can be applied in several ways:

1. **Clearing and Programming Crystals:** Using crystals is a highly effective way to ground and energize the client or self during a Reiki session. I personally use a large black tourmaline near the base chakra if I feel the person will need some grounding during the Reiki session, or if they have trouble grounding out through the muladhara or root chakra. I also use quartz crystal over the crown chakra area, or have the client hold healing crystals such as rose quartz or amethyst. If you want to use crystals, take a workshop on them, or refer to such resources as Melody's *Love Is in the Earth: A Kaleidoscope of Crystals*. Once you have your crystals, you can then use your Reiki SHK to cleanse the crystal by simply holding the crystal in your hands for several minutes, sending in SHK. It is also highly effective to put the crystal in a bowl of salt water in sunlight for a few days and enhance the process by putting the SHK into the crystal once a day. This should be done in the bowl of water when you first buy the crystal.

    After cleansing, use the CKR symbol to "set" the crystal with a specific intention such as purifying, manifesting, or grounding. Also intend whether this crystal is solely for personal use or for use with clients. Visualize the CKR entering the crystal with the specific function of enhancing the intention. Make sure you remember the intention and use the crystal only for that purpose. If you wish to change the intention, simply clean the crystal again and reprogram it using your intention with CKR. You should also clean the crystal every few weeks, as it absorbs muddled or negative energies over time and should remain clear for proper use.

2. **Clearing Negative Thought Forms and Creating Affirmations:** See Exercise 7.1

3. **Cleansing a Space:** This can be done when you want to create sacred space (See Exercise 6.2) or are simply clearing a space, such as a room, home, or garden. You can send Reiki to the space using SHK for clearing for several moments, followed by energizing it with the power symbol, CKR.

4. **Food, Water, and Medicine:** By clearing food, water, and medicine with SHK and then charging with CKR, you can effectively cleanse them of any toxins or negative side effects and enhance the positive qualities. When I give Reiki sessions to my friend

who has cancer, I often pass the symbols into the chemotherapy bag to positively affect the treatment while minimizing the nausea and pain.

5. **Garden Plants, Trees, Rocks, and Various Natural Environments:** Using the Reiki and the symbols, you can practice on everything and anything in the natural world. In my Reiki Warrior courses I strongly encourage students to work with the natural environment as a way to stimulate intuition, ground, open up the aura with sunlight and clear air, and find a personal connection with the Earth. I usually hold a "garden class" in which I have students study plants, crystals, seeds, and water both with the ordinary five senses as well as with our other perceptions. An integral part of the Reiki Warrior path is the recognition that everything has an essence or spirit aspect. Studying both the physical or ordinary attributes of flowers and water as well as the non-ordinary feeling or qualities helps improve our ability to more deeply understand ourselves as well as our clients.

6. **Pets and Animals:** Just as with the plants, you can also apply Reiki to pets and animals around you. They respond very naturally to Reiki and will often move around to show you where they need healing. I have experienced numerous animals coming to me, running even, putting their body up against mine and showing me exactly where they need Reiki. This is also a great practice and can easily be used with symbols as well.

7. **Clearing Technology:** I know this one sounds funny, but just try it! Oftentimes broken technology is surrounded by a negative thought form that can be cleared and reenergized using the Reiki symbols. Just as temples and churches are filled with repeated thought forms of prayer and reverence, other things also cultivate certain qualities around them. When we use our technology and continuously project a negative or positive mind set around it, it can affect the machine and its functionality.

The Time-Distance Symbol

The final symbol learned in Reiki Two is the time-distance symbol and is associated with the electric purple of Reiki. This is a longer kanji symbol that consists of several older characters taken from the Japanese language; it is also expressed as HSZSN. Here we see the distinct connection of Reiki to Japan through its first practitioner, Mikao Usui. This symbol is primarily used when practicing time-distance healing. In order to use this properly, the student must be able to visualize all three of the Reiki symbols very clearly. In the process of sending, the third symbol is used both to connect with the recipient as well as to begin the movement of the Reiki from the healer to the recipient. In other words, the time-distance symbol works like both a telephone and the wires. The sender is lifting up the phone, accessing the line, and beginning to talk. It is a powerful symbol and, when used correctly, can result in extraordinary healings.

A Personal Story

One of the most significant times I used time-distance healing, coupled with group Reiki, was for the birth of my daughter, Mojave Lotus. I taught my birth assistants both First and Second Degree Reiki. During Reiki Two, the three of us spent three powerful days working with the deeper elements of spirit and body. Through this I continued to practice the art of surrender, listening to the spirit of my new child, who undulated watery wisdoms from within. The powerful distance healing we did together involved sending Reiki energy specifically to the birth. The three of us sat, holding space and sending our intention for an easy, clear birth in the golden purple Reiki light across time. That moment is forever etched in my mind, as the energy of those few minutes certainly transcended the days and months to the moment of birth. When the three of us and my husband came together to welcome my daughter into the world in that same room, we witnessed the very same feeling of intense purple golden light, a wondrous, pure-hearted blessing. Using the symbols and energy of Reiki, I felt that we connected the birthing event with the moment two months prior, forming a clear bond that transcended time and space.

EXERCISE 9.1: *The Process of Sending*

First you must find someone to whom you want to send Reiki energy. As discussed earlier, it is important that you choose someone who wants to receive healing. To do this in an ethical manner, you must ask the person you choose. If asking is not possible, choose a past incident of your own or simply send to the Earth or a troubled spot on the planet that could benefit from general healing.

Now, follow the steps below to send your Reiki healing.

1. Set up the picture of the recipient or prepare to visualize him. Set up painted images of the Reiki symbols to help remind you of your visualization. I have my students first paint and practice with the images to help in memorizing them. In a short time, they will be easy to pull up and use in the mind's eye, but the images are a nice addition to your altar space.

2. Create a sacred space, using the power and clearing symbols, incense, and four directions. See Exercise 6.2: Creating Sacred Space.

3. Turn off the lights and light a candle to focus your gaze. (I often do my sending at night when the spiritual realm is stronger.)

4. Sit in a chair or on a cushion in front of the image of the person or place and candle and do the Grounding Cord exercise (Exercise 1.1) and Auric Cleanse (Exercise 3.1).

5. State your Reiki intention that this goes for good, with palms pressed together.

6. Put your hands up in the air, facing the image, and close your eyes.

7. Visualize a color to get your sending work going and imagine it moving through space toward the picture of the recipient.

8. Send the time-distance symbol and continue visualizing for a few moments.

9. Follow this with the power symbol, then the clearing symbol.

10. Continue sending symbols and colors as needed for ten to fifteen minutes.

11. When you feel enough Reiki has passed to the person, then visualize him healthy and relieved of his illness or issue.

12. Dedicate this healing so that it may help all beings of the Universe.

13. Close the Reiki connection by stating aloud that the session has finished.

14. Take a moment to open your eyes, stretch, do your Grounding Cord, Auric Cleanse, and a protection exercise, if needed.

The following exercise is a beautiful practice to do before or after a sending session. This is the essence of the Reiki Warrior, the firmly rooted Being on Earth, who is able to access the incredibly sky wisdom from above. Becoming a channel of these forces is one of the most beautiful experiences one can have while living on Earth. I always do this practice after a sending session, as a way to connect in with earth and sky, as well as to take a moment to feel gratitude for this rich life experience. Once you are used to doing a longer sitting practice, you can also do this before a sending session to enhance your time-distance Reiki practice.

EXERCISE 9.2: *Earth-Sky Visualization*

Sit in a comfortable, cross-legged meditative position. Keep the spine straight. Close your eyes and concentrate on your breath for a few moments. Focus on where you are sitting, on your buttocks, hips, legs pressing into the ground. Visualize muladhara, the root chakra, as a red disk, slowly spinning. After a few moments, imagine your grounding cord. Visualize the cord extending downward from muladhara into the floor below. Allow your cord to grow straight down, through any rooms below and into the soil. Make sure your grounding cord is a healthy size and color as it moves through the rock, the water, then more rock into the center of the Earth. If the cord is too small, too large, dark or muddled, simply remove the cord and visualize throwing it into the psychic fire. Then replace the cord with a bright, clear color, four to six inches in diameter. Notice how it feels to be connected with the Earth.

Now imagine the Earth energy moving upward. Become a channel for Earth energy to move up through your grounding cord and into muladhara. Allow the energy to rise higher, through your legs and hips, into your spine and back. Notice how it feels as it moves through svadhisthana, the sacral chakra. Visualize the energy moving through your organs, the genitals, the womb and ovaries, and the lower intestines. As the energy rises higher, into manipura, the solar plexus, feel the relaxation and warmth. Visualize the energy moving through the upper intestines, liver, stomach, gall bladder, pancreas, and spleen. Feel the movement up the spine, spreading out through the kidneys. Take note of any colors, symbols, and/or sensations you may experience as Earth energy rises through the body and auric field.

When the Earth energy reaches anahata, or the heart chakra, allow it to move through the heart, into your shoulders, down your arms, and out your hands. Notice any sensations as the energy swirls through your hand chakras. This activates the Reiki energy. Stay here for several moments, breathing the energy deep into the lungs and heart chakra, allowing it to permeate your energy field and body.

Next, bring your awareness to the space above your head, to the sahasrara, or crown chakra. Take a moment to visualize the dark, indigo night sky above you. Imagine the stars sparkling and the moon shimmering as bright, cosmic light moves down into your auric sphere. Visualize the energy from the stars, the moon, the sun, swirling downward, into sahasrara, illuminating your crown, head, and face. Allow the energy to move farther down, through ajna and into your head, the brain, and forehead. Feel the sensation of skylight illuminating the third eye. As you inhale, imagine the sky energy moving down into the face, the eyes, cheeks, lips, jaw, and ears. Feel the clear brilliance illuminating your head and auric field. Visualize the energy moving down into vishudda, the throat chakra, filling up the neck and upper chest. Notice any colors, symbols, and/or sensations as the sky energy moves down through your neck, lungs, and into anahata. Imagine the sky light swirling in your heart, mixing with the Earth energy. Pay attention to your feelings of this fusion, as you open yourself up as a Reiki Warrior channel. Spend several moments in this space absorbing the feelings and cleansing the heart chakra. Take a few moments to be thankful for mixing Earth and sky, to honor Spirit as a creature on Earth.

Allow the sky energy to move through your shoulders, down your arms and into your hands. Raise your hands upward, palms facing away from you and allow the Reiki to emanate outward. If you are Second Degree Reiki, use the appropriate Reiki symbols. Picture an image of the planet, a dear friend or family member, or simply a ball of light; let the Reiki fill the image with bright, clear healing light. After several minutes, release the image into the universe by raising your hands up to the sky and chanting AUM three times. This offering is a special way to show gratitude for allowing Reiki to move through you. After you have released your image, bring your hands to your heart and practice self-healing Reiki for a moment.

Finally, bring your awareness back to your body. Check in with your grounding cord and do an Auric Cleanse and protection if you wish. Bring your hands to the ground, roll out your neck and shoulders. When you are ready slowly open your eyes. Take note of any sensations, colors, or symbols you may have experienced. How did sky energy feel different from Earth energy? How did it feel to send healing energy to others and/or the planet? Another option is to try bringing sky energy down through all the chakras without bringing up Earth energy. You can do this to help heal the Earth by asking her what she wants you to do with this sky energy and how you can honor her. Remember to always re-ground after this exercise.

EXERCISE 9.3: *Full Moon Ceremony*

The full moon is a time of abundance, vitality, celebration, and witnessing the night illuminated by the glowing light of the moon. This is the time to honor projects that have come to fruition, to honor the abundance already present in one's life through gratitude, and to do healing on the self and others, as the healing will be magnified by the intensity of a full moon. Drawing down the moon into oneself for healing is an excellent way to align your practice of working with the Reiki symbols with nature. For this ceremony you need altar items, such as flowers, incense, water in bowls, fruit, and candles, as well as paper, pen, and a small cloth bag.

Once you determine which night is the full moon, set aside space and time for about an hour or more. As in the New Moon Ceremony, Exercise 7.2, use a place that is undisturbed by anyone and where you can give yourself the time to enter into a sacred space. Again, take time to set up a small table as an altar and decorate it with a few items to make the space personal—flowers, fruit, a mirror, candles, incense, bowls of water, and personal pictures or images that mean something to you and enable you to connect in with the Earth and healing. The full moon is also an excellent time to "charge" items—such as crystals, stones, healing wands, and divination tools—with the energy and brilliance of the moonlight.

As you would do for the new moon ceremony, take time to make sacred space. This can be done in your own method or you can use Exercise 6.2: Creating Sacred Space as a guide. Then perform the Grounding Cord visualization and Auric Cleanse and do some self-healing Reiki for several moments to relax and deepen the healing connection within the circle.

The space must then be charged, which is very connected to the presence of the full moon. To bring up the power of the space, you can visualize the moonlight streaming into your sacred space and filling it up. Chant AUM repeatedly, drum, or move to fill the power of the space, to make it potent and charged with energy. Imagine the moonlight coming down into your body, through your crown chakra and spreading out through the rest of you, filling you up with light and love and power. In the Wicca tradition, this drawing down the moon will fill you with healing light that can be used to focus your intentions of healing, abundance, and joy. Imagine your magical items also filling with moonlight, becoming charged by the energy in the sacred space under the moon.

Once you and the circle are full of energy, sit down and begin to practice your Reiki distance healing. Follow the steps given in Exercise 9.1 to send healing to another person. Imagine the symbols flowing down from the moonlight, through your crown and out your hands into the person who needs healing. You can also imagine your family, a group of people that are in crisis, or the Earth as a whole receiving the positive, beneficial Reiki energy. Notice if there are differences in the symbols when you sit in this power-filled space. Do they seem brighter and more intense? Easier to work with? When we put ourselves into a state of non-thinking, as when performing a ritual, we often find it much easier to access the healing energies.

When you have finished sending healing, take several moments to think of all the people, events, and things you are grateful for. Make a list if you wish, or visualize each person and event that you are joyous about in your life. Bless each gratitude with the CKR to enhance its power of openness. Intend to see even more fully the abundance that exists in every moment of your life.

Finally, if you wish, take the time to write down intentions for projects to which you want to bring more energy so they can be enhanced in the power and brilliance of the full moon. Sometimes in sacred space, the intention and energy is so focused that we can empower ourselves and life plans more than usual. One full moon I wrote down a wish to bring my Reiki book into manifestation and the very next day I received an email from my future-editor-to-be wishing to see my proposal! We must be ready for this abundance and gift, so ask and then let go, standing open hearted and open handed to receive. In time, receiving follows gratitude effortlessly and eventually becomes a natural flow in life that may not need rituals, just the simplicity of clear thought. Until that cycle becomes effortless, rituals enable the complex thinking mind a chance to let go and open up to being and dancing with myriad forms of expression.

To close the ceremony, put the written intentions in a small cloth bag and leave them on the sacred altar space for the next weeks or months. Revise as needed during following new moons as done in Exercise 7.2, where you can burn your intentions to be released once they have manifested or if you no longer want something to happen. Notice how your wishes change and use that knowledge to guide which intentions are true-hearted paths and which are mere whims fueled by desire. Feel a final sense of gratitude toward yourself, the natural world, and the Reiki for taking the time to connect in with the full moon. Close the sacred space in your own way, or use the guide for releasing each direction and element. Blow out the candles and sit in quiet moonlit contemplation, feeling full of renewed energy and power for the next month.

There are so many ways to work with your energy and the Reiki symbols. I encourage the seeker to be creative and open to exploring new ways of using them. In my Reiki Warrior courses, I have my students learn and memorize the symbols by painting them and meditating on their form. Other ways one might incorporate the use of the symbols into daily life is to dance them or imagine them moving through the body in a physical way, create three-dimensional forms of the symbols with clay or wire, use them in the auric exercises, and chant the mantras during meditation. Reiki Warriors are not meant to be overly serious, and by playfully experimenting with color, symbol, and movement, we can move further away from our egotistic tendency to take ourselves too seriously. This bit of levity allows more light to flow through and humor to dance lightly upon our days. I will explore more advanced work with the Reiki symbols in Chapter Twelve: Advanced Reiki Warrior Practice.

10

Reason Versus Intuition

Humans have been practicing healing for thousands of years. The first prominent healer role assumed among tribal peoples was given the name "shaman," by anthropologists of the twentieth century. A shaman is likened to a medicine man and was responsible for curing the sick, working with the elements to alleviate times of drought or famine, and providing emotional support for the entire tribe or village.

As human societies have evolved, we have moved away from the more intuitive perspective of the shaman to a time of rational and scientific thinking. Modern approaches to the body by contemporary physicians are based in deductive thinking from a physical perspective. Today, much of our modern medicine is still entrenched in the Newtonian, dualistic view of the world, one that sees the body as individual, physical components that must be addressed separately. Not only are the physical parts and systems of the body divided, the mental and emotional realms belong to another field altogether: psychotherapy.

In contrast, methods of healing that are based on ancient wisdom—such as Chinese medicine, the traditional Indian systems of Ayurveda and yoga, Reiki, and contemporary shamanic practices—do not view the mind as separate from the body. Instead, through a holistic approach, they see the fluid interaction between these aspects of the human being. With Einstein's revolutionary scientific breakthroughs, the modernist approach to the body is shifting into a new arena of understanding. Many people who have been born and raised in the rational, linear societies of the West, primarily using deductive reasoning, are beginning to open up to new ways of thinking reflected in modern science. People are starting to discover that indeed there is more to the body, mind, and emotions than just mechanical parts. I highly recommend that the Reiki Warrior student familiarize himself with deep thinkers such as

Barbara Ann Brennan, Anna Wise, Candace B. Pert, and Fritjof Capra, who explore the connections between mind, body, and emotions through science, experience, and health.

One of the major differences between science and alternative healing lies in the way in which we perceive the world. Intuition is the method of knowing akin to the shamanic practices of ancient times, while reason is the more contemporary, deductive approach. The Reiki Warrior today lives in a modern world and although he uses the more intuitive system of laying-on-hands and Reiki symbols he must still function in the current reality that is usually founded in logical thinking. I firmly believe that by using both the holistic method of intuition combined with the linear approach of the rational mind, the Reiki Warrior can cultivate a disciplined practice that promotes true transformative healing.

INTUITION AND REASON

In order to use these two perspectives effectively, we must examine their meaning more closely. Reason is the critical, deductive, or rational perspective. Based on the scientific method, we approach the world with the idea that nothing is true, that there is no inherent meaning, but there is instead a logical explanation to the various phenomena in the world. Although this idea may appear cold or detached, it is actually very useful in the Reiki Warrior's practice. Instead of jumping into the Reiki practice with blind faith, we are simply testing the theory of Reiki and working with the various results that occur when we do our healing practice. In this way a concrete and stable awareness is cultivated within the practitioner.

Alternatively, intuition is the deeper insight we all possess within. This is the part of us that feels or senses the world around us beyond the mind and its rambling thoughts. Shamans have used this kind of silent knowing since time immemorial to go on spiritual journeys for their clients, finding symbolic answers and decoding them.

There are two important qualities to note within these ancient practices that can be applied to the Reiki Warrior's path. First, most shamans or healers went through an extensive training period that required the apprentice to first encounter, then face, subdue, and transform the deeper ego tendencies. In this way, his silent knowledge, or intuition, was not impeded by personal desire or the ego's subtle manipulations. Second, Carlos Castaneda, who has delved deeply into the warrior path in his series of Don Juan's teachings, succinctly points out that the true "warrior" is the one who has not only developed this power of both silent knowledge and the power of reason, but can also consciously navigate between the two.[57]

Many people, especially in the Western world and the quickly modernizing portions of the East, are currently entrenched in the more contemporary view of the world, using reason and logic. Having experienced the dominance of the rational mind for centuries, our silent knowledge has been displaced or discounted in the current views of modern science. Many of my students from the West have a hard time understanding Reiki and its mysterious method of passing through the body to promote healing. They want to know how and why it works. My answer is always that one must experience Reiki first, not just once or twice, but with much practice. Experience enables the student to begin accessing her own silent knowledge. This state of relaxing or simply being has largely been abandoned by modern society and reclaiming it is an integral part of the Reiki Warrior's path.

A Client Case History

One man who came to see me, like several of my clients, was simply curious about Reiki and its possible effect on him. He was extremely critical of magical systems in general, especially those where the practitioner blindly devotes himself to a path without analysis. Yet, he was also fascinated by the various magico-religious layers that are found in India and persisted in exploring different arenas of thought and practice. I agreed to give him a series of sessions—three altogether over the period of a week—so that he might witness some differences. He did not have any particular health problems, so we did a general focus on his energy field. As I worked on him, I found there to be rigid mental thought forms in his field around his head. I focused on rebalancing the aura and easing the thought forms. His response to the first session was one of deep relaxation and he was mildly impressed with the beneficial result. The second session was much more intense and I worked even more on the rigidity of his field. After the second session, he said he felt very strange and remarked that he couldn't believe how different he felt, as if he had done yoga for two hours. This was mysterious to him, that he might feel so much change in his body from lying on a table for an hour. Later that day he suffered from a severe headache for some time, which then passed, leaving him feeling quite clear. For

57 Castaneda, *The Power of Silence*, 240.

the final session, I focused on grounding him energetically and physically so that he might not feel overwhelmed by the shifts.

The interesting aspect of this series for me was not that he felt a shift, as this is a common experience with my clients, but how amazed he was at his *own* awareness shift. I have found that my most critical clients and students, the ones who are suspicious of "psychic" awareness or intuition, are often the most receptive to those very psychic impressions. It seems that maintaining a healthy level of doubt enables practitioners to make highly acute observations. Also, I believe those with strong tendencies toward a full perspective of reason may actually have an easier time, with practice, in more fully shifting into the realm of silent knowledge.

Using only intuition and relying solely on the insight of the silent knowledge can be limiting, especially when the practitioner has not fully dealt with his own ego tendencies. The intuitive stream of images, colors, and symbols that sometimes appears before the healer's mind's eye may only be projections without the structure of reason.

It is important to understand that intuitive knowledge, while imperative to successful healings, is just one layer of our perception. Many seekers in India are highly attracted to the mystical and revel in psychic phenomena. While this is certainly a fascinating and wondrous realm, we are still viewing the phenomena through our own personal, emotional, and mental filters which, until fully cleared, are affected by our past, our karma, our ego, and our unresolved emotional and mental issues. This is illuminated by the present state of our chakra system, and the process of clearing and activating takes time. By simply witnessing the intuitive insights, Reiki Warriors can cultivate a discerning awareness through non-attachment without being waylaid by mystical perceptions.

A Personal Story

Most of my students have some sort of intuitive awareness that is enhanced with just one Reiki attunement. One of my students from West Africa had a highly intuitive way of working with healing that became apparent during the Reiki Two class. He instinctively knew the way the Reiki symbols should be applied. With almost no guidance from me he simply applied the symbols as needed in the appropriate manner. Many students, myself included, take at least a year to cultivate this kind of knowing. Coming from Africa and from a healing family, his development is based in an alternative type of perception that is often lacking in my Western students. Yet, when I questioned him about this, there was no way he could rationally explain the process, it was simply a matter of knowing. By cultivating the use of reason, he will be able to create a map of his intuition and formalize the silent knowing about the processes of the body.

Another way in which reason can assist our intuitive work is in cultivating discernment. After practicing Reiki for ten years, I have had thousands of intuitive perceptions that have grown with time. At first I could only discern certain colors and symbols. For many years I chose not to reveal too much about what I saw because something like "seeing green" didn't mean very much to me or to the client. After "seeing green" in association with a certain kind of person, I slowly developed what I call an auric vocabulary, which helped to decode the symbolism of the client's energy field. As my intuitive perceptions have become more refined, I not only see colors, I see a multitude of thought forms, organs both physically and astrally, and even hear specific issues in parts of the body. I strongly believe this is a natural state of awareness that many of us have lost or forgotten and that it can be reclaimed with time and practice. That being said, I advise the Reiki Warrior practitioner to not only practice "seeing" colors but use her rational and deductive mind set by keeping note of the available information to form long-term conclusions. Although I am often amazed by my own precise, intuitive perceptions, sometimes I am also wrong! Even with years of practice, it is possible that my own filters are still not definitively crystal clear at every moment. The best way to work with this intuitive knowledge is to ask the clients questions after a session. If you have felt something very specific, ask them and see if it correlates with their current issues.

THE ASSEMBLAGE POINT

Surrounding and interpenetrating our bodies is a complex energy field that exists dynamically with our environment. This energy field is composed of threadlike energy strings, filling up an egg-shaped luminous sphere that surrounds us.[58] The anatomy of this energy field includes the nadis and chakras, which are fueled by the Ki or pranic life force as discussed in Chapter Five: The Chakra System. The assemblage point is the place in the energy field that provides the overall filter for how we perceive the world. Most people's assemblage point is located somewhere in the back of the body. According to Castaneda, the assemblage point can be moved from its position on the surface of the energy field to another position or to the interior of the energy

58 Castaneda, *The Power of Silence*, xv.

field. When this happens, perception shifts and the warrior is able to claim energy and power and find solutions for healing and life situations.[59]

Reason and intuition, the two perceptions we have discussed, are two primary areas that can hold the assemblage point. Most people's assemblage point is not fully on either perception, but partially working through a semblance of reason. This reason, or right-side awareness, is linked to our left brain (since the right side of the body is linked to the left side of the brain), the logical, rational, and analytical part of us. This awareness is akin to the pingala nadi discussed in Chapter Five and dominates the right side of the body, the active, forceful, willpower side that most of Western society is concerned with. Don Juan calls this the *tonal*, or first attention, and it is used in our normal everyday experiences in our work and relationships. The tonal is the organizer of the world and everything we know.[60] The power and strength of the tonal, or left-brain activity, is important for a Reiki Warrior, as it gives a strong form to hold the Reiki energy during healing sessions.

The intuitive or right-brain side is concerned with holistic, synthesizing, and random activity. This is associated with the ida nadi, the intuitive, lunar, and quieter aspect of the energy field. Don Juan terms this knowledge the *nagual*[61], which is our second attention, the unknown, the left-side awareness. The ability to perceive from this point is rare but can be cultivated through the Reiki attunements and practice. Shifting or moving the assemblage point can happen during trauma, taking drugs, accidents, disease, or intense life situations. During these extreme situations we are often able to tap into that deeper, intuitive part of ourselves that enables us to act with speed or clarity. These events come with their own repercussions and may be accidental, but we can also begin to work with this alternate way of perceiving through Reiki practice and meditation.

The sorcerer or warrior is not only able to move the assemblage point fully into the tonal and nagual, but also to shift effectively between the two. This is akin to moving between reason and intuition, between the left and right brain; the ability ultimately leads to immense clarity, power, and balance. Being able to move the assemblage point is the goal of an advanced healer, a place the Reiki Warrior is moving toward. The practice of self-healing and healing others helps to loosen the rigidity of the assemblage point, the fixedness of our current views of the world.

59 Castaneda, *The Power of Silence*, xvi.

60 Castaneda, *Tales of Power*, 121–122.

61 Ibid.

EXERCISE 10.1: *Balancing the Brain Hemispheres*

This exercise can be done on yourself or during Reiki sessions for others. It is a simple and effective way to begin working with the loosening and eventual shifting of the assemblage point. Simply lie down and place your hands in the self-healing position against the back of the head. This time, instead of just passing the Reiki, visualize or imagine the brain inside of your head. Intend balance for several moments and watch what happens. Use CKR to enhance the practice. Oftentimes, when we lie quietly and balance the brain hemispheres in this way, we may go into an altered state of perception that unites the reasonable and intuitive aspects of ourselves. When you feel this shift, you can ask questions and be open to the symbolic messages received to be decoded later. This state can also be achieved through shamanic drumming or rhythmic sounds, various therapies, or light patterning on the eyelids. Such a state of awareness is an incredible tool for the advanced healer and Reiki Warrior.

Robert Monroe[62] is an excellent example of someone who worked with balancing the brain hemispheres, leading to extraordinary travels outside of the body. In this second state, akin to the nagual of Don Juan, much information can be retrieved, spontaneous healings happen, and, even more importantly, we realize that we are conscious beings who continue on after our physical body dies. Monroe mentions the point between the shoulder blades, composed of several fibers of light, which connects our second body to the physical. The point can be likened to the assemblage point. Shifting our awareness to the central part of the energy field will open up new ways of perception that will dramatically enhance our ability to heal effectively.

62 Author of *Journeys Out of the Body*.

Client Case History

I gave Reiki to an older Portuguese woman who was passing through Varkala, India on her holidays. Because she spoke no English and I speak no Portuguese, I had no background about her except that she was feeling some fatigue. When I first laid my hands on her head, I immediately started to hear a small, yet insistent voice stating, "The spleen! The spleen!" over and over again. I proceeded to her spleen area, and worked on both the physical and auric field for some time, then continued with the rest of the session to rebalance and harmonize her energy. Afterwards, we consulted with our translator and I asked if she had any problem with her spleen. She nodded definitively and told me she had recently had an operation on that part of her body, and the spleen had been removed.

A final note on reason and intuition working harmoniously together is illustrated in the above client case history. Knowing the anatomy and physiology of the body should be a crucial part of every healer's path. Using the modern advances of science and its knowledge about the physical systems of the body can only add to your healing practice and help refine the intuition within. The modern-day Reiki Warrior uses the Reiki symbolism to ease the suffering of her clients by cultivating a definitive pipeline between intuition and reason. When both areas are developed, a powerful level of real transcendence emerges.

EXERCISE 10.2: *Partner Perception*

This exercise involves using a partner to enhance the silent perception and intuition within. Partners sit opposite each other and decide who will give first and who will receive. The giver closes her eyes and first decides on an element to send to her receiver. This can be fire, water, air, or earth. The sender must choose how to send this feeling of the element, using imagery, color, and/or memories. She sends for several moments while the recipient does his best to relax and receive. After several minutes, the sender stops and rests for a moment. They do not speak during the rest. After a moment, they exchange roles and repeat the same procedure with a chosen element. After several minutes, the sender stops and both partners open their eyes. At this time they can share what they felt or sensed.

After doing this with elements, explore this same exercise using color, sending in a general way. Then send a particular color to a specific chakra, maybe enhancing your sending using a Reiki symbol. Finally, do the exercise one last time, but try to intuit what the partner needs before sending the chosen color. This is much more difficult because it requires your intuition to be strong enough that you are in a constant communication with it. With time, this becomes easier, more accessible, and even part of your everyday life.

A Personal Story

When working with the partner perception exercise during one of my Second Degree Reiki Warrior classes, an interesting awareness emerged. Before the teaching began, I gave each student a Reiki Two attunement. Sometimes, during the attunement, I am able to sense colors or guides or images that are very powerfully connected to the student in that moment and possibly beyond. One of the students emanated an intense magenta, like a purplish red fire that burned vibrantly throughout his entire auric field. I mentioned this to no one, merely observed the color and energy of the attunement.

During the partner perception, I had the students send and receive colors, without telling each other what they saw in between. The student with the magenta field sent and received from his partner and during this time, I still witnessed the strong magenta color emanating throughout his aura. After the exercise was finished his partner was certain he had sent her a deep, magenta color, which he had. Interestingly she had also sent him this very same color, commenting that no other color could have been sent, that this indeed was simply the energy that was there, in the aura, and was not moving for some time. These moments may seem like simple coincidences, but it is important to know there is a deeper intelligence that connects us all. When we tap into it, these kinds of incidents become more frequent and even common. Soon you may not even be surprised by them!

11

The Human Energy Field

As we progress further on the path of Reiki Warrior, the mind becomes calmer and more focused, allowing certain insights to arise, heightening our perception. The first degree of Reiki seeds the aura with the symbols needed to begin practicing Reiki, and the second degree activates these symbols so the energy flows more easily through the practitioner. Once this happens, a more advanced level of awareness can be used in conjunction with the Reiki symbols.

THE HISTORY OF THE HUMAN ENERGY FIELD

Written knowledge about the human energy field dates back hundreds of years. As mentioned in Chapter Five: The Chakra System, Indian sages contemplated, meditated, and discovered the philosophies that were written down in the ancient mysteries known as the *Vedas*, meaning "knowledge." This inner wisdom knowledge was compiled into a group of texts called the *Upanishads*, which literally means "to sit at the feet." This refers to the nature of the disciple at the feet of his guru or teacher, where this information was transmitted from Master to student.[63] The *Paingala Upanishad*, which contains specific information regarding the human energy field, was written down sometime between the seventh and fifth centuries BCE.

The yogic philosophy classifies three vehicles or bodies of the human being: the physical body, the astral body, and the causal body.[64] Several centuries later, the Theosophy society (specifically, C. W. Leadbeater and Annie Besant) was responsible for researching the noted Vedic texts and delivering the material to the West in the early 1900s. C. W. Leadbeater used

---

63 Definition from *The Oxford Dictionary of World Religions*.

64 Vishnu-devananda, *The Complete Illustrated Book of Yoga*, 15.

the phrase "etheric double" to describe the field that interpenetrates body, mind, and spirit, regulated by the spinning activity of the chakras.[65] We can see this word, *etheric*, used also by Barbara Ann Brennan, as the first layer of the complex system she developed to understand and interpret the human energy field. Brennan takes the idea of the layers even further and draws deep connections between each chakra and seven precise field layers. Each chakra has a certain number of nadis, or energy circuits, running through it, pulling energy into the various layers of the auric field.[66] The number of nadis is also illustrated by the ancient Vedic mandala drawings that symbolically represent each, which are re-created in the chakra table in Chapter Five: The Chakra System.

During the past decade I have worked with certain layers of the aura and found important connections between them and the chakras, and I used these connections in my Reiki Warrior practice. In Second Degree Reiki Warrior we primarily work with the following auric bodies: the etheric or physical body, the emotional body, the mental body, the astral body, and the outer causal body.

The first layer we focus on is the etheric body, the energetic area closest to the actual physical body. This is the layer in which acupuncturists use their needles to tap into the matrix of the energy field in conjunction with the physical organs and tissues. The layer is easily affected by external circumstances, such as too much sun, pollution, and harsh climate, and should be revitalized along with the body during a Reiki session. Using Reiki healing energy on this area is also highly beneficial to stimulate the immune system, balance the endocrine system, revitalize organs, and diminish infection.

The second layer is the emotional body, which contains the fluid energetic movement between the body and the mind. This part of the aura changes rapidly, from day to day and hour to hour. Here energy is expressed through the myriad emotional states and moves around the body in different textures and forms such as globules, streams, spikes, or balls. When a person harbors an excess of a certain emotion—fear, jealousy, anger, sorrow—there may be some rigidity in this layer, so that it can appear dull or brownish colored. Using the Reiki symbols for clearing and then revitalizing is an effective way to begin the process of emotional cleansing in the auric field.

---

65 Leadbeater, *The Chakras*, 2–3.
66 Brennan, *Hands of Light*, Chapter 7.

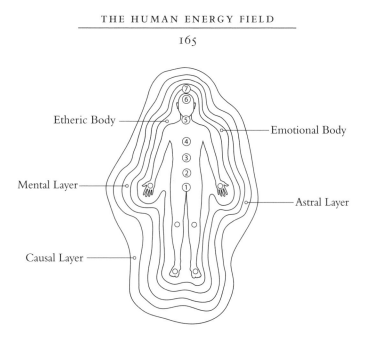

The next important layer is the mental layer, which stores the thought forms and identity constructs we carry around with us. Thought forms are stored packets of energy that exist over various parts of the body. For example, sometimes when I am passing my hand through the aura of a client, I may hear something like "I am not worthy" over her knee. To investigate this further I may ask if she's having knee trouble to see if the thought form has manifested in the body. We can begin to work with releasing the thought form before it manifests as physical dis-ease. Using the time-distance symbol to clear the past cause of the thought form is beneficial, followed by the mental/emotional clearing symbol.

The fourth layer is connected to the higher, spiritual aspect of the auric field. Here is the crystalline layer, which contains the wisdom of the spirit, the higher vibrational aspect of our aura. This is where the Reiki symbols are placed during the attunement process in order to channel the healing energy. The layer is also known as the astral body, which is able to travel during sleep and contains an advanced level of consciousness that is not bound to the lower physical, emotional, and mental states.

The final important layer is the outer layer of the aura, usually referred to as the causal layer. Here, the bands of past lives are stored. Both the astral and causal layers continue on after death, carrying the karmic imprints of this life beyond into the next. Reiki Warrior practitioners are encouraged to first focus on the lower layers before beginning work on the outer, as it takes an extremely keen level of perception to discern the auric qualities of the complex outer layers.

All five aspects of the aura discussed above are interrelated with the chakra system. Certain emotions may manifest as traumas in the nadi connections running through a particular chakra. For example, depression often results in a lack of energy in the muladhara chakra and revitalizing this area is helpful. Another example is found in the knee thought form, "I am not worthy," which may be rooted in the heart chakra. To better understand this interplay between the body, aura, and chakra system, the Reiki Warrior practitioner must develop her own auric vocabulary and practice diligently to form the system that works for her. In this way, no reference list is provided as an "easy" check for the various ailments that can occur. This is because each of us interprets the world in different ways and we must work to develop our own auric understanding of our own field before we can truly analyze the auric fields of our clients.

EXERCISE 11.1: *Self Auric Scanning*

This is an excellent exercise to do both before and after a self-healing Reiki session. Sit in a chair and relax the shoulders and arms. Focus for a few moments on your breath. After you feel relaxed, slowly lift your dominant hand up into the aura, with the palm facing in toward the body. Leave the other hand resting on your thigh. Simply let your hand float around the auric field, being open to any perceptions in the form of color, texture, temperature, or even sound. Move your hand very slowly through the field, noting if it is difficult to move at some places, hotter or cooler. After some time, choose one chakra, for example, anahata, and hold the hand steady about one inch from the body. Allow yourself to feel any perception there. Sometimes, when the hand is one place, you may feel distinct sensations in another part of the body. This is due to the nadi connections running through the aura. Take note of any sensations. Slowly move the hand away from the body, but still over the chakra, seeing if you can sense any different qualities in the part of the auric field that relates to the heart chakra.

When you are finished, write down and draw any experiences you may have felt. Then do your Grounding Cord and a self-healing Reiki session. Afterwards, try the exercise again to see if you feel any differences in the hand as well as the auric field. Again note any observations.

EXERCISE 11.2: *Developing an Auric Vocabulary*

This is an important part of developing your understanding of the auric field as a Reiki Warrior practitioner. Each of us perceives the world very differently and we must learn to develop the intuitive aspect of ourselves through our own method of perception. I am predominantly a visual person. I see various colors, forms, and symbols in my clients' auras. For example, in a person who is not developed spiritually but has a strong potential, I might see colored balls of light that are not yet integrated into the auric field. I might see sharp implements that are "stuck" in the aura from past-life issues, accidents, traumas, or emotional problems. Sometimes I perceive animals or guides that may be helpful to the client to reclaim some lost sense of power. All of these perceptions came over time as I honed my intuition, perfected the art of surrender, and trusted in my innate knowledge. I firmly believe we all have the capability to perceive the world in such a way, although it may take different forms, including but not limited to: physical sensation, sounds or words, images or movie-like projections, even smell or taste.

As a Reiki Warrior, I encourage my students to write and draw the experiences they have for each of their clients. Often, the first impressions are very subtle and fleeting and it requires an attentive mind to remember what was seen. Each time you record your first impression, it will become easier to remember. At first the meaning of certain colors, symbols, forms, or sounds will not be apparent, but with a careful record of your clients' case histories and the perceptions you have about them, you will be able to distinguish, for example, what green "means."

To begin developing your auric vocabulary, simply list several colors and symbols. After each word, such as "red," list all the associations you have with the color. For example: passion, anger, excitement, fire, lava, depth. Notice which colors you have more or fewer associations with. Notice which colors and symbols are a reflection of your cultural connotations of those colors. By beginning to interpret the way you understand the world through symbolism, you can begin to uncover the deeper connection to life through the subconscious, which works deeply with symbols and metaphors.

It is important to understand that you will see other people's auric fields through your own perceptions at first. But with time, you will be able to also see symbols that are directly connected to their experience. Trusting your perception is important. Practicing with a group of healers who intend to work on this level is an excellent way to gain feedback and validation of your subtle, psychic perceptions. You will also notice, as you begin to trust and honor your intuition, it will grow even stronger until it becomes a natural part of your awareness.

A Word of Caution

As the perceptions enable you to understand your clients better, it is very important that you refrain from telling the client everything that you see. Primarily, you are witnessing something that most often pertains to the way in which you, the healer, see the world. This is why I encourage Reiki Warriors to develop their own personal auric vocabulary, to interpret according to their own system of intuition. For example, if I see a green cloud over the heart and tell my client this, the client will attach her own meaning to the green cloud. But if I ask her if she has any feeling in her heart she would like to talk about, then this may be useful to her. This is a delicate balance, as sometimes you may witness something that would be useful to discuss with the client. As a rule of thumb, do not say anything unless the client asks, then use your best judgment to discern what is appropriate for them to hear. If you're not sure, then don't say anything. Too many times I have heard stories of people who went to receive Reiki and were told they had a huge block in their heart, which upset them immensely and they never returned to any Reiki healer. We must remember that although the person may have a block in the heart, this may not be the most useful information in that moment. Maybe the block would have evaporated from just one more Reiki session.

Once our perceptions advance we often want to share this experience, which is a valid feeling. Find a group of like-minded Reiki or alternative practitioners to work with where there is a chance to explore and share what you intuit. We do need to communicate and get feedback in order for our perceptions to grow, but we also must be mindful of our ego tendencies and be very clear about what we say to clients.

Client Case History

Oftentimes I not only see visual images, but feel in my own body what the client is experiencing. One woman who came to see me had some cloudiness in the aura around her second chakra and ovaries. As I laid my hands directly over her ovaries, I felt a severe pain in my left side. I later asked her if she had problems there and she confirmed that the left ovary was sometimes painful and that she'd had problems with cysts there in the past. I worked to clear the cloudiness in the aura and rebalance the right and left sides around her second chakra.

Many of my students have a natural predisposition toward empathy and can feel their client's pains and ills. This empathy is often what calls them to be a healer. It is important to remember to use the Reiki Warrior tools in this case, so as not to absorb the illness from the client. Although this is rare in Reiki practice, it can happen, especially once the practitioner becomes more advanced. Using the Grounding Cord, Auric Cleanse, and protection activities are essential ways to prevent this from happening.

Another Client Case History

One woman who came to see me complained of having pain in her upper back. When I scanned the aura there, I found a sharp and immobile energetic form that my mind's eye perceived as a large sword. The sword seemed to be connected with one of her family members, one who was particularly strong and stern. We spent a few sessions working to heal the area around the sword, then removing it and filling in the space left with revitalizing Reiki energy. Curiously, the sword was not something for her to throw away, but in a certain way, a kind of tool that she needed to learn how to wield properly.

This sword was not a real weapon, but the symbolic message that my mind used to understand what was happening in the client's aura. Several times I have seen various implements in people's auras, implements that can cause very real pain in the body. I have found a distinct difference between items that are very easy to remove and those that take time. Swords, nails, or other sharp things that can be easily removed are usually caused by accidents or emotional outbursts from people who are not connected to us. These are easy to clear and I have seen several people's back pain, shoulder pain, or hip pain clear up in a matter of hours after removing and revitalizing the auric field.

The other kind of implements are those that are more difficult to remove, such as in the case history above, and removal will require a transformative effort on the part of the client. This is because the sword, nail, or block is a karmic imprint from a past trauma connected with some life-threatening event or negative relationship. Too often I have found people to be literally "stabbed in the back" by a person they trusted and attempted to maintain a relationship with. Sadly, most humans are not yet so aware of how our negative words and deeds have such a strong implication on the well-being of others. Many times, as we work through removing these blocks, people recall life situations from years before that had not occurred to them for some time. This helps to release the old emotional issue and repair the aura.

Another Client Case History

Another client came to see me and I perceived a distinct image that I had never seen before. When I was working around his solar plexus area, I found that the entire area was swarming with bees in the aura. This was a bit startling for me because I had never seen them before and did not know how they might react. I felt a definite sense of agitation from the bees and I had the impression they were connected to his homeland. Slowly, carefully I removed my hand from the area and continued working on the session. Afterwards I discovered that bees were meaningful to him. He comes from an area of Africa where bees symbolize a kind of influential energy that, in this case, was protecting him. It seemed the bees had been placed there by family members to ensure he stayed well. This is a case where the symbolism I perceived was not linked to my own interpretation, but relevant to the client's auric history.

EXERCISE 11.3: *Running Colors*

This exercise is good for experiencing the associations between color and the feelings that arise in the body. You can practice this every few months to see if your ability to visualize grows over time and whether feelings associated with the various colors change. You can also use the colors that you feel are healing and vitalizing during your Reiki sessions to aid the healing process.

Sit in your comfortable, meditative position. Keep your spine straight and concentrate on your breath for a few moments. Establish your grounding cord, noting color and size. Extend your cord down to the center of the Earth and allow yourself to connect with Earth energy. Focus your breath for several moments on mingling with Earth, your home. After some time, let the Earth energy rise up and connect with your body.

You will now begin to imagine a series of colors moving up and through your body, circulating through each chakra. Take note of which colors are easy for you to visualize and which ones are harder or impossible to see with your mind's eye. Some colors may stay within a certain chakra while others may move to different parts of your body, chakras, and/or auric field. Simply use the following instructions as a guide to work with color and allow your own sensations to inform you.

Visualize a clear, bright red orb or disc slowly spinning in the root chakra. Allow this clear red—the color of a bright, fresh strawberry—to fill the area, filling your legs and feet, hips and genitals. Notice how the clear red feels for a moment, then allow the red to darken to a deep, ruby red; then even darker to the color of blood; then a red-brown mahogany color; then a dark, rich brown of fertile soil. Watch your reaction to each color as it moves through muladhara and possibly into other parts of your body and/or auric field. Choose a color that resonates with your root area before moving on.

Allow your attention to rise upward, into svadhisthana, the sacral chakra. Visualize a clear, bright orange like the hue of the fruit. Again, watching your sensate reaction to each color, let it shift first into a reddish-orange like the sun at sunset; then, shift into a darker orange, tinged with brown; then a muddy orange like a mud flow; lighten the color so it becomes a medium tan; then beige; allow the color to grow into a more vibrant peach color; then apricot.

As the color moves into the yellow range, shift your attention to manipura, the solar plexus. Visualize the chakra as a bright, clear yellow like the sun in mid-afternoon; brighten the yellow so it is almost white like the center of a candle flame; then darken it again to a rich, corn yellow; let the color shift into a bluish-yellow like the color of sulfur. Notice if you feel this color anywhere else in your body.

Next, move your awareness to anahata, the heart center. Allow the dark yellow color to transform into a yellow-green; then the brilliant, vivid green like the leaves on a tree; allow it to darken so that is a clear, emerald color. Watch your reaction as you move through the several greens of mint, lime, pine, olive, and greenish-brown. See what feels good and what doesn't. Colors that you may not normally like may feel better than you thought—be open to them. Allow other colors to move and circulate through your heart chakra. Visualize a brilliant pink that glows softly; then a more pastel one. Imagine gold swirling and notice how these colors feel.

Now allow your awareness to move from your heart, through your lungs and into your throat chakra, to vishudda. As you do this, visualize turquoise and aqua, the green and blue swirling together not unlike the image of the Earth from space. Breathe in these colors deeply and notice if they are easy or hard to imagine. Now, focus on vishudda and picture a clear, light blue like the color of the sky in midday; lighten the blue so that it becomes clear, like topaz or sapphire; then a pale, pastel blue the color of a robin's egg; then let the color shift into cerulean; then royal blue; navy; and, finally, midnight blue. Notice if these colors pop up anywhere else in your auric field and/or body.

As the color darkens into a deep blue, let your awareness shift to ajna, the third eye chakra. Imagine the night sky, sprinkled with stars and visualize that dark indigo blue. Let the purplish-blue shift even darker into a rich, velvet black and allow yourself to be cloaked in this soft, rich color. Observe whether or not you feel comfortable with black. Then, imagine the stars once again and notice what it feels like to let silver swirl through this chakra and into your body. Allow the color to become lighter, turning into a royal purple; then a bright, clear purple like the color of amethyst.

Bring your attention to the top of your head, to sahasrara, the crown chakra. Allow the purple to shift into an electric purple, then into clear, bright lavender. Fill the space above your head with this lavender and let it rain down into the rest of your auric field and body. Finally, shift the color to white—a clear, bright, dazzling white that brightens your entire being. Notice the different feelings that move through you with white and where it penetrates throughout your chakras.

Finally, do the Auric Cleanse. Bring your attention to the outer boundary of your aura, which should encircle your body approximately two feet above you, behind you, below you, and in front of you like an eggshell. Notice what color(s) it is. Check in with your grounding cord and note the color. Make your grounding cord larger as you pull in your auric boundary and squeeze out any muddled colors that you do not like in your field. After several moments, pop the auric boundary back out and fill your auric field with the same color as your boundary but paler, more pastel. Resize your grounding cord to between four and six inches in diameter and let it be the color you need for the day.

Slowly come back to your body awareness by touching the ground, rolling out your neck and shoulders. Open your eyes and take the time to write down and/or color any of your experiences. Take note which colors made you feel good, which ones you did not like, which ones you felt like you needed. What emotions did you feel in response to red, black, olive green, turquoise? You can use this exercise to choose a grounding cord color each day as well as to determine which colors you may need more of in your wardrobe. Also, colors that cause negative feelings may be useful in determining certain issues that reside in the chakra(s) that are associated with that color. Use your auric vocabulary to help understand the deeper relationships that you hold with color as well as its personal and cultural symbolism.

12

Advanced Reiki Warrior Practice

The following chapter consists of several advanced techniques that will further augment the Reiki Warrior practice. They are intended to supplement the reader's current study of Reiki and to be used in conjunction with a teacher. The student must have a strong practice of Reiki healing on others, have reached a certain level of quieting and focusing the mind, have cultivated awareness, and have some understanding of subtle perception to truly benefit from the techniques below.

EXERCISE 12.1: *Auric Scanning Technique*

This technique follows the same method as Self Auric Scanning but is done on others. When first working with the technique, it is best to practice several times with partners with whom you regularly exchange Reiki healing sessions. After you become comfortable with the technique, you can then use it when giving sessions to clients.

To scan, choose your dominant hand for sensing the aura and keep the other hand at a distance of two feet from the client's body. This helps to stabilize the client's aura and your own receptivity. With the dominant hand (whichever you write with, although you may find the other to be more sensitive in healing—test and decide what works for you), start the scan an inch and a half to two inches from the skin. Start at the head and slowly work your way downward, over the main chakras. As you come to each chakra point, rest your hand there for a few moments, allowing any sensations to arise, like color, temperature, or texture. As you did in the self-scan, allow the hand to move up and away from the body, staying in the area of the chakra as it fans outward, into the aura, like a funnel. Take note of anything unusual and write it down. When practicing with a partner you know, you can ask questions about what you may have felt and see if it makes sense to the person. Be careful not to assume that just because you felt something, it is necessarily in accord with that person's experience. Working continuously over time with one person will help you to discern the various phenomena in the auric field. Once you feel comfortable with the scanning technique, apply it to your Reiki sessions. After you do your Reiki prayer and make your intentions, then scan the client's body, especially if there is an area they want you to focus on. Use that information to direct the healing session, apply the appropriate Reiki symbols as needed, and revitalize the field.

EXERCISE 12.2: *Chakra Balancing Techniques*

This technique is very useful to balance the interrelated connections found between chakras. It is a simple technique that can be done immediately to benefit your clients. I usually teach my Second Degree Reiki Warrior students four main methods of chakra balancing. First is the anahata–ajna bridge, which balances the mind and heart, aiming to heal the throat in between. This helps to activate the balance between the wisdom center of the mind and the compassionate awareness of the heart. The physical heart contains thousands of neural cells that act like a tiny brain to perceive the world around us. Bringing awareness away from the head and down into the heart enables us to use a compassionate approach when working with clients. Balancing these two centers is beneficial for everyone and should be used in most Reiki sessions.

The second chakra balancing method is the balance of the muladhara and svadhisthana, the first and second chakras. Our lower centers of survival, desire, and emotions are often intertwined, resulting in emotional imbalances, frustration, fear, and ignorance. Working with these lower levels of consciousness is extremely difficult because it involves transcending our deeper issues. By working to balance them, we can begin to start the healing process that is often needed to overcome the past traumas, fears, deep-seated pain, and loneliness that all of us carry to some degree or another. Opening and revitalizing the root chakra inevitably leads to grounding, which, when balanced with the sacral chakra, helps us to steady our emotions and center our being. By working with the deeper parts of ourselves through the body, Reiki Warriors can begin to anchor in the higher, transformative vibratory wisdom of the mind that resides in the higher chakras.

We can also note that because these two chakras are located so close together in women, the balancing needed is often even more crucial to our development. Biologically, women are geared toward a love that is based in the physical–emotional connection more strongly than are men. This also means that when women do balance these two chakras properly, heal the traumas that are held there, and begin to activate and integrate the energy between muladhara and svadhisthana, they have the potential to be very strong and successful on the spiritual path.

A third chakra balancing that is highly beneficial for all clients is that of the spine. After the client turns over and you have treated the head, then place one hand on the back of the neck and the other on the base of the spine. This works to balance and energize the entire spine, which is responsible for supporting the body, organs, and tissues. Here, the seeds of the chakras are held in the sushuma nadi, and revitalizing this central channel with healing Reiki energy helps to release blocks and nourish the health of the spine and the entire auric field. I recommend that this important balancing be done on each client in almost every session, short or long.

A final method can be used to fully balance one chakra. For example, in the case of anahata, if it seems especially weak or closed, you can work to bring in sufficient amounts of healing energy by placing one hand over the front of the heart and the other hand over the back. This is a powerful and revitalizing technique that can help to open the chakra.

There are many other possible chakra balancing options as well. As you begin to work more deeply with the auric field, you will intuitively notice how blocks or tears are connected with certain chakras and you can work to re-balance these appropriately. Take note of what you perceive when working with a client over a period of time and you will see how chakras begin to reenergize, heal, and activate over time, causing dramatic and transformative shifts that improve the client's well-being.

Client Case History

A woman came to see me who was suffering from a throat infection that made it difficult for her to swallow. By the time I saw her, she had even lost much of her voice. As I worked over her throat chakra area, I felt a strong impulse to balance the vishudda with the manipura, or solar plexus. She jumped visibly when I laid my hands on her solar plexus, as if someone had hurt her. I asked if she was all right and she nodded, yet tears began to flow from her eyes. I spent the next several minutes revitalizing the solar plexus using the clearing Reiki symbol followed by the power symbol. After some time her tears stopped and a smile played on her face. When I asked her, afterwards, what she had experienced, she told me that she could feel the power dynamic between her mother and her when I put my hands on the solar plexus. With the aid of the Reiki, she was able to witness the emotional pain she had suffered as a child and then heal the trauma. Within a few days her throat completely cleared.

This illuminates how our body sometimes manifests certain illnesses that may not be directly connected to the associated chakra. Various diseases are often a result of certain past karma, and sometimes these deeper issues must be healed before the body can heal. This is an important aspect of being a healer, to work to treat the deeper root cause, and not simply address the symptoms. Otherwise the disease may manifest in another part of the body in another way.

ADVANCED SYMBOL TECHNIQUES

After the Reiki Warrior has practiced working with the Reiki symbols for several months, there are several ways to enhance and develop her healing work using symbols in advanced techniques. Before these can be properly used, the Reiki Warrior practitioner should be able to hold the image of each Reiki symbol very clearly in her mind and be able to visualize blowing or sending the symbol into the client's body and/or aura. The student should take the time to check in with her teacher to verify that she has a clear understanding of the conscious essence inherent in each of the symbols.

EXERCISE 12.3: *Master Lineage Meditation*

One way to work with the symbols is to honor the Reiki Master lineage with them. By taking the time to show respect for the Reiki Masters—those in our lineage, and those who have gone on to other realms—we are dedicating ourselves more fully to the path of Reiki. This also enables us to tap directly into the power of our Reiki Masters, which helps the Reiki to grow and flourish in our lives as Reiki Warriors.

To invoke the power of the Masters, set aside time and space as you would for a distance healing Reiki session. Follow the beginning steps of saying the Reiki prayer and intention. Then visualize each of the Reiki symbols in the space in front of you; imagine them dissolving into a clear light. After the mind is focused on this clear light, imagine some of the Reiki Masters in front of you. Visualize and, even more importantly, *feel* Mikao Usui in the space in front of you, smiling and radiating his love and healing light toward you. After a few moments, imagine that he dissolves into your heart. Then imagine Chujiro Hayashi in the same way, followed by Hawayo Takata and other Masters from your lineage. Again, allow them to dissolve into your heart and feel the radiance and warmth emanating from within as you connect into these clear Beings. After some time, thank the Masters for their guidance and wisdom and close the session as you would any other distance Reiki session.

EXERCISE 12.4: *Using Mantras*

Another effective method to build the concentration of the mind is to use the mantras of the Reiki symbols. As you know, each symbol has a name that comes with it. Mantras are a string of sacred sounds that can be used to help calm the mind and activate more spiritual qualities. During your morning meditation, you may choose to visualize one of the Reiki symbols for several minutes while continuously chanting the associated name or mantra aloud or in your mind. Chanting works to bring clear focus, which cultivates mindful awareness throughout our day and Reiki sessions. With time, deeper meanings associated with the Reiki symbols and their mantras may arise, enabling you to work further with their wisdom.

Another way to enhance your practice is to add the use of a mantra to exercises you are working with. For example, during the Auric Cleanse (Exercise 3.1), while you visualize the muddled or negative energy pouring from the aura out and down through the grounding cord, you can enhance this by also chanting the SHK mantra either aloud or in your mind. When doing auric protection, such as imagining clear, brilliant light surrounding you, add the CKR to further magnify the energy you are creating.

REIKI THREE
giving the gift of reiki

This final section contains a synthesis of the various wisdom teachings I have received, my dedicated practice of Reiki and meditation, and my own connection to the spiritual path. Much of the wisdom is applicable to anyone on any path, not just healers or Reiki Warriors. This section contains less scholarly information and more wisdom that I have gained from experience. It is crucial for you as a Reiki Warrior walking the path to not only learn about the Reiki, do the daily practice, and apply what you have learned, but to open yourself up to the deep experiences that ultimately connect us with our own truth and wisdom, which manifests through each of us in a very specific manner.

This section deals directly with becoming and working not only as an advanced Reiki practitioner, but as a Master and teacher of Reiki. Like the second section, the work with the Master symbol requires one to have had the proper attunement. Still, any Reiki practitioner may benefit from both the wisdom and the techniques. The techniques included can be used by anyone but are specifically designed for healers who are working deeply with the path of healing and are in connection with their spiritual teachers and Reiki contemporaries.

13

Becoming a Reiki Master

The final traditional degree of Reiki is the level of Master. Unlike almost every other type of study throughout the world, this degree and title are available to anyone as soon as they have completed their Second Degree Reiki. Although this may have some small benefit for the student, it is not in the best interest of the Reiki Warrior practitioner to complete his Master degree until he has worked with Reiki for one year (at the very least) and given at least fifty Reiki sessions. It is important that we truly understand our practice before we attempt to teach it. Even more important, the Reiki Warrior Master must be able to hold a strong and concentrated focus while passing the Reiki attunements. Without this capability, the attunements may not work and students are left struggling to understand how to use the Reiki healing energy properly.

Receiving the Master attunement of Reiki Three is a precious gift from the Universe, the Reiki Masters, and the spirit guides. Becoming a Reiki Master is the final stage in learning Reiki from the Master, yet it is also a new beginning as a spiritual leader. Now is the time for the Reiki Warrior to truly walk her talk as she learns to embody Spirit even more fully, with more resonance and greater power. The healing power is believed to increase by a hundredfold from the Reiki Master attunement. Reiki Warriors learn to embrace the now of each moment and how to raise the Reiki energy higher, thus bringing others along on the path. Students who become Masters may find themselves opening up in wondrous new ways after this attunement as they align more completely with Spirit and their life begins to change in dramatic and healing ways. Now is the time for Reiki Warriors to begin accessing their truth deep within, to listen to the quiet voice of intuition and honor it, and to pay attention to dreams and allow them to work more fully in waking life.

REIKI WARRIOR—REIKI GUIDE

In the Tibetan Buddhist tradition, there is a powerful archetype called the bodhisattva, as mentioned in Chapter Eight: A Deeper Commitment. The bodhisattva is a spiritual hero or warrior who contains the noble qualities of courage, fearlessness, devotion, dedication, and the ability to transform. This is because he has already reached a state of enlightenment, a state that is inherent in all of us but we have not yet realized. The bodhisattva has not only realized and attained the ultimate liberation of mind, body, and spirit, but at that moment of enlightenment, he vows to return to the earthly realm to help all other sentient beings to do likewise. In other words, he sacrifices the purity of oneness to help all of us self-realize, to lift beings up from their suffering.

Although this is a noble act often beyond our normal comprehension, there is also a tradition in Tibetan Buddhism to attempt to feel oneself as one of the wisdom deities or bodhisattvas. This is not done in an egotistical way, but instead to motivate the development of the clear, bright seeds of pure awareness and joy that inhabit each of us. By visualizing ourselves as the Reiki Warrior—as one who is full of light, compassion, and wisdom—we begin to become aware of those qualities inside of ourselves.

As Reiki Warrior Masters we are attempting to not only learn meditation, cultivate compassion, and heal others, we are taking on the noble responsibility of teaching others to do the same. By grounding ourselves into the form of Reiki Warrior while also being responsive to the spacious clarity of being, we can open ourselves up to the precious ability to pass Reiki attunements. In this way, we, like the bodhisattva, are choosing to use our Reiki ability to benefit others who are suffering, pulling them up and onto a path that is supportive and empowering.

SPIRIT GUIDES

Another integral aspect of becoming a Reiki Warrior Master is learning to find and trust the guides who can assist us. Teachers come in many forms, both physical and nonphysical. Physical guides are our Reiki and spiritual teachers and, to some extent, our friends and family. Nonphysical guides can come in many forms, including Reiki Masters who have gone on before us, ancestors or deceased relatives, or wise spirit beings. As with anything of the nonphysical, experiences with these beings are subjective and require the practitioner to cultivate a level of discernment. That being said, as you move further along the path of Reiki, work with these spirit guides often becomes inevitable. They may appear during Reiki sessions, in dreams, or in meditation. Try not to expect them or dwell too much on their appearance. Often, their messages carry some significant information and can be used properly during a Reiki session or in your own life. It is important to note that spirit guides do not tell you what to do, they only give clear guidance based in love and wisdom. If you hear other unhelpful or domineering messages, then it may be a lower part of your own mind or an unhelpful entity coming through. The true spirit guide, like a bodhisattva, cares for all sentient beings and aims to ease suffering and promote love, joy, and peace.

Client Case History

I gave Reiki in a series of three sessions to a man who suffered from lower intestinal pain. The pain cleared up quickly, yet I continued to work on this second chakra, which was imbalanced with his heart. Sometime during the second Reiki session, I sensed a distinct presence in the room. I looked up and clearly saw a Being that was faintly glowing sitting directly opposite me. The energy that radiated from this Being was one of pure love. As I had never experienced any kind of spirit guides during a Reiki session, I was astonished by his very real presence. He distinctly told me that he had been there since my client's birth, that he was related to him, and that he would always be there to guide and help. He continued to radiate vast amounts of love and warmth as I continued to do the session. Afterward, the client felt completely rested and rejuvenated. This time, instead of waiting for him to ask questions, I felt it was imperative that I tell him about the guide. His response was that he knew who the Being was, that it must be his twin, who died at birth. He felt absolutely certain and we both looked at each other in awe, filled with the blessing of his deceased brother.

Another Client Case History

I had been working with a client on different levels over the course of several days, including giving readings, Reiki, and teaching her the first degree. We had formed a deep trust and she came in to see me about several issues that correlated with the second chakra. She'd had a series of bladder infections and menstrual problems after stopping the birth control pill, which she had taken for eight years, partly in response to an abortion. At this time I was working with a guide I called "B" for short, a Being I had met during a shamanic journey who was useful in working with very deep, transformative shifts that can happen during a Reiki healing. As I worked directly with slowly opening her second chakra, I called in "B" and felt him come through my back and work through my hands. When this happens, I feel an incredible surge of energy that moves through me in waves, very clear, bright, and joyous. He guided me to put my hands on the two sides of her sacral chakra, one above on the womb and the other below, on her sacrum. I did this and then clearly saw the baby spirit there, the one from the abortion, whom she had never fully let go. He was very beautiful, an indigo sphere inside a brilliant, blue sparkling field. He told me to tell my client that he was okay but he was ready to go now. By this time my client was weeping and her second chakra felt like it was on fire, burning and searing through my hands so hard that I couldn't tell where my hands ended and her body began. I asked my client what she wanted to say to the baby spirit and she said she was sorry, amidst many tears, and that she was now ready to let him go. After that simple but powerful exchange, I watched in amazement as the tiny, brilliant light detached from my client's womb and moved toward a vast light opening, with love and clarity.

During the rest of the healing, I removed a block from the back of my client's heart chakra, opening her up to feel the deeper love that comes from within. Her guides helped at this point, removing the unneeded energy from the spine and then filled her up with waves of golden light. She felt completely shifted and healed afterward. I told her what I had seen, and she smiled, saying she had always felt the spirit was a boy as well. The next few days she moved even more deeply into a place of beauty, openness, and clarity while adjusting to the shifts that occurred in healing the physical body. She remarked a few weeks later that she had changed more in a month than she had in years. I felt deeply honored to be the witness and space holder for such an incredibly deep healing, simply providing the blissful environment for the healing to occur.

EXERCISE 13.1: *Meeting a Guide*

You can use this technique to begin the process of accessing a guide or the deep inner wisdom of your Higher Self. Reiki students of any level can try this practice. Whether you are "successful" or not in actually meeting a guide, it is wise to wait and follow up a few weeks later, allowing anything you have experienced during this time to integrate into your life. Often when we begin to work on the level of visualization, we are entering a deeper subconscious part of ourselves. Although the visualization itself may not be dramatic or life changing in the moment, it can still produce changes in the body, emotions, and mind through the intention to access Spirit.

This visualization will help you to come into contact with a Being who guides you. It may be an actual astral entity that aids you on the healing path, a Reiki Master from the past, or simply an aspect of your Higher Self. Allow yourself to experience meeting the guide without judging the outcome. Know that true guides only offer words of wisdom and do not tell you what to do. Choosing your actions accordingly remains a part of your path, as you—and you alone—are responsible for your own actions.

With the above in mind, sit in a comfortable, meditative position and close your eyes. Keep your spine straight and concentrate on your breath for a few moments. Make sure your grounding cord is clear and straight and breathe in Earth energy if you wish. You may also do an Auric Cleanse. After you are in your quiet, meditative space, imagine that you are walking through a forest. Notice if it is day or nighttime. What do the trees look like? Are they tall or short? Are there other kinds of plants? Notice if you are walking on a path or just meandering through the trees. Is there anyone else there? Any animals?

After some time, you meet a bear. What color is the bear? Is it facing you or turned away from you? You must get past the bear somehow. Remember how it reacts to you, if it does at all. You continue walking through your forest and come to a body of water. Notice how it sounds, smells, and looks. Cross the body of water and continue walking through the woods.

Next, you come across a box. How big is the box? What is it made of? Is it locked? Open the box if you can and look inside. Then, continue on your journey. You come to a clearing. There is a tree in the clearing. What kind of tree is it? How tall is it? How do you respond to the tree? Go around the tree into another part of the clearing. Put your hands on your heart and ask to meet one of your guides if it is possible. Watch as someone or thing approaches you. Notice what s/he looks like. S/he has something for you, which s/he now gives to you. Put it away in a pocket and thank him/her for the gift or message. In thanks, give Reiki to your guide. Hold up your hands and send Reiki. If you are second degree, send the distance symbol followed by the power symbol, then the emotional clearing symbol to the guide. After a few moments, acknowledge that your meeting is now over and bring your hands back to your heart. Sit quietly for a few moments, contemplating your gift and/or message from the guide.

When you are ready, touch the ground and roll out your shoulders. Slowly open your eyes and take note of all the things you encountered. The woods symbolize your life, and the bear symbolizes the animal part of ourselves, which is rooted to Earth. The water represents our emotions, our fluidity with our surroundings, our sensuality and sexuality. The box is symbolic of our inner heart; the gift inside may be some representation of a gift we wish to give ourselves. The tree is the reflection of our true self, our soul and the way it expresses itself in this moment, here and now. These images are only symbols, yet symbols are powerful because they speak to the deeper parts of ourselves, the part that works without language and mental rationality, the part that operates the inner workings of our heart and soul. Loosely interpret what you have seen. If you have simply gone around the bear, it is a time to reflect whether you embrace your Earth, animal power self, or have little connection to it. Remember the body of water. How does this reflect you and your emotional state? Do you dive right in or cross over in a vessel? What kind of box do you have and what sacred gift is waiting for you inside? Remember the tree you saw. What kind of tree was it? Once, I performed this exercise at a transition time in my life and saw a huge, dead, white tree in the desert. The life of the tree was completely gone, dead; it was a time of complete letting go and laying fallow before the rebirth and new growth. Finally, remember your guide and the message or feeling that overcame you when you met him/her/ it. Maybe there was simply a presence of love, or a shining light.

Repeat this exercise every few months and take note of the changes in the way you deal with the earthy grounded part of you, your emotions, inner heart and deeper self. If you continue to work with your guide, s/he may become accessible to assist you during Reiki sessions. You can call in this guide to work with you by simply remembering the loving, clear, light feeling that occurred during your guide journey. Allow that feeling to come into the Reiki session when you begin the healing and notice any difference in the way you work with the Reiki healing.

EXERCISE 13.2: *Advanced Healing through Time and Space*

As a Reiki Warrior Master, you should be able to easily send Reiki through time and space and have a clear sense of how it works, what it feels like to do this, and be very natural with using the symbols. Once you have grasped this, you can move to the next level, which involves sending to other healers. This technique follows the exact same method as time-distance healing, but now you are sending through another healer. This can be done with someone who is giving a normal, hands-on Reiki healing session or to a healer who is sending as well. The only difference in this method is that you set a pre-arranged time with the person who will be doing the main healing. A few minutes into the session, simply follow the steps for time-distance healing, but visualize sending Reiki through the other healer. It is not important to know who or what they are sending their healing to. In fact, not knowing is interesting, because you may glean certain psychic insights into what is happening and check in later. Sending fifteen to twenty minutes is usually sufficient, followed by the normal procedure of closing the session.

As a Reiki teacher, a way to help your second degree students is, like above, to assist them as they practice learning time-distance healing. I usually have my students do a few evenings of practice on their own before I assist. Then, we arrange times and, as with aiding another healer, I wait several minutes before assisting so that they feel the difference between their own sending and being assisted by someone else. During class time we are then able to discuss what the students experienced, which provides good feedback for the class.

Client Case History

During a Reiki Warrior Second Degree course, I arranged for my students to send healing in the evening and I would then come in to assist them so they could feel the power of healers assisting each other. One of my students, a student of Tibetan Buddhism, was doing her time-distance healing practice and I joined a few minutes after she had started. During the healing, as I was sending to her, a very strong image of the Green Tara deity of Tibetan Buddhism spontaneously arose in the space in front of me. I continued to send her the Reiki healing energy, through the Green Tara and into her healing hands. When I told her the experience the next day, we were both amazed—it turns out that her dharma name, or Tibetan Buddhist spiritual name, is Jetsun Dolma, the name for the Green Tara! I had witnessed the essence of my student as her lama had appropriately named her.

Another Client Case History

One of my students was approached by a woman suffering terribly from some kind of unknown psychological ailment. As the client was from a small village in a rural country, she had no way to understand her illness from any kind of Western mind set and the family assumed she was possessed by a spirit. I advised my student to have the family take her to a doctor or even a local shaman, but the family wasn't interested and pleaded for help from my student, who by then was already showing signs of being a promising healer. She agreed to give the woman a Reiki session and asked me to assist her; however, because of the village context that we were living in, it would have been inappropriate for me to work directly with her. Instead, I told the student I would assist by distance. We agreed on a set time and several minutes into the session, I began sending the healing Reiki. This was a very strong session and if my student hadn't been as strong as she is, it could've been too much even for the two of us. I sent Reiki for almost an hour and the time flew by. When I finally closed the session I felt a sense of release and revitalization that usually occurs when passing a lot of Reiki.

The next day I met with my student, who reported that several minutes into the Reiki session, she felt an incredible surge of purple light that she knew was my assistance. She was able to help her client by balancing the energy field and releasing the blocks that prevented her from functioning healthily. It took several more months and various kinds of treatments (including Reiki) for the woman to be completely healed, but a significant start was made that evening by our efforts.

THE IMPORTANCE OF DREAMS

Dreams can be used as signs that reflect our progression along the path of Reiki Warrior. As we begin to practice healing, work with quieting the mind, and developing concentration, we will often be able to better remember our dreams. If we cannot remember our dreams, this may show that we have a limited awareness of the deeper currents of the subconscious and its inner workings. To bring this awareness into our life, we need simply intend that we remember our dreams. Before falling asleep, we can intend to remember them and upon waking, try to remember anything we may have experienced during sleep. With time, we will be able to recall the various images and stories that play out against the screen of our mind. The feelings we have during our dream state are indicators of the subconscious mind states that lie below the surface of our chattering conscious thoughts. Less important are the various images and people we might see in our dreams, as these are usually culled from the collection of events of the day and the past. As inner awareness and lucidity develop during our waking hours, a clear state will likewise grow in our dreams. Until this happens, it is important to focus on the feelings and awareness currently in our dreams as a way to look at strong emotional patterns, suppressed feelings, and current states of reaction. Writing down dreams upon waking (keeping a dream diary) is an excellent way to begin to understand our dream state imagery. As we progress in the Reiki Warrior practice and dreams become clearer, certain symbolic meanings may appear. Like the auric vocabulary, keeping note of the symbols and their relevant meaning in waking life can help develop a deeper connection to other aspects of our being.

Dreams have been crucial to my own growth as a Reiki healer, teacher, and spiritual student. I have been fortunate to receive many affirmations, guidance, and wisdom during my dream time. Many of my dreams have come true, and I have met spiritual masters and received some of my advanced teachings during the night spent dreaming. I strongly encourage students of Reiki to start activating the higher parts of themselves by bringing awareness into dreams and being open to the sacred messages that come through.

EXERCISE 13.3: *Dream Awareness*

One way to begin bringing awareness into dreams is by consistently drawing awareness into your daily life. During the day, notice how life is like a dream, a series of illusory moments flowing one into another. Watch the incessant rise and fall of thoughts, emotions, and activities in your day. This will help to bring deeper lucidity and clarity to the wondrous flow of different emotions and thoughts without becoming attached to them. At the end of the day, recount your activities backward, starting with the most recent activity of getting ready for bed and moving your mind back through the day to the morning. Notice how this may be difficult to do at first, as your thoughts tend to wander off into the memories of the day or tangents associated with people you encountered. With a little effort, you will be able to maintain more awareness during this activity.

Once you have mastered this step, start intending that you remember your dreams clearly. In the morning, write down what you remember and begin building a dream log that can later become a source of information or messages. After you are remembering the dreams clearly, intend that you "wake up" during the dream, or become lucid. With constant awareness cultivated during the day, the likelihood of gaining lucidity during the dream state is higher. One way to do this is to look at your hands several times a day and ask yourself, "Am I dreaming or am I awake?" Eventually you may also ask yourself this during your dreams for a moment, then literally "wake up" in the dream; you can then begin to lucidly control and direct your consciousness during the dream state. Lucid dreaming is a very good sign that you are advancing on the path of consciousness, especially if you recognize your own intrinsic awareness even in your dream state and are able to cultivate that into a more joyous and clear existence.

14

Master Symbols

The Reiki Warrior dons the title of Reiki Warrior Master through countless self-healings, practice with effort on others, and much work with the Reiki symbols. Becoming a Master incorporates the final symbols of Reiki used to enhance the healing practice as well as to pass attunements. Like the previous Reiki symbols, these are kept sacred to the practitioner and are not shared commonly with others who are not using Reiki. In this way the student learns to honor the inner wisdom developed with the Reiki symbols and the consciousness that they carry.

THE MASTER SYMBOLS

The final symbols of Reiki are learned in the Master training course: the Master power healing symbol, DKM; and one used in the attunement process, RK. The Master healing symbol comes in two forms, traditional and nontraditional, and they can be used interchangeably. Personally, I prefer to use the nontraditional symbol because I intuitively relate to its shape and movement, but knowing both is important for the Reiki Warrior Master.

The powerful, traditional master symbol DKM creates a noticeably stronger channel between the physical body and spiritual self. It allows the unlimited wisdom and power of the Universe to manifest directly on the physical plane. The Master symbol is believed to intensify and focus the Reiki energy one-hundred-fold and it can be used in conjunction with all of the other Reiki symbols to enhance physical, emotional, and mental healing. In general, the Master symbol brings greater wholeness, fulfillment, completion. The use of this symbol frees us from old patterns and belief systems, which enables outmoded parts of ourselves to drop away, revealing the inner quiet beauty within.

Because it encompasses all the qualities of the previous Reiki symbols, just using this symbol enables the practitioner to quickly benefit the client and promote a strong sense of well-being. This symbol can be used in time-distance healing to enhance the intensity of the healing power. The Reiki Warrior practitioner can also use the Master symbol in place of the time-distance symbol when sending Reiki energy. Still, it is recommended that the practitioner maintain a close connection with all of the Reiki symbols, as they each have their own unique consciousness. It is extremely important to be familiar with the consciousnesses of the symbols when giving the Reiki attunements.

THE WISDOM OF THE SPIRAL

Spirals are depicted in ancient art as old as Neolithic times. Often the spiral is linked to the image of the snake, speaking of transformation, shedding skin, moving through dark into light. Spirals are universal symbols found in goddess creation, death, and rebirth.[67] The spiral evokes the ancient wisdom of the Earth as it spirals around its axis, simultaneously spiraling around the sun, while the moon spirals around the Earth. The intestines spiral inside our bodies, and atoms consist of whirling electrons just as our chakras move in a circular motion.

The Reiki Warrior uses the spiral as a tool of movement, change, undoing, and re-creating. Practicing Reiki with the spiral symbol links us to the ever-changing quality of the universe that is reflected in the shifts and movements that happen during the healing process. The spiral of the nontraditional Reiki Master symbol is similar to the power symbol learned in Second Degree Reiki. Using the form of the spiral in conjunction with the nontraditional Master symbol holds an immense power, one that is without beginning or end.

EXERCISE 14.1: *Becoming the Spiral*

As a Reiki Warrior, one connects Earth to sky, utilizing the power that comes from both of these spheres of consciousness. To further integrate these spheres we can use the image of the spiral. Use this visualization to empower yourself during morning meditation or after a self-healing practice.

67 Stein, *Guide to Goddess Craft*, 34.

Sit in a meditative pose and focus on the breath for a few moments. Go through the Grounding Cord exercise and the Auric Cleanse. Now imagine the starting point of a brilliant string of light beginning at the left side of your head. Visualize this brilliant cord running across the crown chakra, curling down, along the right edge of the aura and through muladhara, the root chakra. Imagine the string spiraling back up to the ajna, or third eye, then down to svadhisthana, moving through the sacrum. As the glowing cord moves through each chakra, imagine the vortex of the energy point illuminating with brilliant clear light. Continue the spiral back up the left side of the aura, moving through vishudda, the throat chakra, then down again and passing through manipura, or the solar plexus. Finally, visualize the spiral ending in anahata, feeling the clear light opening and expanding the heart chakra. Imagine that the spiral pulls in brilliant, clear energy from the top and moves through the chakras, lighting, clearing, and revitalizing. Where the spiral ends in anahata, visualize the inner, sacred symbol of the nontraditional master symbol like a tiny seed in the heart. Continue this for several minutes and then allow the spiral to come undone, spiraling itself into your heart chakra, and watch it dissolve into clear light. Close the visualization by checking in with the grounding cord and doing a protection exercise (See Chapter Three: Reiki Warrior Tools). Thank the Reiki Masters or Reiki and state aloud or in your mind that the meditation is now finished.

TIME AS A SPIRAL

According to Albert Einstein's Theory of Relativity there is no "fixed reality" because space is not three-dimensional and time is not a separate reality. This means there is a space-time continuum in which we exist and that we are not limited to a linear, form-based existence. Rather, there is a broader context for our existence, one that incorporates aspects of ourselves that transcend time and space and show how we are, indeed, multidimensional beings.

In Robert Monroe's[68] books on consciousness travels outside of the body, he explores the vast realities of our existence, our connections to death, other beings (both human and non-human), and the multilayered realities of consciousness in the Universe.

I have found that working continuously with the Reiki, we can begin to access these incredible depths of consciousness. On a basic level, giving self-healing and receiving Reiki sessions, we start to balance our bodies, minds, and hearts. Monroe also found that by balancing the hemispheres of the brain, advanced, spontaneous out-of-body experiences of the participants of his studies. These altered states of awareness can happen during deep relaxation, which occurs during Reiki sessions. As we advance on the path of passing healing through us, providing these deep relaxed spaces for others, we tap into the multidimensional potential within each of us.

The spiral of time is a part of this multidimensional self. I have found, over the years, that I often revisit aspects of myself with a new lens or focus, which leads me to different understandings. As we grow and learn and experience greater depths of consciousness, we unite the deeper parts of ourselves, forming a vast, continuous Self that is not necessarily relegated to time or space. I have had dreams of the future, revelations of the past, and convergences of moments that are beyond coincidence or even synchronicity. These experiences are continuous glimpses into the ever-unfolding Universe and its myriad of expressions through me and my Reiki healing path.

Working ever more deeply with the power and wisdom of the spiral, the Reiki Warrior can reconnect the ancient wisdom of the past with the current unfolding of the present into the clear direction of the future. In other words, as we learn to become more still inside, to pass the Reiki with clarity, we begin to witness the larger now, that living in the moment is comprised of the never-ending flow of life currents. Similarly the spiral never ends, only continues on into an infinite point that is indiscernible but still there, still existing. Expanding ourselves into light and revitalizing our being with Reiki enables us to embrace our life and path more fully, yet not attach tightly but move and flow like the spiral.

68 Author of *Journeys Out of the Body.*

EXERCISE 14.2: *Healing the Past*

Using the Master symbol, Reiki Warriors can effectively begin the process of resolving and healing past situations, karma, and trauma. This exercise is done the same as the time-distance healing (see Exercise 9.1), only using the Master symbol, which has a stronger effect on the healing. After choosing what to send to, simply replace the time-distance symbol with the Master symbol. Often it will take several Reiki healing sessions to overcome a serious past trauma and the sessions should be supplemented with other forms of healing, counseling, and work with one's teacher and contemporaries as needed.

Other past incidents can be easily healed using the Master symbol, and are often immediately effective. If you have an argument with a friend, a bad exchange with a neighbor or family member, or any kind of negative passing exchange, take a moment to reflect on the exchange and how it could have gone differently with more patience or stillness. Then, use the Master symbol to send distance healing to the situation, not the person—this is not sending a healing to a person but a healing to rectify the connection between you and the person. This exercise also helps to cultivate awareness of our behavior with others and develop humility and awareness of the various negative ways we can treat each other.

A Personal Experience

I have used the above exercise to alleviate a negative connection. There was a woman who lived in my neighborhood who often said harsh things about others and misinterpreted situations in a way that produced a lot of anger. During one incident, I ran into her on the street and we exchanged news; she interpreted something I said as an attack and stormed away in fury. Feeling badly about the conversation and any part I may have had in the misunderstanding, I sent back the Reiki using the nontraditional Master symbol in hopes of relaxing and healing the negative conversation. I ran into her again an hour or so later and, astonishingly, she asked me to join her for coffee, something she had never done before. A healing had occurred and we were able to share coffee and communicate in a clear way that had seemed impossible just an hour earlier.

This story illustrates how fleeting anger and negative emotions can be. By taking the time to look carefully over our own negative reactions to outer circumstances, we can begin to claim our involvement in situations and then attempt to heal them. Healing the past can be almost as effective as dissolving a negative situation in the present moment, and it is an excellent first step in carefully observing our negative patterns.

PAST LIVES

Past lives are a topic of much discussion, speculation, and amazement among healers in various fields. The present view of reincarnation stems from one of the central tenets of Hinduism and was first recorded in the Upanishads sometime around 800 BCE. This view holds the understanding that the soul leaves the body at death and migrates into the next one to continue the fulfillment of karmic debts that keep us bound to the wheel of *samsara*, or "world" in Sanskrit. In the Buddhist view, there is traditionally no soul, but there are karmic winds that similarly keep us connected to samsara until we break free and become enlightened. Because this is such a huge process, it takes many lifetimes to free ourselves from ego tendencies, desire, ignorance, and greed. But with practice, dedication, and the right effort, enlightenment does become possible and we are able to move toward a place that is free of death.

Along with the chakra system, the Theosophists brought the concept of reincarnation to the West. Reincarnation has spawned a vigorous interest among the New Age communities, ones that may also include the study of Reiki. Even though past lives are not verifiable in terms of a rational or scientific perspective, the issue does seem to come up during healing work, whether we believe in it or not. My personal inclination is: if it works use it, but, like other psychic phenomena, don't attach to the experience. For example, we may have vivid recollections of a life story that is very different from our own conscious memory of this current life. If we can use this information in a way that helps and heals us, then this is a valid kind of experience. But if this story becomes something we are attached to and we use it to further our ego tendencies, then it is usually not worth holding on to.

I have had several past-life story recollections over the years, some of them I distinctly connect with and others that do not seem to relate to me in my current life at all. These remembrances are often like an archetypical myth in which various characters play out certain dramas that correspond with issues I am presently dealing with. It is very likely that my mind is composing a vivid tale to enable me to uncover deeper issues in my life path that can remove blocks and restore healing. In the end, whether or not these stories are truly past lives becomes unimportant, but they are another useful method in the Warrior's tool bag.

A Personal Story

When I am able to work closely with a student over a long period of time, I often have them give me a Reiki session to feel where they are at and see how the practice is working for them. One student came to give me a Reiki session and spent the hour working on my body, practicing her hand positions. When she got to my back, a very energetically sensitive part of my body, I felt a sense of apprehension. Then she placed her hands on my waist, I jumped and a ripple of intense energy moved up through my spine. Suddenly, without warning, a very vivid scene played out in my mind's eye. I found myself in the midst of battle, wearing a white gladiator-looking outfit complete with sandals, heavy metal headgear, and even a spear! I was a man and was clearly fighting together with my friend, who is also a friend in this life, against some unknown enemy. He had vivid blue eyes in the recollection, so vivid that when the session was over, I could honestly not recall the true color of his eyes, because they were so blue in the memory. (They are not, as it turns out, blue at all!)

I wanted to fight to the death, to honor my country, but my friend did not want to fight, which I found very irritating. He had a love interest back in his village he wanted to be with more than he wanted to fight. Then there was an intense, sharp pain in the center of my back and I felt myself fall over and die. I floated above the dead body and up into the ether where the recollection waned. The whole story probably lasted only a minute.

My student continued giving me Reiki, having no idea what I had seen. When I sat up and we talked about it, I felt the story was giving me the message that I previously felt I had to die for my beliefs. That is no longer relevant today and I don't need to "die" to prove that my way of thinking is valid. My friend is the other part of me that needed to remember that love is more important than one's beliefs. I have no personal connection to an era of gladiators or fighting, but this is the way certain information was given to me. I cannot honestly say I was that person at that time, but there was an intense shift during that healing process that enabled me to become clearer, which is the more relevant part of the process.

THE FINAL REIKI SYMBOL

The last symbol given to the Reiki Warrior Master, the RK symbol, is primarily used during the Reiki attunement process. The method of attuning students must be learned from a Reiki Master in order to first seed the aura and then activate the healing abilities. The final symbol is used to disconnect or cut the Master's aura from the student's, to prevent the student from relying on the Master to channel the Reiki.

In my own work with the cutting symbol I have found other uses for it as well, such as protection and strengthening. For protection, use RK in rooms, houses, or outdoor spaces after they have been cleansed and vitalized with Reiki energy (CKR and SHK). Simply visualize the symbol to the end of the time spent creating sacred space. When strengthening something, visualize RK entering into and enhancing alternative therapies, including gem elixirs, homeopathic remedies, floral essences, and essential oils.

EXERCISE 14.3: *Cutting Cords*

Cutting cords is an action taken to release someone from your life. By cutting the psychic strings that connect you with another person, you will clear both your life and theirs. To determine who has cords in your aura that are no longer necessary, perform a self-healing Reiki session. Focus on the sacral, solar plexus, or heart chakra with your hand and ask yourself if there is anyone who is draining your power. This may be a person from the past who is no longer a part of your current path. This person may be a friend, coworker, ex-lover, or relative. You may even choose to cut cords from people who are currently in your life so that new, healed cords may form.

Once you are ready to take action, make a Reiki altar or sacred space like the one used for distance healing. Light a candle and sit in a meditative posture, relaxed and alert. Focus on the breath for a few moments. Visualize yourself surrounded by a ring of white light, one that protects and energizes you. Intend protection for you and your Higher Self. Intend that the action of cutting cords be done only in alignment with Spirit and the wisdom of Universal Love. Send a Master symbol to clear the space and align yourself with Spirit.

Now, imagine the person from whom you want to cut cords. Spend a few moments sending them distance Reiki using the Master symbol. Imagine surrounding their aura in a clear bubble of light, intending that you speak with their Higher Self. Imagine your own aura also surrounded with a bubble of light. Visualize yourself and the other person floating up and away from where you sit, into the sky. See yourselves, surrounded by stars, floating in bubbles of light. Ask to see the cords that connect you. Ask the person if s/he has anything s/he wishes to say to you. This dialogue will be coming from the Higher Self, one of clarity and based in compassion. Respond from your heart and explain why it is necessary to now cut the cord. After you feel the conversation is finished, imagine a large pair of golden scissors. Visualize cutting the cord between you and the other person. Again, send distance Reiki using the symbols. Imagine golden light filling up your auric bubble and theirs. Visualize the other person floating off and away, into the space, healing and recharging while you drift back down to your own body and space.

Close the session as you would for a distance healing. Feel yourself reconnect and ground out any excess energy. Slowly open your eyes. Notice any changes in the way you feel. Do you feel like you've reclaimed another part of your power? Check your solar plexus and see if it feels cleared and charged. If the person is one from the past, you should feel a sense of general clearness and energy in the next days. If the person is one from your current life, you should feel newness with that person, a fresh space in which to build brighter and clearer cords.

A Student's Story

One of my Reiki Warrior students, who worked with me for over a year, used the Cutting Cords exercise during the Reiki Warrior Master class. She chose to cut cords with her partner, someone she is very close to but was having certain issues with revolving around negative attachment. After we talked for some time about the issue regarding expectations and fear, we decided to cut the cords. She did the exercise based in love and trust, using her Reiki Warrior skills to cut and heal the cords between herself and her partner. Afterward she felt clear and full of the revitalizing Reiki energy. Later that day, her partner's behavior had shifted significantly, illuminating the effectiveness of the practice. The important part was her ability to let go, thereby momentarily letting her partner go to allow new growth to occur.

EXERCISE 14.4: *Seeding the Future*

This exercise is done to intend specific, positive futures for oneself or others. The main symbol used in this exercise is the nontraditional DKM, as a way to access the spiral of time discussed in this chapter. It is important to remember that this exercise is not done to enhance personal gain or fame, but done with alignment of Spirit and open-hearted joy. In the Tibetan Buddhist tradition, whenever one asks for something it is grounded in the awareness that all actions, speech, and thoughts should be done in the service of helping sentient beings. In this way, if we want to intend something for ourselves, we know it will serve our higher interests and therefore benefit others as we find our own happiness and joy.

To do this exercise, it may be helpful to write a complete list of what you want for your future: a new home, a teacher, money to start a business, etc. Choose something that is personal to you, not something that directly involves someone else, unless they are in complete agreement with what you want to intend. For example, don't use this exercise to seed a certain person to fall in love with you, although you can make a list of qualities of someone you would like to have as a partner. Make a complete description of what you intend for your future, including as many clear and precise details as possible. When you look carefully at the list, then ask yourself, the deepest part of your heart, is this something that will truly benefit me and therefore others? If the answer is a clear yes, then it is in alignment with your Spirit and will help to cultivate positive growth in your life. If you are unsure, then wait a few days and come back to the list. I have noticed that for myself, when I intend something for my future, if it is a precise thing I want—for instance, if there is a real purpose for money or wealth as opposed to wanting just a bunch of money—the Universe seems to flow more easily through me, moving me toward this intended future.

To intend the future, create sacred space. Doing this visualization on a full moon night will enhance the power of intention as the full moon is the time of abundance and everything on Earth is magnified by the moon's strong influence. Once you have created sacred space, sit with your list of your intention. As you would do for a distance healing, light a candle and raise your hands, directing Reiki energy toward the future. Send the nontraditional DKM spiraling into that future, unlocking the myriad possibilities and enabling you to create your own specific future. Then visualize, as best you can, the future you want. If it is a home, visualize the size, the various rooms, the kitchen, the surrounding area. Send several DKM symbols to the visualization and feel the clear Reiki light moving through you. Spend several minutes imagining this future for yourself, clearly sending the DKM and feeling the joy in participating in this future. This joyful feeling will help to enhance the ability to pull the future closer to your present moment.

After several minutes, seal the future image with a final, golden DKM and CKR to enhance the energy of the visualization. Close the Reiki session as you would normally do and release the sacred space. You can repeat this exercise several times over the course of a few weeks or months to bring the future into your present reality. Remember that when the Universe begins

15

Reiki Is Not a Religion or a Business

In Eastern traditions, there is a strong focus on lineage, both familial and traditional. Yet, in the West, our culture has a tendency to primarily value independence of the individual self. Therefore, Reiki, which is now largely a Western tradition, has lost its integrity as a lineage. Still, many people have been able to access the importance of simple and effective laying-on-hands healing. Because many Westerners do not hold a deep religious tradition, they may associate other values with the healing, such as money and a kind of pseudo-religious importance. Although Reiki contains the potential for benefit in one's life, it is important to approach it with the correct view, as a path, not as a religion or a business endeavor.

REIKI IS NOT A RELIGION

Although Reiki can be used as a spiritual practice, it is important to understand that Reiki, in itself, is not a religion. It does not promote any prescribed cultural activity, does not have the specific goal of becoming enlightened or connected to God, and does not require the practitioner to form a certain kind of faith. Reiki is, at its core, simply a means of promoting well-being and health through the use of laying-on-hands. Although many people have beneficial results due to Reiki, this can be viewed simply as a by-product of practice that comes from work in being and stilling the mind.

Reiki is not based in faith, yet a measure of openness is needed to practice. The best approach is to treat Reiki as a theory, one that should be tested by the practice. As a Reiki Warrior, once you put the practice to the test, results follow. A measure of faith then grows naturally and spontaneously because of the results. In turn, this enables you to continue building the practice, bringing more positive results in which clients are healed and transformed.

The Reiki Warrior path is organic and natural, growing in a way that allows for space and openness and does not need to be rushed or pursued unnaturally.

KNOWLEDGE AND WISDOM

A common misunderstanding prevalent in the world of Reiki is the crucial difference between knowledge and wisdom. We often see Reiki courses packaged and marketed in a way that advertise the wisdom a student will gain from taking a simple weekend course. Reiki is easy enough to learn and the use of the title Master after three courses is misleading to say the least. We must not confuse the learning of a new subject, which is knowledge, with the time it takes to build a Reiki practice, which leads to wisdom. In Eastern cultures, the belief is that it takes decades and even lifetimes to accrue the necessary wisdom so that it can be imparted to others in a way that is truly beneficial to the recipient.

When we read literature about Reiki, take the courses, and learn from teachers and Reiki contemporaries, we are simply gathering information, collecting knowledge to build a Reiki foundation. With practice, we start to put this knowledge into use, testing the theory of Reiki. Through the continued practice of laying-on-hands and using the Reiki symbols, certain insights begin to arise in the new stillness of the mind. Knowledge of Reiki remains conceptual until our practice enables us to not only understand but realize the wisdom that is inherent on the Reiki Warrior path. Discovering the ability to cultivate compassion; developing concentration, and mindfulness; and better understanding of the interconnectedness between ourselves, others, and the world are the insights that we are able to reach. These fruits of the path aid us in further help for others and also benefit our own practice through continued inner peacefulness.

SEEING THE WORLD

Another important aspect of becoming a Reiki Warrior is to work toward seeing things as they are and not inventing fantasy or bliss around the varied Reiki experiences. Certainly many of the occurrences are wondrous and interesting in their own way, but like anything in life, they simply rise and fall away. When remarking on one of my amazing visions during a Reiki session, a spiritual friend once advised, "That's nice, but don't get attached because you may never have that experience again." This idea is important for two reasons: First, it is true that our experience is really only one moment in all that has passed and is held in that bubble of the present, which is quickly gone into an unknown future. And second, by attaching to that past moment, we limit our ability to experience things as they are in the present moment. Remaining open and clear allows for new and even more wondrous things to arise as we continue our Reiki Warrior practice.

BEGINNER'S MIND

The beginner's mind is a concept found in Zen Buddhism, which refers to having an attitude of eagerness and openness. This way of viewing the world has a lack of preconceptions when studying a subject, even when studying at an advanced level. Each time we practice self-healing or pass Reiki during a session with someone else, we should try to remember to approach the moment with newness and openness to the healing. In this way, we learn something new each time. Every time I teach a Reiki course, I'm amazed at what I learn from my students, as each person has a story, a personal experience with Reiki that is unique and provides a new perspective. The beginner's mind approach reminds us to come to Reiki fresh and new, open and ready to learn.

During one of my Reiki One classes, I had a student who, although excited to begin learning a healing practice, had no interest or even belief in "seeing energy." Yet, during the Grounding Cord visualization, he experienced, to his surprise, an array of colors and sensations that was new to him. Often, beginners have a strong shift during Reiki One classes because they come with no previous expectations and are open to whatever arises. In this way Reiki Warriors can be inspired by the beginner's mind and aim to be open and without expectations for each and every Reiki healing session.

REIKI IS NOT A BUSINESS BUT A PRACTICE

As Reiki Warrior teachers, we usually charge money to both give sessions and teach classes, and the money is an important part of the Reiki exchange. Yet, a normal business provides a service to anyone who wants to partake. This is not necessarily the case in the Reiki Warrior practice. Especially when teaching Reiki we must remember that it is not a service that should be offered to anyone and everyone. Not all people are on the healing path and it is important to remember that, although Reiki has the potential to affect all areas of our life, the principal method of Reiki is through healing. This fact should be understood by each Reiki student. Reiki is truly a path of spiritual practice, yet is also one of many paths and as such is not appropriate for everyone.

So, instead of treating Reiki as a business, treat it as a practice. Each potential student is someone with whom we can practice our compassion, our surrendering, and our patience. If Reiki Warriors choose to advertise, then intend that each person who responds is someone who is truly aligned with the intention to learn Reiki, with you as their teacher.

KARMIC INFLUENCES

Karma is a Sanskrit word that means "action." In yogic and Buddhist philosophy, karma is the actions of our past lives that play out in this life; it is also a repository of actions from this life that are stored for the next. We can also look at the way our past in this life affects us now, today, and how the way we act today affects our future. The way in which we choose to earn money has a direct effect on our lives and those around us. Our work is an important aspect of our karma, our actions or way of contributing to the world. Reiki Warriors choose to work with the energy of healing, of creating a beneficial environment so that others may experience a shift within. Ideally we create positive karma, but we must honor the Reiki flow. If we begin to use Reiki to gain money and fame, the quality of the Reiki may suffer as the karma of our work changes. Our intention is extremely important here and must be checked continuously to provide the best Reiki possible.

ABUNDANCE AND FLOW

In my own Reiki Warrior practice I have witnessed the inevitable ebbs and flows that are part of the path. All things that are created are impermanent and so the notion of continuous growth is not necessarily the best method to apply to the Reiki Warrior practice. In other words, the Reiki healing practice should not be measured as successful in monetary terms, but instead in terms of quality healings performed, insights gained, wisdom achieved, and quietness observed. As this happens, more of the inner joy and peace within each of us radiates naturally and inevitably attracts more clients and students as the practice grows. This is wonderful, but it is important as a Reiki Warrior to continue to take the time needed to practice self-healing to renew one's own spirit.

Abundance is generally viewed as a positive thing, as something to aim for, but this can often be a burden as well. Having more money, more stuff, more anything can lead to a complicated way of existing that revolves around the abundance itself instead of our own spirit and Reiki healing work. It is important to distinguish between what we truly need and what we desire. Often what we need is more simplicity, quiet, and quality time with the people in our lives and less accumulation of wealth.

EXERCISE 15.1: *Feelings Toward Money*

Take a dollar bill or other monetary note and hold it for several minutes. Notice your immediate reaction to this piece of paper. Do you wish to throw it away? Give it to someone? Store it in a safe place? This immediate reaction illuminates your relationship with money and thus your connection to the material aspect of energy flow. Discovering this connection enables you to transform as needed. If you wish to throw the money out, you may have a negative association with money. Money is merely the physical or material version of energetic flow and is inherently neutral. Our ideas about money stem from our family, culture, and belief systems. The urge to give the money to someone else is rare, a show of generosity that transcends ego. Storing it in a safe place for later use is common, the need to save for a rainy day. None of the reactions are wrong, but it is important to understand our relationship with money so that it will not be confusing when giving healing sessions.

The connection to money also illuminates our ability to be generous and open with others. Once you have determined your relationship with money, try to notice it in other manifestations in your life. Are you giving things away to others, not only things you don't want, but are you able to give away things you love but don't need? Look carefully at the difference between need and want. We are sometimes swept away by our own desire and buy impulsively without really paying careful attention to what we spend our money on. Just as important as being generous and giving offerings is the ability to accept when others give to us. When you receive money for Reiki sessions, take a moment to feel thankful for the gift and place the money in a sacred place on your altar for a day or so. This helps to bring further awareness to the flow of money, which is a flow of energy through our lives.

16

Giving the Gift of Reiki

When Reiki is applied properly, like any spiritual practice, it will result in the landmarks of the spiritual path as so beautifully illustrated by Tibetan Buddhism: the beginning stage, the purification, moving beyond time and space, compassion, and completion. These qualities will surface within the Reiki Warrior through her practice of self-healing, the laying-on-hands for others, and the discipline of time-distance healing; this develops into the gift of giving Reiki to others, the art of healing, and the mastery of teaching.

REIKI AND ITS CONNECTION TO TIBETAN BUDDHISM

Many Reiki Masters find a connection between Reiki and its potential and the wisdoms that have come from Tibet. Although there may be a few loose similarities, we must not confuse the simple art of Reiki healing with the powerful path of Vajrayana.[69] Vajrayana Tibetan Buddhism is considered the swift path, offering enlightenment in one lifetime (or very few), but only through advanced practices and the completion of intense, lengthy training. When we try to apply something as advanced as Vajrayana to something as basic and simple as Reiki, we must remember that it is imperative that Vajrayana Buddhist practice be successfully built upon the preliminary stages and practices of both Hinayana, or narrow vehicle, and Mahayana, the greater vehicle.

In Hinayana, the practitioner works with very basic but often difficult practices to begin to understand the true nature of the mind. This is done by stripping away the normal activities of everyday life and doing only basic activities—such as sitting, walking, and eating—in

---

69 *Vajrayana* in Sanskrit means "thunderbolt" or "diamond vehicle."

continuous meditation. Vipassana,[70] or insight meditation, is one of the main methods used in the Hinayana practice, where students spend ten days in silence, practicing sitting and walking meditation for ten hours a day. After this experience, many people come away with a clearer picture of how the mind really works, racing here and there, responding so quickly to desire and compulsion. Vipassana meditation works for some and not for others. An alternative to this practice may lie in working with the First Degree of Reiki Warrior and practicing daily self-healing sessions and giving healing to others. Although I am not claiming that Reiki practice is the same as Vipassana—as in fact they are very different and simultaneous practice is often discouraged—I have found in my personal experience that the consistent practice of Reiki healing sessions has provided me with a clear view of my mind, similar to the times I practiced Vipassana meditation and Zazen, or sitting meditation. The key here is consistency and dedication to the path. Either way, the importance of first cultivating a discipline, whether it is sitting meditation or Reiki healing, has a profound impact on our growth and eventually, our ability to transform and heal.

Once the discipline of Reiki healing is cultivated, the practitioner naturally moves into a place of compassion and openness that is comparable to Mahayana Buddhism. The Mahayana path is distinctive in Tibetan Buddhism and focuses on dedicating our entire lives—all of our speech, actions, and thoughts—to the benefit all sentient beings. Here we find the powerful archetype of the bodhisattva who, as described in Chapter Eight: A Deeper Commitment, is the spiritual hero who forgoes complete enlightenment until all beings have achieved this blissful state of spiritual advancement. Comparatively, when we learn the Second Degree Reiki Warrior and begin to practice healing of others through time and space, we move into a deeper space of compassion for others.

Another aspect of Second Degree Reiki is the work with symbols and visualization. This is a faint echo of the powerful practices found in Vajrayana Buddhism. In this way, the Reiki Warrior exercises (such as the Grounding Cord, Auric Cleanse, The Process of Sending, and Creating Sacred Space) are all beginning steps toward a deeper, fulfilling practice not unlike the practices of Vajrayana Buddhism. In my own practices given to me by my Tibetan teachers, I have found that the Reiki work enabled me to focus even more clearly and deeply and can be used as a vital stepping stone for the more profound practice of moving toward enlighten-

---

70 *Vipassana* in Sanskrit means "see clearly."

ment. Still, it must be emphasized that Reiki is in no way a replacement for the combination of advanced practices, as true Vajrayana practice requires a proper teacher, certain vows, and focused discipline. Reiki, at its core, is a very simple practice that works to aid the healing of ourselves and others; this is what makes Reiki so accessible.

BECOMING REIKI MASTER

Besides holding the space for more powerful Reiki sessions, Reiki Masters have the unique privilege and responsibility of teaching Reiki to others. The Reiki Master must remain clear and do continuous self-healing in order to channel the attunements effectively. During times of sickness, disease, and disharmony, it is recommended that the Reiki Master take time away from clients and students in order to reestablish her own sense of inner balance, peace, and clarity so as to maximize the effect of the Reiki attunement process. This a useful time to go within and understand the deeper forces at work during illness and disharmony, which inherently cultivates a stronger compassion and deeper understanding of one's clients and students.

When deciding to teach Reiki, you are making a commitment to each student that you attune. A special bond develops with each person you attune and this must be recognized and honored. When a potential student comes to you, spend time talking about the general nature of Reiki and healing. Give them a Reiki session so they can feel the energy and see if it is what they want to learn. When deciding whether or not to take someone as a student, trust your intuition! Sometimes the person may not be an appropriate student for you and you may not be the appropriate Master for her. If this is the case, try to recommend another Reiki Master if you know of one.

As you begin to hold classes, teaching others the value and beauty of Reiki, you must exemplify the Reiki energy. This means you, again, are simply providing the space for your students to learn Reiki. You are not a preacher, but a channel. Allowing students to open and express Reiki in their own way is crucial. As a Reiki teacher, it is your job to simply present the concepts and allow the students to form their own Reiki theory and then test their theories through practice. This also requires you to practice non-attachment, meaning that you cannot control how your students will use the Reiki exactly. Honor each way that students take and use the Reiki and be ever-present for them if they come back with questions, concerns, or the desire for further Reiki degrees.

Each student will come to learn Reiki from you and each student will gain something in common as well as something personal. Each student will also give you something unique in return, some deeper lesson for you to play with. Attunements are strong connections between you and the student and they may continue for months or years. Such connections help in cultivating continuous compassion for yourself and others as you develop powerful Reiki friendships with your students. Although these friendships can be difficult at times, as they require you to be completely honest and open, they are very rewarding and continuously guided through the incredible, enriching power of Reiki.

Finally, as a Reiki Master and teacher, you will find your own way, your own method of imparting the magic and power of Reiki to others. Although the essence of the attunements has been passed down and remained the same, the teachings and the practices have evolved with each teacher and each student. Be open to the ever-flowing nature of Reiki and allow the way to teach to be your own, yet changing as appropriate for each student or group of students.

A Personal Experience

The first major Tibetan Buddhist teaching I attended was one of the most powerful, life changing experiences I've had. On my first trip to Ladakh, a geographical region of political India that is high on the Tibetan plateau, I trekked with a friend through several tiny Tibetan Buddhist Ladakhi villages and over massive mountains adorned with hundreds of prayer flags, piles of carved mani (prayer stones), and stunning views. Ladakh is like a moonscape with no trees on the mountain surfaces, only a variety of stones, dust, and scree while the valleys are fertile with winding rivers and apricot trees, and traditional Tibetan homes. After a six-day trek, we arrived at a sacred monastery in Lamayuru where they had signs posted announcing a weeklong teaching and several empowerments, including the White Tara, Chenrezig or Avalokiteshwara, and Padmasambhava. The festival scene was incredible as hundreds of Ladakhi people trekked in from miles away to participate in chanting together, enjoy the lama masked dances, and receive the sacred teachings and initiations. There were few Westerners there and the teachings were in Tibetan, translated into Ladakhi, and finally into minimal English. Therefore, most of my experience was through feeling instead of through literal meaning. We chanted Om Mani Padme Hum together hundreds of times, drank sacred saffron water, received blessed strings, and opened our upper chakras, the same that are seeded during Reiki attunements. In the final Padmasambhava empowerment, the Rinpoche[71] (the head lama leading the ceremony) came down from the dais and walked carefully through the crowd, blessing us with a large crown as the massive Tibetan horns blew loudly across the mountains. The air was crystal clear and a brilliant, massive rainbow appeared with the most vivid purple color I have ever seen. I felt completely opened up and filled with vital life force, similar to the Reiki attunements I had received a few years before. This was a crucial link for me on my path of exploring spirituality and I have since taken what I learned from my Tibetan Buddhist teachers and infused it into my Reiki path.

EXERCISE 16.1: *Breath of Fire*

The purpose of this exercise is to bring in more energy during the attunement or initiation process. The exercise can be practiced from these instructions but it must be learned from your Reiki Master in order to use it with the attunement properly.

To do the Breath of Fire, also known as the Fire Dragon Breath, first you must practice the mulabhanda, or "root lock." The mulabhanda involves squeezing the muscles of the perineum, the area between the genitals and the anus, together to form a kind of "lock" or contraction. The feeling is as if you are physically holding the urge to urinate, and then locking it up even further. Women have several layers of muscles in this area and can effectively lock the area of each layer successively. This is akin to the Kegel exercises recommended before and after birth to help strengthen the pelvic floor muscles. With practice, you can eventually seal off the downward flow of prana or Ki, resulting in increased energy flow within the body and auric field.

After the mulabhanda has been practiced, the next step is to practice the khechari mudra or "tongue lock," by simply placing the tip of the tongue at

71 *Rinpoche* means "precious one" in Tibetan and is used to address highly revered masters of Tibetan Buddhism, a lama that has reincarnated for several lifetimes.

the roof of the mouth, just behind the teeth. This effectively keeps the energy flow within the body without leaking.

To practice the Breath of Fire, practice mulabhanda and the khechari mudra simultaneously, then inhale deeply and hold the in-breath for a few moments. Then visualize the Reiki power symbol in the space in front of you. After you see it clearly, unlock only the khechari and blow over the symbol, slowly and clearly, without releasing the root lock. Practice this several times until it becomes a natural and rhythmic exercise. You can use this while passing attunements, as you blow the various symbols into the auric field of your students. The practice will enhance the power and energy of the attunement.

THE ATTUNEMENTS

Each Reiki Degree has a certain series of attunements specifically designed to open and clear the energy channels of the body and auric field. Below, we explore the significance of the Reiki degrees through the various attunements given for each level of Reiki Warrior.

First Degree Reiki Warrior: The Seed

The first degree of Reiki is a gateway. Reiki Warriors are entering the temple of the Dragon where the breath of Spirit plants the seeds of Reiki in the student's aura during the attunement process. This is a time of personal choice for the student, a time for the newcomer to Reiki to embrace the power of self-healing into one's life as well as intending to embrace Spirit in all aspects of life. This is also a time to heal and align all aspects of self beyond the physical body, including the emotions, the mind, the aura, and the spirit.

Reiki One often introduces meditation to students. If a student has never practiced meditation, the Reiki Master must introduce the basics of following the breath, allowing thoughts to pass through the mind, and simple visualizations. The Reiki Warrior path includes the basic tools for grounding, clearing, and protecting the aura using intention, visualization, and physical exercises.

The Reiki Master shows the student how the laying-on-hands method is a way to focus the mind and encourage the meditative process. The Master encourages opening and being, as these are crucial to passing Reiki through the body. The student is encouraged to test the theory of how Reiki works by practicing often. The attunement may take a few days to move through the student and the Master must be physically and mentally available during the twenty-one-day clearing process.

Reiki One weeds out the non-healer from the healer. Although everyone would probably benefit from at least learning Reiki One, not all people are intent on being healers. The Reiki One attunement is, in some ways, a test to see if the student is dedicated to the Reiki path. The attunement provides only the Reiki seeds and it is up to the student to water those seeds through daily self-healing practice. By doing this for at the very least twenty-one days, only then will the student have gained enough mental and emotional harmony, confidence, and auric energy to learn Reiki Two.

A Reiki Warrior Master must decide if the student is ready for Reiki Two after twenty-one days. It is essential for the student to really want Reiki Two training. She should be asking for it and show that she is dedicated to the healing path. On a practical note, the student should have little or no problem visualizing the grounding cord and cleansing the aura, or at least be able to hold the mind steady for several minutes. This steadiness is necessary for someone to practice Reiki Two with any success.

Second Degree Reiki Warrior: The Activation

During the Reiki Two attunement, the Reiki seeds or symbols are activated through the Breath of Fire. This is a deeper commitment to the path of healing using Reiki, and the focus shifts from self-healing to healing others. The student learns to connect to the world in a larger context through the time and distance healing.

Reiki Two is the heart of Reiki in the sense that it takes Reiki from a simple laying-on-hands method to the powerful use of symbols. The Reiki symbols are an intelligence that holds different aspects of consciousness to be used in the healing process. The symbols have been passed down and used for over a hundred years and although there have been slight changes to their form, their essence has remained intact. They are the key to unlock the power of Reiki, which is done by inserting them into the student's aura during the attunements. It is crucial to remember that Reiki One is the seed and Reiki Two is the activation of that seed, as the student now learns how to use the Reiki intelligence.

In Reiki Two, there are fewer facts for the student and more practice. The Reiki Warrior Master must set aside several hours to use the symbols in different ways. Make sure that students become familiar with and accustomed to the different qualities of energy that each symbol holds. Use diverse methods to show all the ways the symbols can be used. Have the students do more creative activities like painting the symbols, charging crystals and plants, and more advanced visualizations.

Reiki Two facilitates a time for deeper interconnectedness with others. The essence of this class is about exchange and opening. This class is even more colorful and open than Reiki One. Students are encouraged to be more creative in their healing sessions by using crystals and pendulums and trusting their intuition more when laying-on-hands. They learn how to heal aura layers and practice chakra balancing.

Again the Reiki Warrior Master must be present both physically and mentally for the student as she goes through the twenty-one-day cleansing process. Often this process is less dramatic than the Reiki One attunements, but it may have a deeper emotional and mental impact on the student. Students are encouraged to use the symbols often, to again practice daily self-healing for twenty-one days, and to practice several distance treatments.

A Student's Experience

During one of my student's attunements, I "accidentally" passed the Reiki Two attunement during the first degree course. She had a very strong reaction to the attunement and was seeing brilliant violet light almost immediately. Although her reaction to the attunements was somewhat strong, it was not uncommon. When I observed her giving her practice Reiki sessions, I noticed how strongly it moved through her and the power of the session was considerably greater than with most Reiki One students. At that point, I suddenly realized that I had practiced the Breath of Fire during her attunement, thus activating the Reiki symbols before seeding them. I don't think there are accidents really, and the student was able to handle the Reiki flow, although the strength difference was quite significant.

Third Degree Reiki Warrior: The Manifestation

Reiki Three is considered the true gift, the gift of full power and the ability to pass it on to others. Reiki is a lineage and becoming a Master links the healer into the line of Masters before him. Reiki Three is treated with love, faith, reverence, and humility. It is the time to learn about honoring power and developing in-depth on the spiritual path. A Reiki Master is capable of giving great healings and teaching others.

Passing the Reiki Master attunement to students should be a rare and precious event. Before going on to the Master attunements, each Reiki Two student must wait a year at the very least and should attempt to give twenty-five to fifty Reiki sessions. It is extremely important that the Reiki student has an in-depth understanding of Reiki before teaching it to others, and this can only happen after much practice. The Reiki Two student should have a strong desire to teach and pass on the Reiki to become a Master. The Reiki Warrior Master should have an incredibly clear idea as to why and how the student identifies with Reiki, uses Reiki, and what her spiritual path looks like. It is highly recommended that the Reiki Warrior Master give the Master attunement if she has taught the student the other degrees as well or has a very strong assessment of the student's previous teachings and practice methods. Yet, if a student has a great connection with Reiki and has been practicing for some time and has a strong desire to teach, the Master degree should be considered. Reiki Mastery should be prized, but not coveted.

During the training, the Reiki Warrior Master should be available for several weeks or months. Although the attunement is shorter than the previous degrees, the student should be working toward becoming Master for some time before the class. The student will assist Reiki One and Two classes. She is taught the power of intention and how to focus with greater clarity and awareness as the power becomes more refined. Masters-in-training must give many healings and keep notes so they can more fully comprehend the aura, chakras, and layers.

The Master class is very clear and beautiful. Oftentimes the students connect directly with guides and Reiki Masters. The class includes advanced auric work, creative visualizations, and powerful psychic healing tools. The Master symbol can be used for different things like accessing creativity, powerful distant healing, invisibility, accessing dreams, and meeting healing guides.

Again, be present for your student following the attunement. This is considered a twenty-one-day activation period and the student should wait at least this long before passing on her first attunement. Have the student pay close attention to synchronicity and dreams during this time. She should also be doing her advanced auric work and self-healing daily. As Master/teacher, now is the time to let your student go. Let her follow her own path as contemporary Reiki Master and grow in the ever-abundant flow of Reiki.

EXERCISE 16.2: *Golden Sun Healing*

The visualization enhances the flow of the aura, utilizing an often untapped resource: the golden light above us that connects us to the sacred parts of our Spirit. The exercise can be used anytime to call on deep healing, to seal in shifts after a session, or to recover from a trauma or emotional letdown.

To practice the Golden Sun Healing, sit in a meditative posture, keeping the spine straight and shoulders relaxed. Focus on the breath for a few moments. Watch your thoughts come and go without attaching to them, allowing yourself to relax deeply into the present moment. Visualize your grounding cord and auric boundary and perform your Auric Cleanse. Now, focus on the crown of your head. Bring your attention to the top of your aura, several inches above the sahasrara, or crown chakra. Imagine there is a brilliant, shining golden sun in the space above the crown. Visualize the glowing light extending out and down, illuminating the entire auric boundary. Take several minutes to visualize the warming, healing sun energy moving down your aura and through each chakra. Visualize the chakras successively lighting up with gold light. See your body and internal organs alight in the warming gold, as if the rays of the sun are warming your aura and body, healing you. Imagine the gold energy circulating down through all seven chakras, filling your aura with warm golden light. Visualize the grounding cord as gold and connect to the Earth. Allow the gold light to permeate your aura and being for several minutes. Use the Master symbol to enhance the circulating gold light. Notice where more gold energy collects, places in the body and/or aura where more healing is needed.

After several minutes, bring your head to the ground and visualize the remaining gold light draining out and into the earth. Notice any places where the gold remains for continued healing. Imagine the grounding cord in a color that suits you, sit up, reground, and slowly open your eyes. Notice what you feel as you sit up. You should be revitalized and energized from this gold sunlight. Use this exercise as needed to bring about deep, nurturing healing in your aura and body.

17

Healer as Teacher, Healer as Master

As a Reiki Warrior Master and teacher, I have been assisting people for more than a decade to access the inner part of themselves. This is the true message of Reiki: that once we start to awaken, we are able to pass on the gifts that we ourselves enjoy. Healing is an excellent path that cultivates compassion, to give to others both individually and through the community. Each time I give someone a Reiki session, I feel more fulfilled, closer to my own natural and joyous existence.

REMEMBER THE REIKI WARRIOR TOOLS

The Reiki Warrior tools—offering, intention, grounding, trust, clearing, and protection—are just as important for the teacher as they are for a practitioner. Continuous work with these tools and their practical applications will form a ground upon which to build a strong foundation for your teaching work. Each tool can be applied to your students and classes.

Begin the Reiki class by making an offering to the Reiki Masters who have gone before you, to the students who give you the opportunity for new growth, and to the Earth for providing such a wonderful place to practice our healing gifts. This can be done with the students or on your own before the class starts.

Forming intention is the most important tool for a Reiki Warrior Master. This aligns the clarity of focus for teaching Reiki. Even more important is having the student form his intention as well, to illuminate how focused and dedicated the student is. The power of intention is like an arrow headed toward the future. Encouraging a student to define and verbalize his clear point of focus for the Reiki class will considerably enhance his Reiki experience and benefit his practice. I have my students say aloud what their intention is before we officially start the class. This gives students a chance to hear where other student are while opening up to the clear purpose of learning Reiki.

The remaining four Reiki Warrior tools should be used by the Reiki Master continuously throughout the class and during contact with students. Grounding keeps us focused and relaxed while teaching. Remembering we are in form allows for us not to become carried away with the title of teacher or Master and to more easily connect with our students. This also enables the flow of the class to follow smoothly and in a progression where each idea and technique builds upon the one before. Teaching students grounding exercises, such as the Grounding Cord, is an excellent way to get them out of the fantasy of the furious mind and into the present moment.

Trust or surrendering is the inherent Reiki Warrior tool of Reiki practice. This is valuable in opening up to the Reiki energy within as a teacher and allowing ourselves to teach in a way that best suits each student or each class. Every time I teach, I find that I learn something new from my student, a unique perspective emerges that adds to the depth of my understanding of Reiki. This also, like the Reiki session, provides the tool for teachers to simply allow the attunement to occur without expectations. Each student will experience receiving the attunement in a distinctive way and this should not be judged or interpreted, simply experienced.

I have found that each class is different and I must continuously trust the direction or way that the class moves. Luckily, in India, we have more time and openness to allow the spontaneous needs of each student to be addressed. During one of my recent first degree courses, I affectionately nicknamed the course my "water class," because we had to allow more space and fluidity during the three days, as each woman spiraled deeply into emotional processing that required more time to adjust to the attunement process. Interestingly, during the time they take to draw what they experienced during the first Grounding Cord exercise, they all drew water underneath the Earth's surface. I have been teaching the Grounding Cord exercise for several years and none of my students have ever drawn the water, although I mention it in the visualization! And each of them drew the water, which was sublimely and, at times, difficultly, expressed through the following days of tears and shifts and transformative healings.

I have also found that attunements can be varied as well, depending on the student and his/her guides. I have learned to deeply trust the attunement process and go with the flow, so to speak, to allow whatever needs to happen during the initiation to take priority over my attachment to following any specific attunement process. This flexibility allows for an even deeper connection to form between the student and the incredible, powerful energy that is Reiki healing.

The tools of clearing and protection are used to assist in the attunement process and during the class. It is important to emphasize the students' ability to access the Reiki themselves through consistent practice and not to rely on you as the teacher or Master. Doing the Auric Cleanse and protections before and after classes helps you to remain present for students but with a detachment that enables you to have perspective of their progression. Occasionally it is necessary to use the Cutting Cords exercise to free the student and yourself from any limiting patterns that are inhibiting further growth.

A tricky relationship that crops up from time to time is the student who is also a friend. Of course, it is inevitable that some friends are students and some students become your friends, but mindfulness of the relationship should be maintained. During Reiki courses, I aim to treat all students equally or according to their needs, regardless of personal friendship. Redefining a relationship or taking space is sometimes necessary to encourage others to grow as needed on their spiritual path. Sometimes, being a teacher and seeing what a student will benefit from does not coincide with friendship, which can create a difficult situation. Trying to see the bigger picture and maintaining your integrity is at times more important than placating a friend's ego. This is a test of the true Reiki Master and the use of the Reiki Warrior's skillful perception in working to benefit others and their healing path.

A Personal Story

One of my students, whom I trained for over a year, was excellent at learning the form and practice of Reiki but struggled with the art of surrendering. As time went by, we became friends as well as spiritual contemporaries. During the series of Reiki Two attunements, she worked very well with the symbols, had good concentration, and was gaining benefit from her healing practice. Yet, due to certain expectations she held, one of the attunements did not go to her liking and she asked several times for me to "re-do" the attunement. I knew with certainty that the attunement was as it should be and that saying no to her was an important lesson for both of us. In her repeated requests to receive the attunement again, I finally decided that I would agree if she asked more than three times. But by the fourth time we approached the topic, she had surrendered to the way it happened, allowing it to be as it was, in its own quality instead of trying to change it. This showed me as a teacher that I should trust my intuition, as I believed she gained some wisdom from the interchange, and to accept things as they are without trying to fit them into her expectation.

BE A LIVING EXAMPLE

Becoming a Reiki Warrior Master encourages us to work even more deeply on the process of opening, allowing, and surrendering. As we continue to open to our Reiki clients through the process of healing, we tap into the ever-abundant inner source within. This source, this clarity, is the Reiki that unites us with all things, all Beings, all that is living, that has lived, and that lives on in other dimensions. The Reiki Master symbol is the activated seed that will begin to break down deep barriers that keep us from being completely open and full of love.

As we become more integrated into Spirit, it will be easier to see others' pain and problems preventing them from being happy. It is crucial now to be a living example for people. Instead of offering advice or trying to change their minds, simply allow them to express their feelings and offer a Reiki session instead. Allow them to access their own pain. By acting as a mirror to reflect back others' issues, you are allowing the person to exist as they are without trying to change or dominate their issues. Allowing them to simply be will inevitably lead to greater healing. By holding your own light and being a living example, you will become less involved in others' dramas and less interested in stories that are not about healing, becoming, or opening. This will allow others to access their own inner source of clarity and joy in your presence, during Reiki sessions, and in classes.

At times, people may have certain expectations or demands on you that are actually inhibiting to both your growth and theirs. Here, the Reiki Warrior must remember to honor the integrity of Spirit and act in a way that, in a larger perspective, is more beneficial instead of falling into the trap of doing what others want you to do. Since I spend much of my time in India, I am constantly coming into contact with travelers who are seeking some kind of spiritual insight or wisdom. Occasionally people come to see me and wish to learn a Reiki degree very quickly and with a certain kind of urgency. Although I may be tempted to teach them, it is really not the most beneficial manner, especially if they will be traveling on in a short amount of time. We must remember to honor the quiet wisdom of the Reiki and not be swayed by outer circumstances.

DEEPER RESPONSIBILITY

Becoming a Reiki Warrior Master also means that we are fully responsible for all of our actions. Now, when things fall apart, we learn to accept that life is not a perfect, rigid plan, but a flow from one moment to the next. Each action has a reaction and as we become more aware of this, we can work with the higher vibrations of Reiki Warrior Mastery. We begin to see how each of our actions and interactions with others is not a one-way street, but an exchange between both parties. We begin to use the gift of the Reiki Master to connect, honor, and be grateful for each person who comes into our life. Even when there are aggravating or irritating people in our lives—as there are bound to be—we can use the wisdom we glean from Reiki practice to approach each moment with awareness and clarity. Responsibility is really the ability to respond and not to react to things—to respond with a sense of appropriateness to each situation, to bring Reiki more fully into every corner of our lives.

THE ART OF SPACIOUSNESS

By bringing Reiki into each moment, we open up to the brilliant clarity and spaciousness of the ever-present beauty of life. When we give a Reiki session or teach a Reiki class, we become continuously more aware of the quiet beauty that emerges when we are still, receptive, and open. This spaciousness allows for deeper insights to arise, for a quality of being to come into our lives, a quality that allows the interplay of life and its colors to arise, then fall away. The binding nature of attachment, aversion, and ignorance begins to wear away like an old shoe, as the ego tendencies lessen their hold over our actions, speech, and thoughts. This shift takes time and is a continual process; it is not just a leap from unhappiness to spiritual enlightenment. Reiki is one of the many ways to open and become clear, to honor the true art of surrender.

EXERCISE 17.1: *Listening*

We spend so much of our time racing from one activity to the next, moved by the myriad desires, ideas, and thoughts that inhabit our thoughts. In order for our minds to slow down, first we must slow down our bodies; this is done by the practice of giving Reiki sessions to both the self and others. Then we must become aware of our speech and the way we communicate with others. Often we rush to say something to others, anticipating the end of their sentences so we can share our knowledge. Using the art of spaciousness, we can instead try allowing space to become part of a conversation instead of cramming idea after idea into the heads of the people with whom we communicate.

For this exercise, take one full day and dedicate it to listening. Remove the tendency to tell our story in response to others' stories and simply allow their story to be told. Remain quieter and bring spaciousness into communication in your life. Notice how hard it can be to do the simplest things in life. Also notice how rewarding it can feel to hold the space for someone to express herself instead of constantly comparing stories or outdoing each other's experiences. Try this practice once a week, to take a full day to honor others by simply listening. Not only honor people, but the sounds in your life, the music that drifts through the days, the information that we miss when we are so busy chattering in our minds and voices. Try the exercise with family and friends, those you are closest to, and really *hear* them, let them find their true voice as you honor your own.

A SENSE OF HUMOR

As a Master, a teacher, a healer, and a human being, it is essential that we retain our sense of humor. My own teachers, students, family, and friends are always showing me how I continue to take myself too seriously in a way that prohibits growth and openness. By reminding ourselves that we are in this funny, messy process of life, we won't get overly disturbed when things go awry. We don't need to feel guilt or shame when our students just don't get the Reiki. Instead allow that to be their experience, even laugh at our own need to "make" them understand. Likewise, we should remember not to take our "mystical" experiences too seriously either, as these, like all phenomena, simply come and go. Remember that humor indicates lightness and that as important as it is to maintain discipline, concentration, and healing, the ultimate goal is one of openness and lightness.

THE LONGER NOW

In today's modern world, people are racing around building vast collections of things, technology, ideas, degrees, therapies. I have met many healers who have a business card listing so many therapies, so much knowledge, so many qualities . . . but I wonder how much wisdom comes through all this stuff. Whether we are on the "spiritual path" or not becomes irrelevant if we are still functioning based on our ego desires. Our ego simply gets caught up in all of our spiritual practices and little benefit is gained.

But, if we take the precious quality of time and apply it to our practice, many benefits will be gained. Reiki is such an incredibly simple art form, so simple that I think its beauty is often overlooked by the need to fill up our resume with sophisticated healing techniques. Focusing on the simplicity of laying-on-hands, using the concentration of a few symbols to direct our intention, and literally allowing light to pass through us, our ability to grow, heal, and embrace life becomes tremendous. As this happens, our capacity to see the larger perspective also becomes relevant. The *now*-ness of each moment grows to incorporate more of life and Earth, more awareness of other lifetimes, and a deeper understanding of our multidimensional self.

As this element of time is used to open more and to surrender, when we do apply ourselves to doing and acting, it is with mindfulness and increasing awareness. This awareness creates activity that is filled with clarity and spaciousness, which inevitably—without us even trying hard—honors ourselves, other people, the Earth, and our environment. Becoming Reiki Warriors is just that: a becoming, a life in process, where the path is the goal and the journey is its own reward.

Conclusion: Claiming the Warrior Within

This book provides the Reiki practitioner with the tools and guidelines needed to train students in the ways of the Reiki Warrior. Reiki Warriors approach Reiki as a practice. They are on a path of learning the lessons of Spirit encased in human form. Reiki provides a *sadhana* (a method for applying daily spiritual practice) by healing through laying-on-hands. Reiki Warriors cultivate compassion, an essential part of the spiritual path, through continuous exposure to people in need of healing. The practice of Reiki also aids in learning non-attachment, loosening the ego, and embodying the power of becoming a living example. Inevitably, if one practices Reiki regularly on oneself and others, she becomes ever more attuned with Spirit and uses Reiki in all aspects of life. The Reiki Warrior is one who truly sees this practice as a discipline, remaining grounded and centered in her practice, cultivating discernment, and understanding the profound spiritual connection between Master and student.

Once the time has been taken to work with Reiki effectively, adding other therapies is quite useful for clients. Because Reiki is such a simple art form, it can be used with a variety of other healing arts: acupuncture, aromatherapy, massage, shiatsu, and journey work. Once you have learned the basic techniques, experiment! Test the theory that is Reiki. Watch clients open and surrender to your healing hands on the table. Pay attention to the shifts and the ways they grow and how the mind can loosen and open. Watch your own ego lessen its hold on you as you explore the varied dimensions of Reiki and the healing arts. As Reiki takes over your life, notice how it opens up to include everything from your food to money, to your children, to school . . . even to the way you make love! Reiki is about honoring Spirit and allowing it to move through you, so that as we begin to come closer to death, we are more and more filled with light.

As the world moves further into the twenty-first century, we are increasingly surrounded by the reality of pollution, overcrowding, climate change, and natural disasters. Taking the step to begin understanding ourselves and exploring healing is becoming as crucial as breathing. These threatening world situations are forcing us to work more deeply on opening the heart and connecting with each other, to transcend the dualistic nature of good and evil, to find a place of health and harmony and wellness among the ever-shifting tide of culture on our planet. Practicing the Reiki Warrior path is a good way to honor that part of us that is walking on Earth, the part of us that has a form and a body and must relate directly to other human beings, animals, plants, and our environment. Reiki also gives us the opportunity to express that part of us that is always searching for more—more happiness, more joy, and more love—by enabling us to experience the infinite wisdom of healing that comes through the now of each moment, through our incredible ability as human beings to look up at the stars and wonder where we came from and where we are going.

I will conclude with a quote from the Dalai Lama, Tibet's exiled king who endlessly promotes peace on this planet, even in the face of great violence and adversity:

"We are all here on this planet, as it were, as tourists. None of us can live here forever. The longest we might live is a hundred years. So while we are here we should try to have a good heart and to make something positive and useful of our lives."

Appendix A

Chakra Questions

The following questions are intended for the Reiki Warrior student to more deeply explore the chakras and their inner workings.

Chakra means "wheel" in Sanskrit. What does this mean to me? Draw an image of a chakra.

Which chakra do I identify with most and why? The least?

Take a moment to visualize a patch of flowers in the sunlight. Notice what sensory stimulus comes to mind first. Can you smell the flowers? Do you see the flowers and sun clearly? Can you feel the sunlight on your skin? Identify which senses are predominant and explore this more as a way to enhance your extrasensory perception.

Muladhara:

Do I feel safe in this world? What do I need to feel safe?

Hold a note (money) in your hand. Ask yourself: How do I feel about this money? Do I want to hold it close or throw it away? The initial reaction is a clue about your connection to money. Write down the answers and transform negative associations into positive affirmations. How can I transform my idea of money into one of energy?

Put your hands on muladhara. Ask yourself: How does my vagina or penis feel to me? Do I identify with this part of my body as a part of my being? What do I feel here?

Svadhisthana:

What is my secret, creative dream?

What do I desire? Am I afraid to receive my desires? Why?

Make two lists, one labeled "masculine" and the other "feminine," and write down the characteristics associated with these labels. Which traits on the lists do I admire? Which ones do I dislike? How can I bring these two aspects of myself into balance?

Manipura:

What is my personal power and how do I express it?

Do I give away my personal power? To whom? Put your hands on manipura and ask yourself: Is there anyone or anything I no longer need to give my power away to? Visualize yourself surrounded by a golden light. In front of you is that person or thing, also in a golden light. Look to see if you are connected by any psychic cords. Ask them why you are still connected. If this connection no longer serves you, imagine a large pair of golden scissors cutting the cord, freeing both you and the other person or thing.

What do I want to transform in my life? How can I do this?

Anahata:

What is my definition of love? Compassion?

How do I give myself love?

Sit in a meditative position and breathe into your heart center. Imagine a clear light emanating softly from your heart. Now visualize someone you dislike or who has hurt you in the past. How does this affect your heart center? Try to look at this person objectively. What in their life context has caused them to act hurtfully toward you? How did you respond? Now imagine breathing in the negative feelings from the person, the anger/hate/mistrust generated by your relationship. Visualize this dark energy going into your breath, into your lungs and filling the heart center. Allow your heart center to purify this negativity, clarifying the situation with compassion. Let the clear, bright light in your heart absorb the dark negativity and transform it. Imagine a warm, brilliant light filling your heart and slowly exhale this light into the ones who will benefit from healing energy. After several moments, forgive the person if you can and release them.

Vishudda:

Do I communicate clearly with others? Do I listen to them as much as I speak? How can I communicate more effectively?

Close your eyes and ears with your fingers. Listen to the silence in your consciousness for ten minutes.

What does the term "Higher Self" mean to me? Do I have dialogue with my Higher Self? How can I better honor this part of me?

Ajna:

Think of a dream that has stuck with you for many years and write it down. Why do you think you remember this dream often? How can you manifest the elements of the dream's lessons into your life?

Think of a time when your intuition spoke to you about an event or person but you did not listen. Write this experience down. Why did I not heed my intuition? What happened when I didn't listen? How can I cultivate my intuition?

Sit under the full moon one night with a bowl of water and a candle. Meditate for several minutes and then ask a specific question and pour the melted wax from the candle into the bowl. Let it cool, then look at the image and interpret the symbol that emerges. Can you find some meaning?

Sahasrara:

What does spirituality mean to me?

Where do I feel most connected with Spirit? What activities in my life honor Spirit?

What is my spiritual truth? Why is this my spiritual truth?

Appendix B

Chakra Journey

This technique is useful when we are faced with obstacles that are unknown or obscured by our emotions. This partner exercise enables us to go even deeper than the Chakra Check Visualization in Chapter Five. It is a good method for times when we need clarity and direction in our healing path.

This exercise involves two people, a facilitator and a recipient. The process is as follows:

1. The recipient lies down with their eyes closed and relaxes, and the facilitator sits beside the person with a note pad and pen.

2. The facilitator asks the recipient to breathe into and focus their awareness on each chakra, one at a time, asking specific questions that are connected to the consciousness of that energy center. The recipient breathes into the area and asks him/herself the questions inwardly.

3. The recipient is then asked to speak whatever sense impressions come to mind in relation to the question. These can be images, colors, symbols, thoughts, feelings, sensations, dialogue, etc. The idea is to speak the immediate impressions without analyzing them. The process encourages intuitive responses.

4. As the recipient speaks these impressions, the facilitator writes them down for future reference, making sure to clarify and read back anything that was not heard clearly. A few sentences is sufficient.

5. The facilitator then directs the recipient's focus to the next chakra and repeats the process with all seven major energy centers.

6. At the root chakra, the facilitator asks the recipient to put his/her hands there and breathe into the energy center. The recipients asks, "Am I safe?" and "How can I be safe?"

7. At the sacral chakra, again the recipient puts hands there and breathes, then asks, "Do I know and use my creativity?" and "How can I use it more effectively?'

8. At the solar plexus ask, "Am I worthy?" and "How can I be worthy?'

9. At the heart center: "Do I give and receive love?" and "How can I give and receive love?"

10. Throat chakra: "Am I open?" "What am I not saying now?" and "How can I express myself more effectively?"

11. Forehead chakra: "What do I need to know now?"

12. Crown chakra: "What is my spiritual path?" and "How can I pursue my spiritual path?"

13. Once the facilitator has moved through the process, the recipient remains with eyes closed and relaxed as the facilitator reads back what was spoken. As this is being done, the recipient places his/her hands on the corresponding chakras and adds any further impressions that may arise.

14. After this process is completed, the recipient looks at the information. Together, the recipient and facilitator try to encapsulate the sentences into one phrase or word that summarizes the impressions. The idea is to contain each chakra with a particular key phrase or symbol to clarify the issue or story that is being told by the chakra. By journeying through the chakras in this way, the individual can access certain insights into the chakras and their stories. The recipient can then further his/her own healing work using the key phrase.

15. The recipient can then take this information home and use the key phrase or symbol to work even more deeply with the chakras. Meditate on each chakra for one week, exploring its story, listening to how it is in balance or not and what can be adjusted. Use Reiki self-healing, the Reiki symbols, and visualizations to enhance each chakra's balance and healing process.

Appendix C

Reiki Confidential Client Survey

Name: (Last, First, Middle) _____

Date of Birth: _____ Age:_____ Sex:_____

Address: _____

City: _____ State:_____ Zip:_____

Telephone:_____

Reason for Reiki Visit: _____

_____

Any Allergies: _____

_____

Any Chronic Health Problems: _____

_____

What Medications Currently Taking: _____

_____

How Would You Rate Your Health on a Scale of One to Ten?: _____

Why? _____

_____

List any Fears or Phobias: _____

_____

I, the undersigned, do understand that this Reiki Session is for relaxation and information shared is for the purpose of education only. A Reiki practitioner does not replace a regular family physician or diagnose or prescribe any course of treatment.

Signed _____ Date _____

Thank you!

Appendix D

Reiki Clinic Guidelines

The following list is a set of guidelines used by the Free Reiki Clinic in Baltimore that I worked at. This list can be used to help set up your own Reiki clinic. I also encourage students of Reiki to find a Reiki Share, or group of practicing Reiki healers who participate in a share group to exchange Reiki, healing methods, and stories. If you can't find one, simply start your own!

The objective of the clinic is to educate the public about Reiki and offer treatments on a donation basis.

1. Time

It usually takes about thirty minutes to give a full Reiki treatment when working with a group of two or more practitioners. Please keep in mind that the client may need more Reiki than we can give them in one session. Feel free to recommend subsequent visits to the clinic (or private sessions if a more customized approach is desired). Practitioners are encouraged to have business cards and/or brochures with them to hand out to interested clients.

2. Sacred Space

Reiki is all about creating a sacred space within ourselves and around those we are treating. Respecting this space means being aware of the atmosphere we create at the clinic. Keep conversation to a minimum. Speak quietly and only in reference to the client and their issues.

3. Responsible Communication

Think before you relay any impressions you receive to the client. Always word them as positively as you can—if you cannot relate positively, then do not say it!

Be careful not to prescribe or promise healing: you are then practicing medicine without a license. Use phrases like, "This may help relieve your headache," instead of "This treatment will definitely help your headache—it sounds like sinuses—you should also probably take some allergy medicine." Remember that you are responsible for everything you tell the client. Or simply describe the energy that you feel and ask: "I sense a lot of energy around your face. Has something been going on for you there?"

4. Closing Circle

We finish working on our last clients a half hour before closing so all practitioners can participate in the closing circle. This is important for clearing and grounding the Reiki practitioners and the clinic space.

THE CLIENT'S EXPERIENCE

1. Sign-In

Clinic coordinator greets client and pulls client information form.

If new client, have them fill out information form.

Clinic coordinator gives client estimated waiting time.

2. Table Protocol

One person for the table's group gets the next client's form.

Introduce self to the client and find out about the goal of today's session.

Show client to table.

Introduce the other practitioners.

3. Begin Reiki Session

Give client feedback (keep positive) if wanted.

4. Closing

Help client up from table slowly.

Show client back to waiting area.

Give any further impressions if appropriate.

Show them the donation box.

"If you would like to make a donation to support the Reiki Clinic, there is a box here. Thank you!"

5. Paperwork

Record any notes on client information sheet.

Return sheet to clinic coordinator.

Exercises

Glossary

Ajna: Unlimited power. Forehead chakra located between the eyebrows. This chakra is associated with insight, perception, and intuition and is seeded and activated during Reiki One and Two attunements, respectively.

Anahata: The pure sound made without any two things striking. Heart chakra or center located at the center of the chest associated with love and compassion, which is seeded and activated during Reiki One and Two attunements, respectively.

Archetype: A symbol or image found cross-culturally that evokes deep emotional connection by embodying universal meaning. For example, the Warrior.

Asana: Pose or posture held comfortably. Poses for meditation and bodily control.

Assemblage Point: Point of awareness and perceived reality.

Astral Body: Associated with the fourth layer of the aura, this body can travel during sleep and leaves the body at the point of death.

Atma: The individual soul, the Self, the eternal principle.

Attunement: The specific initiation ritual that is given to students of Reiki. The attunement process effectively clears the body, energy channels, and aura and seeds them for the healing Reiki energy.

Aura: Human energy field that surrounds and interpenetrates the body. The aura contains the chakras and nadis, or meridians.

Bodhisattva: A spiritual hero or Enlightened Being who reaches enlightenment, then forgoes its full benefits until all sentient beings have reached enlightenment as well.

Breath of Fire: A technique used by a Reiki Master during an attunement to enhance the process.

Buddha: Literally means "awake." A buddha is someone who has awakened to his true spiritual nature.

Causal Body: The outer layer of the auric field. This body contains bands of information that record past lives and effectively holds their karma, passing from one life to the next.

Chakra: Wheel of light or spinning disc. The energetic organs are located at various plexuses throughout the body and work to revitalize the physical body and the energy field.

Chakra System: The system of the chakras, comprised of seven main chakras and several minor ones, which are treated during a Reiki session.

Chi: Energy or life force. Also known as Ki or Prana.

Deity: God or Goddess. A pure being that manifests certain qualities that can be evoked to raise power, transform negative into positive, and receive blessings.

Dharma: Means "to uphold." The teachings and wisdom of the Buddha, as in the Buddha dharma.

Emotional Body: The second layer of the aura, which contains the emotional energetic content of the human energy field.

Empowerment: A Tibetan Buddhist process that works to aid students on the path to enlightenment. The process consists of three elements: preparation, purification, and the conclusion to seed the student with various deities to assist in spiritual practice.

Energetic Layers: The subtle qualities of the aura or human energy field that comprise the etheric, emotional, mental, astral, and causal aspects of the human being. This is a complex and multidimensional aspect of ourselves that transcends time and space.

Etheric Body: The first layer of the aura, closest to the physical body. This layer is directly affected by external sources as well as internal.

Gassho: To place the two palms together. The Namaste or prayer position in India, this position symbolizes respect and also activates the ten meridians of the body.

Granthi: Knot. Three protective mechanisms located in the sushuma that only open once a practitioner has achieved a sufficient level of purification.

Guatama Siddhartha: A spiritual teacher from ancient India who founded Buddhism. He was born in the sixth century BCE.

Hatha Yoga: The path of yoga that first pays attention to the physical body through asana, pranayama, and meditation practices, which give rise to the awareness of Spirit.

Hinayana: The small or narrow vehicle. One of the foundational aspects of advanced Buddhist practices.

Ida: The nadi to the left of the sushuma whose qualities are akin to the moon or lunar aspects of life and associated with intuition, the feminine, and cooling.

Karma: Action or deed. The cause-and-effect law of the Universe in which each thought, word, and action has a resulting cause. Seeds of yesterday or past-life karmas bear fruit today or in future lives.

Karma Kagyu Lineage: One of four main lineages of Tibetan Buddhism.

Khechari Mudra: Position to lock in energy by folding the tongue back and pressing the soft palate of the mouth behind the teeth.

Ki: Universal energy. Also known as Chi or Prana.

Kiko: Japanese form of Qi gong. Physical and meditative exercises to enhance well-being through body, mind, and breath.

Kundalini: The union of the masculine and feminine principles. The manifested power of the universe that resides in all humans, resting at the base of the spine in muladhara.

Kundalini Yoga: The practices, meditations, and techniques used to activate the powerful potential of spiritual energy.

Lung: "Wind" in Tibetan. Oral transmission received during empowerment process.

Mahayana: The large vehicle of the Tibetan Buddhist path that focuses on compassion through the open-hearted dedication of working to help all sentient beings.

Mandala: Circle. A symbolic representation of the universe that is visualized to enhance spiritual practices.

Manipura: City of gems. The chakra located at the solar plexus and concerned with will power, setting boundaries, fire, and mental energy.

Mantra: Instrument of thought. Series of sacred sounds or syllables that, through repetition and reflection, can bring powerful spiritual insights.

Mental Body: The layer of the aura that comprises thoughts, mental activity, and thought forms.

Meridian: Energy channel located in the aura or energy field.

Mudra: Seal. Used with Hatha Yoga postures as a way to seal energy into the body; also, hand gestures that can affect the energy channels of the body.

Mulabhanda: Root lock. This contraction of the perineum is used to seal in energy and bring up the vital life force more strongly into the body and aura.

Muladhara: Foundation. The chakra located in the base of the spine, just inside the perineum in men and below the cervix in women. This chakra contains qualities of survival, fear, and grounding. Used in Reiki Warrior to connect with the Earth and ground the student.

Nadi: Yogic nerve. Energy channel in the aura; same as meridian.

Nagual: Left-side attention associated with intuition and awareness through symbolism and dreams.

Om: Also AUM; the Universal sound of Creation that manifests in all things.

Paganism: The ancient way of practicing religion that is rooted in the awe of nature, ascribing deities or qualities to the natural forces. Wicca is a form of paganism.

Paingala Upanishad: Sanskrit text from seventh to fifth century BCE that contains precise information regarding the human energy field.

Pingala: The nadi to the right side of the sushuma whose qualities are akin to the sun or solar energy. Associated with the active, fiery, logical, and masculine.

Prana: Vital life force akin to Ki or Chi.

Pranayama: The science of breath control used in Hatha Yoga.

Reiki: Spirit-guided energy or life force used to promote healing.

Rishi: A seer or sage.

Sacrum: The lower back area of the body where the triangular-shaped sacral bone sits. Also the location of the second chakra.

Sadahana: Spiritual practice.

Sahasrara: Thousand petals. The crown chakra located at the top of the head, which has the potential for a thousand nadis to run energy through it. This is the union point for the Kundalini energy from the muladhara which, in enlightenment, ascends and unites with the sahasrara.

Sanskrit: Ancient Indian language of written texts including the Upanishads, Vedas, and Bhagavad Gita. The alphabet is composed of fifty letters, which are considered to be sacred sounds; each sound corresponds to a petal of the chakra mandalas.

Satori: A glimpse or fleeting witness of enlightenment. Oftentimes it marks the beginning of the spiritual awakening process.

Shakti: Power, energy, female Goddess, female power. The energy that rests around muladhara in the base of the spine waiting to achieve union with Shiva, the presiding principle of sahasrara, or the crown chakra.

Shaman: One who enters an altered state of consciousness to acquire knowledge and power for divination and healing.

Smudge: To cleanse or clear space or the aura using smoke such as sage or cedarwood.

Solar Plexus: A large plexus of sympathetic nerves located behind the abdomen. Associated with the third chakra, manipura.

Sunyata: Emptiness. The Tibetan Buddhist term for the unification of wisdom, bliss, and luminosity that is the essence of the universe.

Sushuma: The central nadi that runs through the spinal cord. Upon awakening the Kundalini energy, the Shakti rises up through the sushuma to unite with the crown chakra.

Svadhisthana: Dwelling place of the Self. The second chakra located just above the pubic bone, in the sacrum, associated with sexuality, sensuality, creativity, and the balance of masculine and feminine.

Tantra: Web. The vast network of practices that include Kundalini Yoga. Also linked to Vajrayana Buddhism.

Tendai Buddhist: Buddhist sect in Japan to which Mikao Usui belonged. They follow the Lotus Sutra teachings.

Third Eye: The all-knowing eye or ajna chakra.

Thought Form: A crystallized structure found in the mental layer of the aura. Contains certain deeply held beliefs about oneself and place in the world.

Tibet: The highest country in the world and host to two principle religions: Mahayana Buddhism and the indigenous Bon religion.

Tibetan Buddhism: The Buddhist path that includes the practices of Mahayana and Vajrayana, including monastic functions and yogic practices.

Tonal: First or normal attention that we use in day-to-day life, associated with left-brain activity.

Universal Life Energy: The fluid energy that connects all living things. Ki.

Upanishads: The Sanskrit texts that complete the Vedas, known also as Vedanta. Esoteric teachings transferred from guru to disciple in ancient India and still today.

Usui, Mikao: The founder of the system of Reiki.

Vajrayana: Thunderbolt or diamond vehicle. The Tantric aspect of Mahayana Buddhism, or swift path.

Vedas: Knowledge. Collection of ancient knowledge in Sanskrit.

Vipassana: To see clearly or penetrate an object thoroughly. A primary practice of Hinayana Buddhism and foundational practice of Mahayana Buddhism. Together with tranquility (samatha), it represents the two-fold dimension to Buddhist meditation practices.

Vishudda: Pure. The chakra located in the throat, associated with higher aspects of listening and communication. This chakra, along with ajna and anahata, is seeded and activated during Reiki One and Two attunements, respectively.

Warrior: One who walks with impeccability, fearlessness, and a courageous open heart.

Wicca: To "bend" or "shape." A form of contemporary paganism that is based on the ancient Celtic and European system of spirituality. Wicca focuses on the Goddess, the elements, earth seasons and directions, and moon cycles to effectively "shape one's life into being."

Yoga: To "yoke." The union of spirit into form. The philosophical path of going within to discover spiritual nature.

Zen: The instant awareness. Pointing directly to the mind. Clarity.

Resources

Bowker, John, ed. *The Oxford Dictionary of World Religions*. Oxford: Oxford University Press, 1997.

Brennan, Barbara Ann. *Hands of Light: A Guide to Healing Through the Human Energy Field*. New York: Bantam Books, 1987.

Buddhananda, Swami. *Moola Bandha: The Master Key*. Bihar School of Yoga: Yoga Publications Trust, 1996.

Capra, Fritjof. *The Tao of Physics*. Berkeley: Shambhala Books, 2000.

Castaneda, Carlos. *The Power of Silence: Further Lessons of don Juan*. New York: Simon & Schuster, 1987.

———. *Tales of Power*. New York: Simon & Schuster, 1974.

———. *A Separate Reality: Further Conversation With Don Juan*. New York: Simon and Schuster, 1971.

Gerber, Richard. *Vibrational Medicine: New Choices for Healing Ourselves.* Santa Fe, NM: Bear and Company, 1988.

Harner, Michael. *The Way of the Shaman*. New York: HarperCollins, 1990.

Judith, Anodea. *Chakras: Wheels of Life*. Mumbai: Jaico Publishing House in arrangement with Llewellyn Publications, 2007.

Karagulla, Shafica, and Dora van Gelder Kunz. *The Chakras and the Human Energy Fields*. New Delhi: New Age Books, 1989.

Kelly, Maureen J. *Reiki and the Healing Buddha*. New Delhi: Full Circle Books, 2001.

Krishna, Gopi. *Kundalini: The Evolutionary Energy in Man*. New Delhi: Shambhala Publications, 1967.

Leadbeater, C.W. *The Chakras: An Introduction*. New Delhi: Indigo Books and Cosmic Publications, 2003 (updated version; First Edition, 1927).

Lübeck, Walter. *The Complete Reiki Handbook*. Trans. Wilfried Huchzermeyer. Twin Lakes, WI: Lotus Light Publications in cooperation with Schneelöwe Verlagsberatung, Germany, 1990.

———. *Rainbow Reiki*. Twin Lakes, WI: Lotus Light Publications, 1997.

Lübeck, Walter, Frank Arjava Petter, and William Lee Rand. *The Spirit of Reiki: The Complete Handbook of the Reiki System*. Twin Lakes, WI: Lotus Light Publications in cooperation with Schneelöwe Verlagsberatung, Germany, 2001.

Marieb, Elaine N., Jon Mallat, and Patricia Brady Wilhelm. *Human Anatomy and Physiology*, 5th ed. Redwood City, CA: Benjamin/Cummings Publishing Co., 2007.

McLaren, Karla. *Your Aura & Your Chakras: The Owner's Manual*. New Delhi: Shri Jainendra Press, 1998.

Melody. *Love Is in the Earth: A Kaleidoscope of Crystals*. Wheat Ridge, CO: Earth Love Publishing House, updated 1995.

Mitchell, Karyn K. *Reiki: Beyond the Usui System*. Oregon, IL: Mind Rivers Publishing, 1996.

Monroe, Robert A. *Journeys Out of the Body*. New York: Doubleday, 1977.

Motoyama, Hiroshi. *Theories of the Chakras: Bridge to Higher Consciousness*. New Delhi: New Age Books, 2001.

Petter, Frank Arjava. *Reiki Fire*. Twin Lakes, WI: Lotus Light Publications in cooperation with Schneelöwe Verlagsberatung, Germany, 1997.

———. *Reiki: The Legacy of Dr. Usui*. New Delhi: New Age Books, 1998.

Pert, Candace. *Molecules of Emotion*. London: Pocket Books, 1997.

Radha, Swami Sivananda. *Kundalini Yoga*. Palo Alto, CA: Timeless Books, 1978.

Rand, William Lee. *Reiki: The Healing Touch*. Southfield, MI: Vision Publications, 1991.

Saraswati, Swami Satyananda. *Asana, Pranayama, Mudra, Bandha*. Bihar, India: Yoga Publications Trust, Bihar School of Yoga, 1989.

———. *Kundalini Tantra*. Bihar, India: Yoga Publications Trust, Bihar School of Yoga, 1984.

Sharamon, Shalila, and Bodo J. Baginski. *The Chakra Handbook: From Basic Understanding to Practical Application.* Trans. Peter Hübner. Twin Lakes, WI: Lotus Light Publications in cooperation with Schneelöwe Verlagsberatung, Germany, 1988.

Sivananda, Swami. *Kundalini Yoga.* Shivanandanagar, India: Divine Life Society, 2001.

Stein, Diane. *Essential Reiki.* Freedom, CA: Crossing Press, 1995.

———. *Guide to Goddess Craft.* Freedom, CA: Crossing Press, 1987.

Stiene, Bronwen, and Frans Stiene. *The Reiki Sourcebook.* New Delhi: New Age Books in association with John Hunt Publishing, 2003.

Villoldo, Alberto. *Mending the Past and Healing the Future with Soul Retrieval.* Carlsbad, CA: Hay House, 2005.

Vishnu-devananda, Swami. *The Complete Illustrated Book of Yoga.* New York: Three Rivers Press, 1988.

Wise, Anna. *Awakening the Mind: A Guide to Harnessing the Power of Your Brainwaves.* New York: Tarcher/Putnam, 2002.

Woodroffe, Sir John. *The Serpent Power.* Madras: Ganesh and Company, 1928. Reprinted 2003.

Yogananda, Paramahansa. *Autobiography of a Yogi.* India: Jaico Publishing House, 1946; Reprinted by Self-Realization Fellowship, 1998.

Websites

Deacon, James. "James Deacon's REIKI PAGES." www.aetw.org *Provides comprehensive research into the ever-evolving Reiki history.*

Medlej, Joumana. "A (sharp) look at Reiki symbols." CedarSeed. www.cedarseed.com/air/reiki.html. *Interesting article on Reiki symbols and their possible origin.*

International Center for Reiki Training, The. www.reiki.org. *An excellent resource of Reiki news, articles, and contacts.*

Audio

Eno, Brian. *Ambient 1: Music for Airports.* Polydor Records, 1978.

———. *Ambient 4: On Land.* E.G. Records, 1982.

———. *Thursday Afternoon.* E. G. Records, 1985.

Index

Free Catalog

Get the latest information on our body, mind, and spirit products! To receive a **free** copy of Llewellyn's consumer catalog, *New Worlds of Mind & Spirit,* simply call 1-877-NEW-WRLD or visit our website at www.llewellyn.com and click on *New Worlds.*

LLEWELLYN ORDERING INFORMATION

Order Online:

Visit our website at www.llewellyn.com, select your books, and order them on our secure server.

Order by Phone:

- Call toll-free within the U.S. at 1-877-NEW-WRLD (1-877-639-9753). Call toll-free within Canada at 1-866-NEW-WRLD (1-866-639-9753)
- We accept VISA, MasterCard, and American Express

Order by Mail:

Send the full price of your order (MN residents add 6.5% sales tax) in U.S. funds, plus postage & handling to:

Llewellyn Worldwide
2143 Wooddale Drive 978-0-7387-1445-5
Woodbury, MN 55125-2989

Postage & Handling:

Standard (U.S., Mexico, & Canada). If your order is:
$24.99 and under, add $3.00
$25.00 and over, FREE STANDARD SHIPPING

AK, HI, PR: $15.00 for one book plus $1.00 for each additional book.

International Orders (airmail only):
$16.00 for one book plus $3.00 for each additional book

Orders are processed within 2 business days.
Please allow for normal shipping time. Postage and handling rates subject to change.

MAGICK OF REIKI
Focused Energy for Healing, Ritual, & Spiritual Development

CHRISTOPHER PENCZAK

What is Reiki? How has this Japanese healing tradition evolved over the years? How are modern magick practitioners using Reiki energy in their spells and rituals?

Christopher Penczak answers these questions and more in his groundbreaking examination of Reiki from a magickal perspective. The history, mythos, variations, and three degrees of Reiki are discussed in depth. Penczak also suggests way to integrate Reiki and magickal practice, such as using Reiki energy for psychic development and with candle magick, crystals, herbs, charms, and talismans.

978-0-7387-0573-6, 288 pp., 7½ x 9⅛   **$16.95**

Reiki for Beginners
Mastering Natural Healing Techniques

DAVID F. VENNELS

Reiki is a simple yet profound system of hands-on healing developed in Japan during the 1800s. Millions of people worldwide have already benefited from its peaceful healing intelligence that transcends cultural and religious boundaries. It can have a profound effect on health and well-being by re-balancing, cleansing, and renewing your internal energy system.

Reiki for Beginners gives you the very basic and practical principles of using Reiki as a simple healing technique, as well as its more deeply spiritual aspects as a tool for personal growth and self-awareness. Unravel your inner mysteries, heal your wounds, and discover your potential for great happiness. Follow the history of Reiki, from founder Dr. Mikao Usui's search for a universal healing technique, to the current development of a global Reiki community. Also included are many new ideas, techniques, advice, philosophies, contemplations, and meditations that you can use to deepen and enhance your practice.

978-1-56718-767-0, 336 pp., 5³⁄₁₆ x 8   **$13.95**

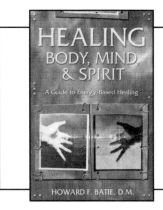

Healing Body, Mind & Spirit
A Guide to Energy-Based Healing

HOWARD F. BATIE

Remove diseased energy patterns before they make you sick. Want to know the root cause of physical disease? Look to the faulty patterns in the etheric body (aura) or higher energy bodies. Performing healing work on these energy levels can often keep disease from becoming a physical problem.

Energy healer Howard Batie discusses several energy-based healing techniques that have repeatedly demonstrated a positive effect on his clients. You will learn how to develop your own sensitivity to energy and open yourself as a channel for healing energy. You'll discover the surprising origins of disease, including infections, viruses, trauma of injuries, and emotional and mental illness.

978-0-7387-0398-5, 312 pp., 6 x 9   **$16.95**

Unlocking the Healing Code
Discover the 7 Keys to
Unlimited Healing Power

DR. BRUCE FORCIEA

Have you wondered why traditional medicine as well as herbs, homeopathy, and other alternative practices all work? They are all linked by a universal, mysterious field of energy that is alive with useful information. This healing information flows from the source to us across four channels, and anyone can learn how to activate these channels to heal injuries and recover from illness.

Bridging the gap between traditional and alternative healthcare, Dr. Bruce Forciea introduces seven keys to unlocking this unlimited healing power. His techniques, useful for both patients and practitioners, help you choose and apply complementary healing methodologies—such as creative visualization, vitamins, herbs, magnets, microcurrents, light, and chiropractics. True stories, including the author's own experience with recovering from chronic illness, highlight how numerous people have found relief using this groundbreaking program for healing.

978-0-7387-1077-8, 216 pp., 6 x 9   **$14.95**